Beyond Control

Beyond Control

A Mutual Respect Approach
to Protest Crowd–Police Relations

VERN NEUFELD REDEKOP
and
SHIRLEY PARÉ

BLOOMSBURY ACADEMIC

First published in 2010 by:

Bloomsbury Academic

An imprint of Bloomsbury Publishing Plc
36 Soho Square, London W1D 3QY, UK
and
175 Fifth Avenue, New York, NY 10010, USA

CIP records for this book are available from the British Library and the Library of Congress

ISBN 978-1-8496-6004-4 (Cloth)

e-ISBN 978-1-8496-6017-4

This book is produced using paper that is made from wood grown in managed, sustainable forests.
It is natural, renewable and recyclable. The logging and manufacturing processes conform to the
environmental regulations of the country of origin.

Printed and bound in Great Britain by the MPG Books Group

www.bloomsburyacademic.com

Contents

Part Two: The Mutual Respect Paradigm in Practice

Foreword

By Archbishop Desmond Tutu

Dissent. Marches. Protest. Violence. Public order policing. Repression. I have witnessed all of these. Protests, called toyi-toyi in South Africa, have been important, not only in ending Apartheid but also for the emergence of full democracy and the development of South African culture today. These phenomena raise important questions about the dynamics of a democratic society.

Foundational to how I make sense of such phenomena are the twin lenses of Ubuntu and Reconciliation. Ubuntu comes from my African roots and highlights how our lives and humanity are tied up with one another. My Christian roots emphasize reconciliation through the promise of profound transformation when former enemies can escape from their resentment and hatred, visualising the humanity of the other and a common future together.

My own experiences colour my interpretation of these things. During the Apartheid era I stood with those calling for justice. Though at odds with the political power of the time, a dissenting voice needed to be heard as it was expressed in many ways. One of these was through our activities with protest crowds. As one privy to the inner workings of government in the new South Africa, I saw how difficult it is to establish an orderly society, especially when so many still experience injustice.

What is refreshing about *Beyond Control* is the vision for the kind of society in which protesters and police recognize their mutual humanity as well as how both are needed for a democratic society to function well. This is *Ubuntu* applied to a contentious aspect of community life. Police and protesters are indeed connected. Governments, as targets of protest; bystanders, who watch; and media, who cover these events, are all part of a web of relational systems centered on protest crowd activities.

In the *Mutual Respect* paradigm and case study of the seminars in Ottawa, there are promises of the possibility of reconciliation in the wake of mutual hurt. There is something magical in face to face encounters that take place in a safe environment. I saw this again and again during the Truth and Reconciliation Commission. Those who lost loved ones at the hands of repressive police could open their hearts to forgiveness of the very people who had hurt them profoundly. Not that there is a formula nor that it happens easily, but seeing the humanity in the heartfelt witness of the other has a profound impact.

We all live with our own truths—what we know by way of our own experience and reflection on that experience. At times our truth is crucial for another whose past has intersected with ours in a conflictual way. The sharing of truth can lift burdens and open new relational possibilities.

Protesters and police who have confronted one another through the violent actions of batons, tear gas, rocks and Molotov cocktails have their own truths of how they experienced the event. When Redekop and Paré recount the story of protesters who suffered tear gas at the Quebec Summit of the Americas and exchanged their truths with those police who launched the tear gas, I can well imagine the redeeming impact of their mutual insights into the lives of each other.

Beyond Control is an important book for any who wish to look beyond simple partisanship to the complex set of relations and roles that make democratic institutions work. This book provides police and protesters with deeper insight and understanding of each other's motivations and how their tactics can positively or negatively impact their relationship. I believe this book presents an opportunity to better understand that our lives are tied up with one another and it makes sense to put in place discursive structures that allow us to talk with one another about issues of justice, democracy, and making the world a better place.

July, 2009

Acknowledgements: Vern Neufeld Redekop

Little did I know that when Dan Clapin, director of development for Saint Paul University (SPU), invited his friend Richard L'Abbé for a meeting to discuss an endowed chair in conflict studies it would open up a whole new world of meaning and action; namely, the relationships between protesters and police. 'Can you do something about crowd control?' was L'Abbé's innocent question. It came from his hope, as then CEO of Med Eng Systems Inc.[1] that a more irenic relationship might evolve between protesters and police. At the time, I was President of the Canadian Institute for Conflict Resolution where we had developed a methodology for Community-Based Conflict Resolution using Third Party Neutral (TPN) training as an intervention, even in such challenging places as Rwanda and Bosnia and Herzegovina. Without hesitation, I answered in the affirmative and so began a journey, the result of which is this book.

My first step was to enlist the support of Shirley Paré. A retired officer with the Canadian Forces, she had taken Third Party Neutral training along with my seminars on deep-rooted conflict, reconciliation, and community-based conflict resolution. As someone with experience in a command and control environment, she complemented my own experience with community action and development. Within the methodology of community-based conflict resolution is a 'gathering process' whereby representatives of key stakeholder groups are invited to a training session such that there is a good balance of whoever needs to be there. Shirley was a master at principled gathering and the success of the seminars with protesters, police, government, media and the community was due in large measure to the quality of her work in this regard. She further assisted with the seminars, the advisory council meetings and eventually the writing of the book. At every step we talked through the ideas, debriefed on meetings, and planned how to proceed together. We have attempted to write a book that is balanced—we entered critically yet empathetically into the worlds of protesters and police in the hope that each would better understand the other. Shirley has played a key role in sensitively ensuring that the book does not take sides. I am deeply grateful for the opportunity to work with her on this project.

To Richard L'Abbé I owe my thanks for the initial research grant which made it possible for us to test our theory through what became participatory action research. Further funding came from the Canadian Police Research Centre, thanks to the efforts of Julie Graham, and the Canadian Ministry of

---

1   Note that since then Med–Eng Systems has been sold to another company; the line of police protective gear, described below as an example of what is on the market, has been discontinued but the Med–Eng brand is still used for some products. Richard L'Abée is not involved in the new company.

the Solicitor General. This made possible additional development work as we conducted the Strategic Leaders Seminar and tried out our process as a preventive intervention leading up to the G20 meeting of finance ministers in 2001.

Trish Blackstaff and Julia Fleming deserve special recognition for their courage in participating in our second seminar as representatives of the protest community. Both had been at the receiving end of tear gas at the Quebec City Summit of the Americas and were passionate in their commitment to the social justice issues that were the focus of protest. It was not at all straightforward for them to join the Strategic Leaders seminar with the very people who had fired the tear gas and confronted them in protective gear. We are grateful they did and for their subsequent contributions to the development of the paradigm.

On the policing side, Gary Nelson, then with the Ottawa Police, and Peter Henschel of the Royal Canadian Mounted Police (RCMP) were key to the success of our research seminars. Not only did they support the initiative from the start, they became active members of the Advisory Council. They were the ones who noted that 'for this to go anywhere in the policing world, it needs the support of senior officers.' This prompted our plan for a seminar for leaders; as soon as the decision was made each got on their cell phones and called their bosses, who, on their recommendations agreed to participate in the three-day session—a significant time commitment for senior officers.

As we continued to reflect on the significance of lessons learned and the corroboration of our application of my own theoretical work on deep-rooted conflict in this domain, it became clear that more thoroughgoing historical and conceptual work was needed. This led to an examination of the history and interpretive models used in the understanding of protest, crowds, and policing. Eli Sopow, who had a history of protest (he protested with Greenpeace before it was called by that name) and of consultation work with police, wrote his doctoral dissertation on public protest. He kindly shared his insights and corroborated the ideas we were developing. Wishing to include cutting edge theoretical work around complexity theory and developmental levels of consciousness, I consulted with Deborah Sword and Richard McGuigan who had done their doctoral research on each of these respectively. They subsequently reviewed those portions of the book in which these ideas were presented and we happily made revisions in response to their constructively critical comments.

Also to be acknowledged are the significant number of police, protesters, journalists, and community leaders who participated in our developmental processes. Without them the basic understandings of this book would not have emerged. They are represented in the short essays in chapter twelve. Those who contributed deserve special thanks: Gary Nelson, representing the police; Julia Fleming and Carl Stieren, protesters; Leonard Stern, then a reporter and now an editor with the *Ottawa Citizen*; Peter Coffin, then the Anglican Bishop for Ottawa and now retired, is a community leader with international experience; and Raymond Laprée, is an academic with expertise in group dynamics.

This book has gone through a number of peer reviews and I am grateful for the anonymous comments that prompted refinements along the way. It was Caroline Wintersgill of Bloomsbury Academic who managed the final processes leading to publication. It was a joy working with her as we cleared various hoops and did the final polishing of the manuscript. She joins with us in the hope that this book will eventually make a difference on the ground.

Archbishop Desmond Tutu was most gracious in contributing the foreword. His perspective, coming from South Africa, frames this work in a most meaningful way.

Among Canada's First Peoples there are teachings that stress beginning with oneself and letting insights grow like ripples to include ever more people. With this in mind, I must thank my lifelong partner Gloria for providing that community of closeness wherein I could experience the dynamics of dissent, protest, and re-emergent order. These dynamics distinguish institutions—from marriage to organizations to nations—where conflict is dealt with in a mutually respectful way that inspires creativity.

My hope is that protesters, police, bystanders, journalists and politicians will each enter empathetically into the lives and perspectives of one another as they are presented below; that seminars, workshops and other discursive structures will be set up to encourage mutual understanding and the creative development of helpful scenarios; that insights from this book will help in the emergence of healthy democracies out of current repressive regimes; and that messages bursting out of a passion for justice and community well-being will be communicated effectively without there being loss of life or violent paroxysms on either side of the protest line.

Vern Neufeld Redekop
August, 2009

Acknowledgements: Shirley Paré

This work is the culmination of my practical inauguration into training as an intervention. Through the lens of protest crowds and security I came to fully appreciate the power and efficiency of community-based conflict resolution and experiential learning. The journey has been gratifying and spiritually rewarding.

First and foremost I acknowledge my mentor, colleague and friend Vern Neufeld Redekop and his seemingly effortless talents and ability to conduct this project. I admire his eternal optimism and am grateful for his positive support. Vern developed the model of identity based conflict, thus providing a foundation and common language for people in conflict to discuss emotional issues. Additionally, he truly believes in the principles of community based conflict resolution and is skilled in applying those principles in any situation.

Secondly, I must acknowledge the participants in our training sessions. They came with hopes for a better future and participated from the heart. From our wonderful participants we were able to develop an intervention for Ottawa at the time and a model for the future. I am enriched by their presence and participation.

Thirdly, I am grateful for the participation of the members of the Advisory Council chaired by Vern and coordinated by myself. Initial members included Daniel Clapin, Saint Paul University (SPU), Julie Graham (then of Canadian Police Research Centre), Peter Henschel (Royal Canadian Mounted Police), Raymond L'Aprée (then of SPU), Gary Nelson (then of Ottawa Police), and Jean Robichaud (then of Med Eng Systems) later Peter Atak (activist), Trish Blackstaffe (unionist) and Leonard Stern (journalist) joined the Council.

Management, academic and administrative staff at Saint Paul University went out of their way to support the project. They were most cooperative and helpful. I am grateful for their support.

Finally, there is a myriad of people who contributed selflessly to the project. Most importantly, I am indebted to my husband Michael for his technical and personal support.

Shirley Paré
August, 2009

Introduction

Societies worldwide, and the communities within them, are caught in a constant interplay between the needs for continuity, on the one hand, and change, with the stimulation and growth that accompany it, on the other. The public interface between these competing needs often manifests itself as the boundary between protest crowds and police. Some protester movements are resisting change, which they perceive to be harmful, and others are pushing for change to address what they perceive to be injustices embedded within the current situation. Police use a range of tactics—from repressive use of force to negotiation and many in between. Their relationship to their political masters ranges from being fully directed by political leaders to relative independence. In any case, police are active within communities in a way that brings them in direct contact with protest crowds. The protest crowd–police relational system is the primary focus of this book. The book examines the interface between crowds and police from the neutral perspective of community-based conflict resolution.

People nest their identities within a variety of groups based on kinship, ethnicity, values, religion, and calling—all of which are manifest at the community level. Community itself has taken on a complex set of meanings in the information age—ranging from geographical communities to communities of interest—that can bring together people with common values who may be spread around the world but linked through the internet. These diverse aspects of community are significant when dealing with protest crowds. Regardless of the type of community, protester engagement with issues often implicates their identities. This means that the values that motivate them are backed by a combination of rational argument, moral principles and emotional vitality.

Given the emotional engagement with the issues and the propensity of many of the players to resort to violence, the relationship between crowds and police includes features of deep-rooted or identity-based conflict. During our work, we have discovered that exposing the underlying conflict in an honest and open dialogue has the potential to transform the relationships and create space for more effective and safe, non-violent protest for all. In Part One of *Beyond Control* we present theoretical research on both protest and policing interspersed with state of the art theories of identity-based conflict. Part Two tells the story of our Ottawa experiences which we present as a case study.

So, what happened? In the summer of 2000, we were given the challenge of addressing the issue of violence between protest crowds and police. Our community and others like it were facing escalating violence during international meetings and the accompanying demonstrations. What we observed was a conflict of cultures and a dearth of meaningful dialogue. Strategies for 'success' abounded on both police and protester sides and there were plenty of negotiations but no real dialogue. The anger and underlying needs of those in 'violent' conflict at the coal face of the demonstrations went largely unrecognized. The more the violence escalated, and escalate it did, the more angry everyone became until eventually the demonstrations became more about the violence during the protests than the issues the crowds were protesting. Demonstrators went out of their way to challenge the authority of the police and police erected barriers and deployed tactical troops in riot gear with Tasers, water cannon and other 'less than lethal weapons' to keep the demonstrators under control. Chaos reigned.

As experienced process leaders and professionals in community-based conflict resolution, we had developed the discipline of treating people equally and coming across as neutral about the issues. We were practitioners with little experience in either the protest or policing communities and we brought fresh perspectives to the challenges. We could provide a safe space for meaningful dialogue and had developed a methodology whereby the deep-rooted anger could be expressed with minimal hurt to either side.

Neutrality is never easy. Those who were intent on putting us in one corner or the other certainly found reasons to do that. In fact, we were accused of being on both sides of the issues as is usually the case when strong emotions and little trust are involved. The emotions and lack of trust were so strong in the beginning that it was difficult to convince enough representatives from divergent sides of the conflict to be in the same room together. By the end of our project, we were unable to meet the demand for participation in our processes.

Our work in the field and the subsequent research uses an interdisciplinary methodology of deep-rooted conflict, reconciliation and community-based conflict resolution that is applied to the protester–police relational system. As such, it is not meant to provide a strategy for either side to win at the expense of the other. Rather we wish to look at the phenomenon as a conflict, a conflict that can take on a structure of violence or a conflict that can take on a structure that enhances creativity, justice and mutual empowerment.

Both public order policing and protest have developed over time; hence in our research we found it necessary to trace their histories, paying particular attention to paradigmatic changes and how each has understood their role and has been understood by others. An insight emerged from this historical reflection that both protesters and police are necessary for a well-functioning democracy. If both are necessary and both need to be effective to avoid the worst alternatives—violent anarchy or violent tyranny—the question arises, 'What is to be the nature of the relationship between them?' Relationships can never be prescribed; however, paradigms of what relationships could be can guide the imaginations, actions, and principles that help mould the patterns of how groups relate to one another. This book explores paradigms past and proposes future possibilities.

From our knowledge of several widely respected conflict theories, we knew that emotional reactions that fuel conflict and violence happen when needs are threatened. We also knew that violence on one side is returned by violence 'with interest' from the other and this results in an ever increasing spiral of violence. Our interest and our focus in meeting the challenge of how to imagine a protester–police relationship that allows both to fill their role with integrity was to find a methodology for exposing the underlying needs of participants on all sides of demonstrations regardless of roles. Additionally, we were interested in facilitating a process so that the divergent communities developed the requisite expertise to provide a platform for protesters to express the intense emotions associated with the important issues they wanted to address without resort to violence.

In describing our approach in Ottawa we believe we have produced a model whereby communities worldwide can adapt their own process for facilitating non-violent protest. It is a methodology for creating meaningful dialogue in confrontational situations where there are strong emotions and little trust. We recognize and acknowledge that there are members of the protest community who believe that destructive violence is the only way to get their message across. This book is not for them—or then again, maybe it is.

The insights that resulted from our intervention pointed to the need for more research and theoretical development. In turn, delving into public order policing and protest crowd literature helped us to see what we did in the early years of the new millennium in a fresh light. Hence, the theoretical research is presented first in Part One and is grounded for the reader with examples from our experiences as well as the documented cases of others.

In Part I we introduce the key players in the drama of the protest crowd–police encounter. The dominant parties are protesters and police to be sure but the picture is not complete without introducing bystanders, media and the targets of protest—with each of these the plot thickens as conflicts become more complex. The conflict theories we use to make sense of conflict are applicable to all players in the various relational systems. We have chosen to alternate the introduction of the parties with the presentation of theoretical perspectives that help us understand emotions, scapegoating, power structures, and reciprocal violence. These conflict theories feed into a description of the mutual respect approach that concludes Part One and which we advocate as a vision for productive relationships between police and protesters.

The story of the challenge and how we responded is told in Part Two. The initial action took the form of training as an intervention and eventually participatory action research. The subject of the training was deep-rooted conflict, a concept that the participants applied to the context of protests. We collected data during seminars and this data informed our research. We interpreted our data through the lens of the conflict theories with which we are intimately familiar and have been presented in Part One. Thus the book is positioned right at the nexus of theory and practice. As such, it could be read in two ways—beginning with either Part One or Part Two.

Part Two begins by telling the story of our project, a series of process seminars that brought together representatives of the various stakeholder groups. We present our story as a case study that illustrates a model for the methodology we recommend. We examine the links between lessons learned through these events and subsequent development of ideas and understandings. Part Two goes on to give voice to representatives of the different groups as they share from their own perspective what is significant in the protester crowd–police dynamic. Finally, it suggests what can be done at the community level to build constructive relationships between police and protesters, drawing on the early portions of the intervention model.

The combination in one manuscript of comprehensive overviews of both protest and public order policing academic literature along with our practical application of interdisciplinary conflict theories is unique in the field.

Our Context: Rooted in Canada with a Global Perspective

We live and work in Canada, a country with a unique place in the global community. We are geographically adjacent to the United States, the most powerful nation in the world, with whom we share many cultural affinities and apart from whom we take pains to distinguish ourselves. We emerged out of the British Empire yet retain a viable French legacy making us a vital player in *la Francophonie*. We have an indigenous population that has preserved a complex mix of tradition, creativity, and cultural development, on the one hand, and struggled to overcome a legacy of forced assimilation and loss of land, on the other. As much as any other country we have welcomed immigrants from the global community and encouraged them to keep their customs and languages. Within our corporate psychological make-up, we bear the marks of both power and vulnerability, of victor and victimized. All these factors have shaped both what we protest about and how our police have evolved.

Though we cannot escape the specific context out of which we view the world, we hope that the present work will be useful in many societies. We have tremendous respect for the complexity of different cultures. Each culture looks at acts of protest differently. However, the world has shrunk and mimetic contagion does not respect the fine points of culture: protest and police practices are replicated globally. Moreover, the conflict theories that form the foundation of our work have been demonstrated to be useful to people from countries around the world.

Nothing can take the place of dignifying all individuals with the intrinsic value that accrues to them by being part of the human family. Nor is there a substitute for respect for the stories, imaginations and personal space of people. There is a blow to our collective well-being when people are designated as anything less than fully human. Stereotypes and disparaging language are the first tools of human atrocity. The bottom line message for protesters and police is that there has to be mutual dignity and respect. Within this context, we present an ethical vision of blessing that means that if relationships were framed such that parties would truly contribute to one another's well-being the world could become a better place. Dignity, respect, mutual blessing—the rest is truly commentary.

For some people, 'blessing' is a problematic word since it is associated with religious institutions and may not resonate positively with people. This is understandable; hence we will provide some background on the etymology of the word and how it is technically defined in this book. The English word 'blessing' translates Hebrew and Arabic words *berikah* and *barakat* respectively. These Semitic words connote the orientation, attitude and actions meant to enhance mutual well-being. We will use it to designate *the mutual concern for, and actions that reciprocally enhance the well-being of those within a relationship.* We find no other word works as well for the concept we wish to describe.[2]

We make reference throughout the manuscript to concepts of complexity and levels of consciousness. Both of these theories have been developed in interdisciplinary ways and we are just beginning to see how relevant they are to the issues talked about in this book. Complexity and chaos theory links us to broad systems theory that emphasizes our interconnectedness (Sword, 2003). The connections among us are so complex that we cannot think in linear cause and effect terms. Any action can set in motion a myriad of consequent actions and events. As soon as we do anything, the effects are out of our control. At certain times, there is a convergence of events such that one small action can have a huge impact. Richard McGuigan has shown us that those with a well developed level of consciousness are able to handle complex conflicts creatively (2003). We have great hope that these theories will bring clearer insights into the relationships associated with protest crowds, thus raising the level of consciousness and hence a capacity to prevent a spiral of destructive violence.

More than anything, it is our hope that the pages that follow will inspire the parties involved, in any country and any culture to get together for honest dialogue. There is nothing that takes the place of a free, open and honest flow of meaning. From the First Peoples of Canada we learn the importance of coming to dialogue with a good mind. They use the smoke of smoldering sweet grass, cedar, tobacco or sage to wash their minds so they think good thoughts, their ears so they hear good things, their mouths so they say what

---

2   For a complete discussion of the issues involved in using 'blessing' in this context see Vern Neufeld Redekop, 'Teachings of Blessing as Elements of Reconciliation: Intra- and Inter-Religious Hermeneutical Challenges and Opportunities in the Face of Violent Deep-Rooted Conflict,' in Mathieu E. Courville (ed.), *The Next Step in Studying Religion: A Graduate's Guide* (London: Continuum, 2007, 129–146).

will be constructive, their eyes that they will see what is important ... and so on. The emergent willingness to engage in dialogue with an open spirit is the beginning of creative understanding and mutually beneficial exchange. We know that this is not easy; distrust abounds along with memories of past hurts. The threat of an angry crowd and the bruises of batons leave emotional memories. By presenting brief histories of protest, crowds and policing and our analyses of theories that help understand their dynamics we hope to provide a framework and vocabulary that will enhance mutual respect.

PART ONE

Protest Crowd–Police Dynamics

Overview of Part One

Our first chapter examines what is at stake in protest crowd–police dynamics; namely, the character of the society in which they take place. In chapter two, we trace the evolution of protest crowds over the last two centuries. This entails separate analyses of protest and of crowds, including how perceptions of each have changed through time. This prepares us for an examination of the role of emotions in crowd dynamics in the chapter three. Chapter four introduces the police, providing a history of protest policing as it evolved with the Metropolitan Police of London, showing a convergence of policing trends in established democracies, and delving into some of the ethical issues raised by protest policing. We then take a theoretical step back from the immediate scene of protest in chapter five as we consider scapegoating and hegemonic structures as ways of comprehending a sense of 'otherness' in relational systems. In chapter six we introduce the remaining groups with a stake in protest crowd–police dynamics: targets of protest, bystanders and media. Chapter seven explores reciprocal violence drawing on the mimetic (imitation) theory of French thinker René Girard and chapter eight develops the concept of mutual blessing as it shows how a relational system can be structured so that the parties enhance each other's well-being. The combination of historical inquiry, introduction of stakeholders, and theoretical background will come together in chapter nine as we discuss three different paradigms of protester–police dynamics. These three paradigms will be presented as building on one another, with each successive paradigm representing another level of consciousness and a greater capacity to deal with complexity ending with the Mutual Respect paradigm or approach. Chapter ten looks at the relationships among protest crowds, police, and political leaders, situating the Mutual Respect approach within the context of evolving forms of democracy.

1. What is at Stake?

Images of tear gas, flying bricks, water cannons, Molotov cocktails, '"Darth Vader"[3] suits,' and balaclavas speak to the reality of violence in protester police dynamics in recent years. 'Diversity of tactics,' blockades, civil disobedience, snake marches, and, in the case of indigenous peoples, 'illegal' (from the Government perspective) logging and fishing indicate a powerful motivation on the part of protesters to do anything to announce and address perceived injustices. 'Less than lethal weapons' become part of the arsenal of police who may use 'soft hats' backed up by 'tactical squads' to reinforce cordons defined by fences or barricades; these may be used to corral and hold protesters for a time. The boundaries at the interface between police and masses of protesters are visibly physical; at the same time, they are at the edge of what is legal, culturally normative, and ethical within a democratic, or even proto-democratic, society.

This chapter sets examples of demonstrations from the recent past in the context of the impact of social movements on public order policing from as early as the eighteenth and nineteenth century. We outline some of the current challenges that show by example that the way protest crowds are treated reflects the society they represent. We conclude this chapter with an outline of underlying motivations and perceptions of those involved and the democratic way of life that is at stake should the protester–police conflict continue to escalate.

Since the 1960s, protest crowds have been significant agents of social change in modern times. They helped to convince Richard Nixon to pull the United States out of Viet Nam. They put environmental concerns on the political agenda and raised cautions about nuclear energy (Epstein, 1993). More recently, building on a sensitivity to social justice on the part of past generations and motivated by an awareness of social inequities exacerbated by market fundamentalist inspired globalization (Barlow, 2001; Soros, 2002), protest crowds shut down the Multilateral Agreement on Investment (MAI) talks of the World Trade Organization (WTO) in Seattle (Goodman, 2002; Paré, 2003). Since that event, anti-globalization protesters have been

---

3   Darth Vader was a character in the Star Wars series of movies; he wore dark protective gear that covered his whole body including his face. This term has been used by protesters to describe police riot gear.

present at major summit gatherings. Building on Gandhian teachings and the experiences of the 1960s and 80s they have used techniques of non-violent direct action (Boulding, 1999; Epstein, 1993; McAllister, 1999), including mass civil disobedience (Barlow, 2001; Epstein, 1993; Killam, 2001). Within countries that formed the former Warsaw Pact, protest crowds were key in bringing down communist regimes (Grix, 2000), and in the last decade protest crowds turned back corrupted elections in Serbia in 2000 (Joyce, 2002), Georgia, during the Rose Revolution, and Ukraine during the 2004 Orange Revolution. In all of these cases, police action has varied from repression with lethal weapons (even the National Guard killing students at Kent State University in the 1960s), to crowd control using an arsenal of less than lethal weapons (Redekop, Paré, 2001), to management of crowds using intelligence, public relations and planning, to laissez faire in the case of Serbian crowds who invaded government buildings in protest against Milosevic's election tactics.

Contemporary protest crowds have a pedigree that extends back to the eighteenth century when food riots in England and France (Bouton, 1993; Randall, 2000; Rudé, 1999) gave way to larger social movements (Klandermans, 1997) that shaped the American Revolution, the Industrial Revolution and the French Revolution. In 1829, with the passing of Robert Peel's 'Bill for Improving the Police' in and near the Metropolis of London, policing was developed in England, in part to reduce reliance on military force (Manwaring-White, 1983); since that time 'public order policing' or protest policing (Sopow, 2003) has been an on-going aspect of police work. In United States, the right to protest is so much valued that the First Amendment to the Constitution guarantees freedom of assembly and expression (Gora, Goldberger, Stern, & Halperin, 1991; M. Welch, 2000). In the 1860s and 70s, crowds were enough of an item that theorists Gabriel Tarde (1890) and Gustaf La Bon (1895) published theories about crowd behaviour, ascribing to crowds emotional, irrational behaviour (McPhail, 1991). Even Karl Marx weighed in on the subject (Hayes, 1992). The 20th century saw the emergence of the discipline of Sociology around collective behaviour and beginning in the 1960s trenchant critiques of the earlier theorists with the use of empirical methodologies (McPhail, 1991). Recent scholarship has provided more precise ways of looking at who is in protest crowds (McPhail, 1991; Sopow, 2003) and has invoked chaos and complexity theory to describe crowd dynamics (Sword, 2003).

At this time, we are at a critical juncture with regard to protest crowd–police relations in that there could be either a turn toward greater mutual violence or the evolution of attitudes and communication processes that would result in creative collaboration. The internet, facebook, twittering, and other e-communications make it possible to organize larger and more sophisticated protest crowds who can coordinate actions globally (Barlow, 2001; Deibert, 2002) and can in an instant bring out the masses locally, as was seen in protests following the 2009 election in Iran. The moral vision of protesters has exemplified higher levels of consciousness as they campaign for the well-being of others, including those with no voice or life-enhancing systems on which all of us depend (James, 2002; Jasper, 1997). New forms of political militancy are evolving, particularly among youth (Peterson, 2001). Vested interests of corporations and governments are vaster (Barlow, 2001; Soros, 2002) and yet more vulnerable than ever. Police capacites for management, coordination and intelligence gathering are greater, and the quality of their protective gear and range of less than lethal weapons have been on the increase. Perceptions of injustice are now global in scope since migrating populations have carried their conflicts with them and the internet provides first-hand reports of atrocities that are instantly available in most of the languages of the world.

How crowds are managed has a lot to do with the type of society we live in. Crowds have played an important part in the historical democratization of the social order and how they behave and are managed largely reflects the health of democracy in a country. The more democratic a society is, the more the right of assembly, protest and dissent is respected.

Historically, the action of crowds at key points has launched given societies on a whole new trajectory. Consider the crowds gathered in Boston in 1774 to protest what they considered were unjust changes in taxation of tea. The protesters complained about lower taxes on tea—the protest was organized by Boston's wealthy smugglers who stood to lose out because of Britain's reduction of import taxes on tea (Ferguson, 2002). Their action, emptying a ship's cargo of tea into the harbour, was a bifurcation point, in the language of complexity theory, as it marked the launch of the American Revolution resulting in the independence of the Thirteen Colonies from Britain and the formation of the United States of America.

Likewise, the French Revolution, which included crowd action in 1789, radically changed the power structure of French society. Gandhi's crowds in India helped his drive for independence from Britain. Closer in time, it was the action of crowds in the Philippines that helped to end the corrupt dictatorship of Marcos and those in East Germany that brought the Communist regime to an end.

On the other hand, how crowds have been managed has also had dramatic historical consequences. Consider the crowd gathered in Tiananmen Square pressing for democracy in China. The massacre and repressive measures ensured the continuation of Communist control over the population for years to come. Often the actions that are chosen to control a crowd can reflect the very injustice that the crowd is trying to communicate to the political leaders.

It is also possible that police go out of their way to facilitate the effective communication of protesters. During the G-8 Summit at Kananaskis, Alberta in 2002 police set up a store front office in Calgary to meet with protest organizers to facilitate communication. In many cities in Europe and North America, protest marches are planned with police. In some cases, plainclothes detectives, who are known to protest leaders, work together with organizers to solve practical problems.

There are many types of crowds; however, this book focuses on crowds gathered to protest a perceived injustice. The qualifier 'perceived' is not meant to cast doubt on whether the injustice is real or not; rather it signals the significance of perception as a motivator for those assembling to protest as well as the response by security authorities. The injustice may be as passing as how a referee made a call during a sports event or as far-reaching as the toxic impact of pollution on the global ecosystem. Perception is real in its consequences. The stakes of the issues at hand may threaten the way of life of millions.

Protesting crowds have their own dynamics. As we worked on the crowd project, we identified different groups that interacted with one another: activists organizing the crowd; the governments, institutions or businesses that are the focus of the protest; the security services that intervene; the media personnel who frame the issues and actions for the general public; the immediate bystanders whose property and personal safety is affected; and finally, society as a whole. The dynamics may involve violence, and violence always proceeds from and evokes emotional reactions. In our experience, in the case of many demonstrators, the motivating force is their frustration over the lack of acknowledgement of their concerns and issues, and the perception of a heavy-handed means of control. Police can be frustrated when a crowd does not respond to orders to move and when they sense they are caught in the middle between political leaders and angry crowds. As for the media, they may be frustrated by the lack of a good story and are often drawn to action that makes good visuals or a front-page story. Some protesters see the media as enemies; some police see the media as advocates of protesters. The immediate bystanders can feel victimized by the proximity to the demonstration and impact of it on their lives. Target groups look for protection and the freedom to conduct the business at hand without disruption.

When violence is introduced, it breeds more violence. As one activist put it, 'more tear gas, more rocks.' On the security side, the more rocks and Molotov cocktails that are thrown, the more gas is used to disperse the crowd. On both sides, violence is imitated and returned with interest. One police officer said, 'When aggression meets aggression you have to go all the way down that road, and you get an escalating response.' The dynamics of 'crowd control' can appear to support the interests of politicians, businesses or other groups who might benefit from conducting their business uninfluenced by those who disagree. Similarly, crowd organizers have their own interests, which are defined in relation to those activities they see as unjust. Everyone has a significant piece of the puzzle—an understanding and a role. There is mutual interest in working together and society, as a whole, must participate.

One activist pointed out to us that for those concerned about global issues, crowd–police dynamics are very much a side-show and then added that given media coverage as it is, 'the side show has become the main show.' The main show for her should be having a voice regarding global issues. From a different perspective, a government official asked, 'What makes protesters think that they (the activists) have a right to have a voice at a gathering of elected representatives?' Observations and questions like these show the need for concerned parties to sit down and talk.

Crowd dynamics are significant because the stakes are high. They involve life and death, public order, the quality of life within society, the legitimacy of institutions of governance, and ultimately the health and well-being of the planet for future generations.

This chapter has shown that protest crowds have affected the political agenda of democratically elected governments for centuries and continue to do so. The way crowds have been managed reflects the society they represent. As conflict between protesters and police escalates the political messages become secondary being taken over by the protester–police conflict itself. Effective protest is an essential part of a vibrant democracy. On the other hand, where there is capricious authoritarian rule or widespread corruption that extends even to the police, dissent and protest are violently repressed.

The next several chapters integrate our growing knowledge of protest with conflict theories illuminating the underlying deep-rooted conflict inherent in the violence witnessed in demonstrations. In revealing the deep-rooted conflict to the divergent stakeholders in our training sessions we provided a framework for dialogue and non-violent interaction that promised to both enhance the effectiveness of the protests and to reduce the need for reciprocal violence during demonstrations. This framework led to mutual understandings that spawned insights for all concerned. Some of these insights demanded further research for their validation. We are pleased to share the research results to date.

2. Introducing Protest Crowds

Protest crowds reflect a conjunction of acts of protest, not all of which involve crowds, and crowd dynamics, not all of which involve protest. As such, their activities are complex actions drawing on two converging histories of meaning-making activities, or drawing on the concepts of Bernard Lonergan, two social recurrence schemes. Since the primary focus of protest crowds is to protest, we will first present an analysis of why people protest; then we will examine crowd activity and how it has been understood. After looking at the phenomenon of protest crowds in general we will provide frameworks to analyze the moral consciousness of crowds, types of protest crowds, constituent sub-groups in crowds, and organizational factors involved in protest crowd behaviour. We will end this chapter with an overview of how crowds have been designated or identified concluding that they comprise complex systems which function at the edge of chaos.

Protest

The word 'protest' is derived from the Latin words *pro*—forth or before and *testis*—witness (Barnhart, 1971). A protest is a bold statement of what one has come to know; through time it has taken on the connotation that the bold statement is an objection to the status quo. An appropriate synonymous phrase would be 'expression of dissent.' The word 'dissent' has Latin roots, *dis* and *sentire*, that translate into 'thinking or feeling differently' (Barnhart, 1971); adding it to the verbal field of protest emphasizes that one role of protesters is to bring new thoughts and feelings to public discourse.

There are many forms of protest and dissent that do not involve crowds (Sunstein, 2003). Some of these are written (letters and e-mails), some take the form of a phone call or a private and discrete conversation, some are individual and public like a letter to the editor or an opinion expressed over the radio or by an individual at a public gathering (Sopow, 2003). Dissent may take the form of taking a position at variance with the dominant view. Protest may also take the form of a symbolic action like chaining oneself to a tree.

A protesting or dissenting crowd involves a collective bold statement that it objects to the policy or action of an individual or group that is the object or target of the protest. This protest takes place in a given context and the context includes a number of relational systems (Redekop, 2002). A relational system can be thought of as something that brings individuals or groups into contact with one another such that their interests are mutually affected. In the instance of a protesting crowd the following relational systems are part of the context:

protest crowd–target;

protest crowd–bystanders;

protest crowd–media;

protest crowd–protest crowd (where two crowds are on separate sides of an issue);

protest crowd–society; and

protest crowd–police.

If we take seriously Cass Sunstein's case that dissent enhances the quality and effectiveness of organizations and nations (2003), it becomes clear that within the broader context of the *protest crowd–society* relational system, the protesting crowd, by offering a dissident voice is enhancing the quality of life for the wider community. In this sense protest is in and of itself a good thing. Where this may not hold, is when the dissenting voice is deliberately misleading, false or inducing hatred against a segment of the population or if the very actions of the protesting crowd are violent and destructive, causing serious injury, death and significant damage.

The way in which protest or dissent adds to the quality of a relational system is not straightforward; sometimes the dissenting ideas point clearly to a better way; sometimes they point out dangers that have been overlooked; sometimes they unmask injustices, but in other instances their role is to get other parties to think creatively about how to address points raised by the protest.

Some scholars suggest that one of the conditions needed for people to engage in protest is that there is reason to believe that they will be effective in changing a given situation (Rucht, 1999; Sopow, 2003). While not denying that this is a significant factor, we would argue that there are three over-riding reasons that would motivate a protester even if the prospects for change would be dim.[4] First, the very act of protest gives voice to an inner sense that things are not right. It allows for the speaking of protesters' perception of the truth—their beliefs and knowledge shaped by their values. This gives the protester a sense of agency; it is one way to start taking action to change what is problematic. Jonathan Grix uses Albert Hirschman's framework of *conditional loyalty, exit,* and *voice* to analyze how protest crowds contributed to the breaking down of the Berlin Wall and the eventual dissolution of the German Democratic Republic (Grix, 2000). When people have a sense that all is not right and that the dominant public truth does not correspond to the table truth that they share within the niches of their friends, family or special communities, they may continue living without dissenting in a situation of *conditional loyalty,* meaning that they are loyal to the system within certain tolerable bounds. If the situation becomes intolerable they can either *exit* the society or they can give *voice* to the truth they perceive; in either case, they gain a sense of agency—in other words they find satisfiers for the identity need for action (Redekop, 2002). State repression of dissent during the era of the GDR meant that it took considerable courage to give voice to the truth and the consequences were severe; hence there was a high level of tolerance among the population for what was thought to be not right. Through an extraordinary coming together of events, conditional loyalties evaporated and protest crowds grew so quickly that the status quo was rapidly, completely and unalterably changed. In this case, a massive number of protesters built on the efforts of those who had chosen to give voice to the truth of what was wrong even when the prospects for change appeared remote.

Second, besides a need for agency, protesters take action in the face of insurmountable odds because of an overwhelming sense of injustice. Intolerable conditions dictate that *someone* has to *do something* about it (Sopow, 2003). The need for meaning is so strongly threatened (Redekop, 2002) that regardless of potential threats to personal security, people protest (Barlow, 2001).

---

4   This resonates with new social movement theory, which emphasizes that participants gain a sense of
     identity and belonging through their involvement in protest movements (Sopow, 2003).

Third, it may be that people have given up on prescribed ways of having political input and even though there are no guarantees of success, protest actions are seen as a more likely way of having an impact than through traditional means. Abby Peterson points out that

> [y]oung people are pushed to the margins of power within society— prohibited from speaking as moral and political agents. They are restricted from speaking in those spheres where public deliberation shapes social policy and refused the power to make knowledge consequential with respect to their own individual and collective needs. (Peterson, 2001)

Peterson goes on to show how this feeling of marginalization contributes to militant protests. Peter Joyce frames protest crowd activity as one aspect of extra-parliamentary political action. He puts this into the context of extremely low voter turnout reflecting a sense that voting will make little difference in the situation (Joyce, 2002).

These three conditions—need for agency, intolerable injustice, and the futility of other means of having a voice—point to motivations derived from the interior dynamics of protesters at the individual and collective levels. These complement the exterior side of the reality expressed in the desire to make a difference, that is, a difference that can be observed.[5] Having looked at the protest crowd through the lens of protest, let us now look at it from the perspective of crowds.

Crowds

There are numerous categories of crowds, or to use the preferred designation of Clark McPhail, temporary gatherings (McPhail, 1991). These include sports crowds, crowds gathered for cultural events, crowds watching a spectacle, crowds gathered for recreation, and the list goes on. We are referring in this book to temporary gatherings for the sake of protest. More particularly we are referring to protest crowds that are large and significant enough to involve a police presence and where there is a potential for a violent confrontation. That means that over 90% of crowd activity is outside the purview of this book.

---

5   The interior–exterior distinction is based on integral approach of Ken Wilber (2001).

When it comes to large, significant protest crowds, there are two different paradigms that emerge. The paradigms can be examined by way of three mutually reinforcing axes:

Collectivity	Individuals
Emotional	Deliberate
Riff-Raff	Responsible

Gustaf LeBon was the most popular of crowd theorists from 1895 until the 1920s, with his influence continuing well beyond that time (McPhail, 1991). He argued, using concepts from the left end of these axes, that when people joined a crowd, they lose their individuality as they are transformed into anonymous parts of a larger collective (Le Bon, [1986]1930). Given the anonymity of the crowd, people do things that they would never do individually or in a situation where they might be recognized. This collective, made up primarily of the riff raff of society, he argued, is emotional; he likened it to an hysterical woman, with all that that meant in Freudian Europe. There is no real rationality. The crowd, he said, wants a strong leader in the same way as an hysterical woman wants a strong man. There is evidence that Hitler and Mussolini were strongly influence by LeBon and patterned their leadership of crowds after his writings (Hayes, 1992; King, 1990; Rogers, 1998). The crowd, in this paradigm is subject to a contagion whereby everyone acts together to do the same thing. They work together in a way such that various functional activities—unfurling banners, chanting, charging a police line, lying down and 'playing dead'—contribute to the same end. LeBon-inspired discourse about crowds introduced the concept of 'mob' for which the concept of mindless action was even stronger. Politically the designation of protest crowds as mobs made up of thoughtless people at the bottom of society was used to discredit the actions of protest crowds (Hayes, 1992).

Since the early 1960s this paradigm of crowds and crowd action has been systematically attacked by historians and sociologists using empirical methodologies. George Rudé in his classic work, *The Crowd in History: A Study of Popular Disturbances in France and England, 1730–1848*, shows, using prison records of the eighteenth century, that participants in protest crowds of that era who were arrested were not the irresponsible riff-raff that theoreticians had suggested but rather they were working people and artisans—people with a stake in society (Rudé, 1999). Clark McPhail, in his *Myth of the Madding Crowd* systematically dismantles the LeBon perspective and the permutations of that paradigm propagated by Robert Park and Herman Blumer (McPhail, 1991). After observing hundreds of protest crowds in the 1970s and 1980s he argues that people do not join protest crowds as anonymous individuals, rather they go to the crowd gatherings with family and friends, they talk with one another in the process and they preserve their sub-groupings throughout the process. Likewise he shows that they are deliberate about joining the crowd and that they continue to make thoughtful choices about what they do during process. Nor are their motivations to protest all the same.

Using a quantitative methodology, Eli Sopow goes further than McPhail in differentiating the various types of crowd participants. He distinguishes among passive protesters who support a cause by signing petitions, using the Internet and writing letters; active protesters, who attend peaceful protests; and volatile protesters who support illegal action and are 'inclined to engage in violent action such as destruction of public property, attacks on police, and the use of ideologically-laden, pejorative language such as calling police "pigs." ' (Sopow, 2003) This latter group forms a tiny minority of protest crowd members; however, in some circumstances their actions may be imitated by others. Similarly Bert Klandermans describes a funnel effect with a logical flow chart showing how only some of the sympathizers of a movement are targeted by mobilization attempts; only some of these are motivated to participate; and only some of these actually participate (Klandermans, 1997).

The two paradigms need not be mutually exclusive. It may be true that people decide to join a protest crowd in the deliberate manner described by McPhail, Klandermans and Sopow. It may also be the case that in the course of a large and major protest event there may be sub-dynamics whereby clusters of participants get carried away in collective action and do things they might not otherwise do. Ken Wilber argues for an integral approach to understanding phenomena (Wilber, 2001). He describes two intersecting axes forming four quadrants. The horizontal axis is between individual (above the axis) and collective (below); the vertical divides interior(left of the axis) aspects of phenomena from exterior aspects (to the right). For him, an integral approach includes looking at things from the perspective of all four quadrants. Crowd analysis, from the perspective of *exterior*-individual, would include the perspective of empiricists like McPhail and Rudé. The *exterior* collective perspective would include Le Bon and Canelli both of whom also try to grasp the collective *interior* using a methodology akin to psychoanalysis. Individual and collective *interior* perspectives come from Maude Barlow and Tony Clark who write from within the protest movement and theorists like James Jasper and Eli Sopow who explore the inner emotional and ethical factors that motivate members of protest crowds. From Wilber's (and many others') perspective, the individual and collective interior 'spaces' will give rise to multiple meanings and interpretations with respect to the crowd members' understandings of the protest issues. That is, different individuals in the crowd will have different reasons for being there and those observing the crowd will have different views of what they perceive are the primary issues driving the crowd action. Given the complex assortment of motivating ideas, a given crowd is vulnerable to manipulation by more sophisticated meaning makers, who have their own agendas and may be able to use symbols with broad appeal within the crowd to intensify emotions.

In addition, even though people may choose to join a large protest crowd deliberately, in the course of the temporary gathering there may be extraordinary circumstances that prompt a limited group of crowd members to get carried away in collective action. René Girard has developed a theory of scapegoating whereby, when things are chaotic, violence is in the air, and there is the potential for reciprocal violence, a community or crowd can decide on a scapegoat and vent all their pent up frustration on the scapegoat (Girard, 1989). This he describes as violence of differentiation (more on this in chapter five). Various crowd theorists show how protests can become focused on particular individuals about whom the crowd becomes united; they become scapegoats responsible for the ills of their community (Gonzales, 2001). Hence, without embracing fully the perspectives of Le Bon, we can envisage sub-groups within a crowd getting involved in violent collective action. One example is when a group within a volatile crowd comes across an empty police car and gets carried away in its destruction. This perspective complements the observations of Deborah Sword who argues that protest crowds exist at the edge of chaos (Sword, 2003). When crowds are at the edge of chaos, there may be a number of ways in which that chaos produces a new alternative. One of those may be through shared violence, another may be through the positive response of the target, another may be through factors that contribute to disassembling. The chaos itself creates many options over which there is little real control by any of the players. Small responses may have large consequences.

Protest crowds assemble because members are convinced that there is either something wrong with the status quo or there is a potential change in the works that they find untenable—in either case there is *something* to protest. They may not agree about what exactly that 'something' is but they are in sufficient agreement to be at the same place at the same time. Frequently, this *something that is wrong* is framed as an injustice (Klandermans, 1997; Sopow, 2003) invoking values derived from moral consciousness (Jasper, 1997). We turn now to an examination of the types of moral consciousness that might motivate people to temporarily gather to protest.

Moral Consciousness

Within the literature on protest crowds, moral consciousness is approached in a variety of ways. James Jasper argues that through history various types or levels of moral consciousness have been present. After examining Jasper's categorization and taking a brief look at oppositional consciousness, we will make the connection between types of moral consciousness, stages of development and levels of consciousness as developed by scholars such as Kegan, Wilber, Piaget, Kohlberg, Gilligan and others. At this point we are concerned with moral consciousness as a motivator for protesters; we will return to the concept of levels of moral consciousness in subsequent chapters as we relate the concept to conflict between protesters and police.

James Jasper distinguishes three types of moral consciousness that motivate protest: deprivation of immediate needs, a demand for citizenship rights, and a desire for justice for third parties. These have evolved, from Jasper's perspective, chronologically. From the mid 1700s on there were widespread protests over the price of basic foods in England and France, often referred to as the Flour Wars (Bouton, 1993). In this case people were directly affected by the policy that they protested against. Not only that, they were affected at the level of physical survival, they were not able to get enough to eat. They felt that not only were the prices not fair, but they had a right to get enough food at affordable prices. What started back then was a concept of moral economy—economic life[6] was starting to be held accountable to a moral standard, a concept that continued to evolve (Randall, 2000). With the industrial revolution came the realization that working people collectively were not getting fair treatment; Jasper's second type of moral consciousness emerged around citizens' rights. Out of this realization came the labour movement and the use of collective action to get rights for working people. There was also a demand for increasingly inclusive suffrage. In England throughout the nineteenth century more and more people got to vote as a result of changes prompted by effective protest (P.A.J. Waddington, 1991). As there was a realization that groups of people had rights that were not recognized, members of these groups used public protest to affect change. An example of Jasper's citizenship protest was the civil rights movement in the United States during the 1960s. His third type of moral protest involves such things as anti-nuclear protest, environmental protest, animal rights protest, and disarmament protest. In each of these cases it is not so much that the particular needs or interests of protesters themselves are threatened but that the rights and interests of wider populations and even the ecosphere are threatened.

Corroborating Jasper's thesis, Mansbridge and Morris develop the concept of oppositional consciousness (Mansbridge & Morris, 2001). They describe the dynamics by which an oppressed group becomes aware of the sources and forms of their oppression. Out of this consciousness comes a desire to work for change and this frequently results in protest crowd activity. This theoretical structure they apply to people with disabilities and sexual minorities. The concept could be extended to show that those who develop an oppositional consciousness, which is characterized by a capacity for critical thinking, will find themselves in solidarity with those oppressed for another reason (Cummings, 1993). Examples are the WTO and G8[7] protests that include a wide range of causes from 'save the whales' to 'gay rights'.

---

6   Economic life is the outcome of moral growth—moral growth is influenced by economic life—it is a dialectical process. It is, also, a developmental process.

7   The Group of Eight G8, and formerly the G6/7 or Group of Six/Seven, is a forum, created by France in 1975, for governments of eight nations of the northern hemisphere to deal with major economic and political issues facing their domestic societies and the international community as a whole: Canada, France, Germany, Italy, Japan, Russia, the United Kingdom, and the United States; in addition, the European Union is represented within the G8, but cannot host or chair. 'G8' can refer to the member states or to the annual summit meeting of the G8 heads of government.

Building on Jasper's concept of a third type of moral consciousness, we would suggest that the idea of protesting for the interest of some Other could be further differentiated between third party concern for victimized groups, animal species or a specific endangered forest or waterway, on the one hand, and systemic consciousness, on the other. Just as protesters in the 1980s saw the potential of global destruction in the event of a nuclear war, protesters in the 1990s and beyond have seen the potential of widespread injustice and destruction through what is loosely referred to as globalization. Their moral imperative to turn things around comes from an awareness of systems dynamics and the realization that what happens in one part of the world can have dramatic consequences in another area of the world (Barlow, 2001). What drives many of these protesters is a passion to care for the earth and all its people and living species. Among the protesters may be a range of types of moral consciousness in that both their awareness of what is happening and the interconnections may be structured differently.

Interestingly, when we look back in history from the perspective of types of moral consciousness it becomes clear that Jasper's third type of moral consciousness was already evident in 1787 when a group of 12 men assembled in London to organize a protest movement against slavery and the slave trade. They had a third party empathetic interest in others and they had a concept of systemic injustice that led them to organize their protest strategically, in many geographical locations. The passion of their convictions was so strong and infectious that they sustained their protest efforts for several decades until the British slave trade was brought to an end (Hochschild, 2005). With these examples in mind, we can see how the discourse around Jasper's types of moral consciousness can be understood within the broader context of developmental levels of consciousness.

Levels of Consciousness

The concept of levels of consciousness emerged from developmental psychology. Initial studies of children's cognitive and moral development led to insights that adults have a capacity to think at different levels. We move from a pre-occupation with our own survival, to a concern for those who are part of our group (ethnic, religious, national), to toleration for plurality, to a sense of being connected to everyone and everything, to a profound grasp of transcendence in which reality is seen as a unified whole. As we develop capacity at ever new levels of consciousness, we still plug into all of the other levels at the same time.

At each level of consciousness we can experience the same event differently because we create different meanings for what is happening (McGuigan, 2006). We notice different patterns, see different linkages, and include different perspectives in how we explain and integrate what is happening.

Levels of consciousness can be used with regard to individuals and groups. In this case, a protest crowd might have people functioning at different levels of consciousness. They may be united in protesting a given action but their reasons for protesting, their understanding of the issues, and their sense of where the protest fits into an overall strategy might vary considerably. Likewise, police and others implicated in crowd dynamics could function individually at varying levels of consciousness.

This conceptualization builds on theoretical work by Kegan, Wilber, Piaget, Kohlberg, Gilligan, and a host of other scholars. More recently, Richard McGuigan has contributed to our sense of the relevance of levels of consciousness thinking to the domain of community-based conflict of which the protester–police relational system is just one example. Through careful research he demonstrated that when confronted with complex conflict, those with a well-developed level of consciousness can handle the situation creatively. Those who do not have this capacity are overwhelmed and actually revert to a lower level of thinking (McGuigan, 2006). The dynamics between protesters, their targets, police, media and bystanders can be very complex. There is the temptation for many of the players to revert to an angry tribalism in which they think only in terms of the rightness of their own groups. This suggests that the moral reasoning behind the impetus for a protest crowd to assemble may be at any of a number of levels of moral consciousness and that the level of consciousness of members in the crowd may also be at any of a number of levels of development. This further suggests that there may be many types of crowds and, indeed, our experiences support characterizing crowds according to several dynamics.

Types of Crowds

The following analytical spectra provide a starting point for looking at the dynamics of any particular crowd. The different sides of the polarity need not be mutually exclusive. For example, a well planned, orderly protest march may become chaotic and violent when the way is blocked or when those with another agenda within the crowd assert themselves. Or there may be a crowd with characteristics in the middle of each axis.

Types of Crowds

Analytical Spectra

Orderly		Chaotic
Peaceful	Non Violent Direct Action	Violent
Planned		Spontaneous
Cohesive		Fractured

These spectra help to analyze a particular crowd at a particular time. The same crowd might be at different ends of the spectrum regarding the different polarities. For example, it may be orderly, yet violent, gathered for protest in a well-planned manner and very cohesive. Another crowd could be the opposite—chaotic, yet peaceful; spontaneous, yet cohesive. Additionally, the crowd can change dramatically over time, notwithstanding that the same individuals or some of the same individuals may be present. How this happens and what influences both the behaviours and changes in behaviour requires an understanding of underlying emotions and needs, concepts we cover in chapter five. Furthermore, the impact of needs and emotions on behaviour is determined in part by the level of consciousness of those involved.

Some crowds demonstrate a sense of order and peaceful presence. For example the crowds holding vigils in several Eastern European countries in the twilight period of the Soviet Empire were massive, yet highly self-disciplined with scarcely a trace of violence. People gathered to show by their presence that they wanted change. Other crowds are boisterous and chaotic in which everything seems out of control; one example is the crowd in Belgrade in 1997 that brought down Milosevic as it stormed into government offices, doing considerable damage. Some crowds gather spontaneously and some are planned months in advance with buses taking demonstrators to the crowd site. Sometimes crowds are cohesive and sometimes they contain sub-groups very much at odds with one another. Peaceful protesters usually try to distance themselves from those who believe that violence is necessary to make their point or who participate purely for the violence itself. There is also a stream within the protest crowd movement that draws on Gandhi and Martin Luther King, Jr. to advocate non-violent direct action. Direct action involves a combination of a dedication to truth and justice, the discipline to take provocative action without being drawn into violence, and the creativity to know what kind of action might have strategic value. People in the same crowd may be protesting for completely different reasons and may be committed to different tactics. Those with the same reasons may differ on tactics and those using the same tactics may be doing so for different reasons. The many permutations make for a complex situation.

Certain types of crowds recur and a crowd culture develops with similar actions becoming anticipated for that crowd. Crowd cultures have developed around summit gatherings as the same organizers prepare for each subsequent event. This does not mean each event is the same; rather, similar types of actions tend to recur. This similarity may or may not be deliberate; however, routines and values evolve with lessons learned and networks of communication used to pass on the elements that comprise a particular crowd culture. For example, those who have experienced 'routine' demonstrations in repressive regimes report that there is often an expectation that the demonstration will become violent, this violence is anticipated by everyone involved and the scene plays out as if there was a script. In some countries, the use of horses, water cannon, and even ammunition can become the norm and an expected part of participating in a demonstration. Some demonstrators are willing to risk dying for their cause. On one occasion, pro-Palestinian demonstrators in The Hague, Netherlands were seen laughing at being chased by police on horseback. Bystanders at the same scene ranged from being disinterested to being downright afraid. Many protesters went to the Summit of the Americas in Quebec (April, 2001) fully prepared for pepper spray. Others who had experienced only peaceful protest were overwhelmed when tear gas and water cannon were used as a means of crowd control.

Protest crowds assemble because there is a passion, mild or wild, driving people to make a statement that all is not right with the status quo or that proposed changes are not desirable. In other words, there is a difference of opinion about what should be done for the public good. Where there has been sustained commitment to a cause, protest crowds have played a major role in initiating social change. Protest groups like the Chartists[8] of nineteenth century

---

8   The Chartists represented working class English who petitioned and demonstrated for electoral re-
     form. Their Charter failed to gain the support of the Parliament—it posed a threat to the self-interests
     of those in power—and failed to get the support of the middle classes who were content with the
     status quo. Nonetheless, it was a powerful force that resulted in an increased awareness of social

Figure 2.1 Sub-groups within Protest Crowds

England, while they did not succeed in the short run, over subsequent decades succeeded in getting all but one of their proposed reforms enacted. Changes such as those of the Chartists have moved society in the direction of social justice, increased suffrage, and new levels of democratic fairness. In contrast, protest crowds like those organized by National Socialists[9] in the 1920s and 1930s paved the way to a repressive regime. Since the 1980s, protest crowds have played a significant role in regime change (e.g. former Warsaw Pact countries, Philippines). In still other venues, professional crowd organizers have managed to put environmental concerns on the global agenda.

Protest Crowd Sub-Groups

Protest crowds are not homogeneous. The following diagram indicates three different sub-groups within a protest crowd. Each of these, in turn have sub-groups within them.

At the centre in the diagram above (Figure 2.1) are those concentrating on protesting against what they believe to be injustices—they tend to be the mainstream activist groups. They are the reason why there is a crowd there in the first place. Some people on the periphery in the diagram concentrate on violence and others are simply there for moral support. However, it is not that simple. Among the active demonstrators are those who are full-time staff people working for organizations focused on environmental, human

issues and created a framework for future working-class organisations. The People's Charter contained the following objectives:
- Universal suffrage for all men over the age of 21
- Equal-sized electoral districts
- Voting by secret ballot
- An end to the need for a property qualification for Parliament (so that constituencies could return the man of their choice, rich or poor)
- Pay for members of Parliament
- Annual election of Parliament

9   Refers primarily to the ideology of the *Nationalsozialistische Deutsche Arbeiterpartei* (*National Socialist German Workers Party*, or NSDAP) under Adolf Hitler.

rights or other social justice issues. There are people working on logistics, organization, protest methods, and communications. Labour unions, religious organizations, community cooks and volunteer community medical teams may be part of the protesting group. Many volunteers become part of the networks supporting activist organizations. Another group within the crowd consists of individuals, not formally members of any organization, but with passionate feelings about the issue. There may also be visitors from other countries who fall into the same groups—professional organizers, members of networks, and independently concerned citizens—and who may join the demonstration.

Most, but not all, crowd participants are peaceful. Among those demonstrators with violent intent there are generally four types. There are activists who at one time were committed to non-violence but who found non-violent means ineffective at communicating to either their targets or through the media to the general population. These people feel that the causes for which they are fighting are so significant that drastic means are necessary to produce results. There are also people who call themselves anarchists, a word derived from the Greek word for 'no rulers.' Anarchists range from those who believe in a Utopia, with no laws or rulers, to those who wish to violently overthrow the existing order. One grandmother activist attending one of our sessions described herself as an anarchist and distinguished her brand of anarchism from some of the others. She told us about having talked with some of the youth Black Bloc[10] anarchists and saw them as marginalized young people who feel isolated and want to be part of a tight family of activists. The following quotes from this group provide some sense of their perspective:

'Black bloc' is not an organization but a tactic that is historically rooted in the militant anti-fascist movements of Europe ...

The wearing of black clothes and facemasks is a major strategy in black bloc tactics. The aesthetic is a rejection of materialism and the lure of consumer glorification. In tactical terms, wearing black as a group or

---

10   A **black bloc** is an affinity group that comes together during some sort of demonstration, or other event involving class struggle or anti-globalization. Members wear all black. Black clothing and masks are used to make the bloc appear to be one large mass, promote solidarity, create a clear revolutionary presence (usually associated with anarchism), and also to avoid being identified by authorities. Black blocs are differentiated from other anti-globalist groups by their routine use of vandalism and property destruction to bring attention to their opposition to multi-national corporations and the support perceived to be enjoyed by these companies from Western governments.

a block means that we all look the same, making it harder for police to target individuals. It also provides us with some personal safety in the face of potentially violent police troops ...

People who criticize politically motivated property destruction as violent must think broken windows can feel pain and scream like people do when they are shot with rubber bullets ... As anarchists, we do not advocate mindless destruction, and we simply ask that the movement be open to a diversity of tactics. (Warcry, 2001)

A third group of people comprises those who are fascinated by violence for its own sake. A fourth element is made up of those who like the rush of being a part of a violent mob—the opportunistic violent. They think of it more as an excuse for a big party or a big riot. Whatever the motivation for violence, those who use it believe that their actions are legitimate in the circumstances.

Sometimes *agents provocateurs,* who feel it is in their interests for a crowd to be violent—either to make a point or to discredit a crowd—stir up violence within a crowd; those predisposed toward violence are susceptible to this. This phenomenon is particularly acute in a corrupt democracy where any means needed are used to keep a certain group in power. Where there are protests against the corruption, if they can prompt a crowd to become violent, it becomes illegitimate and police action against the crowd is justified. In this situation, for a crowd to be effective it needs training in non violence, internal security to surround and contain the *agents provocateurs*, and effective witnesses.

Among the peacefully intentioned, the moral supporters may have some relationship with the activist protesters or they may feel that generally the activists deserve support. Some just come out of curiosity. They may be friends and relatives of protesters or people who heard about the crowd action on the news and feel that they should be there to support the cause. There may be grandparents coming with their young grandchildren.

The dynamics of the demonstration can result in people shifting from one group to another in response to their experiences. Repressive security measures may prompt some activists, committed to non-violence, into a violent frame of mind. What moral supporters see and hear might make activists of them. Bystanders may even get caught up in the experience and become violent. On the other hand, violence on the part of fellow protesters might also discourage some activists from being part of the crowd, not wanting to be identified with particular tactics.

The mimetic theory of René Girard helps to understand these dynamic shifts. As he demonstrates through countless examples, people have a tendency to imitate the desires of others. In the case of those who join in the violence, we can understand it as mimetic contagion. People want to belong, they want the same sense of justice to be done and they want to join in the excitement. There may also be mimetic rivalries that develop between sub-groups within crowds. (Chapter seven provides a succinct overview of mimetic theory in the context of crowd dynamics.)

In addition to the activist demonstrators, violent protesters and moral supporters described above, there is another potential group involved in protest crowds, namely, outside instigators. In some instances, the State may encourage violent crowd action against a targeted group. For example, *Kristallnacht* or The Night of Broken Glass, was a massive, coordinated attack on Jews, organized by the Nazis, throughout the German Reich in 1938. On November 9, mob violence broke out as the regular German police stood by and crowds of spectators watched that night and all the next day as Jewish homes and businesses had their windows broken and goods stolen. Other examples are repressive regimes that use crowds to target minorities and political opponents.

The various groups may come together spontaneously but in instances of major protest crowds they are generally well organized.

Organization

Organization is essential to mounting a significant public protest. If we think of protest as 'boldly speaking out a truth, belief or ideal to which one is a witness,' for there to be a large protest crowd a shared truth must come from somewhere. A communication system enables participants to first share and refine a protest message and then share the knowledge that at a given time and place there will be a temporary gathering.

To borrow terms from Grix, protest crowds may be single niche or multiple niche (Grix, 2000). People from a given niche who decide to engage in protest activity become an affinity group. Unions or identity groups (e.g. based on ethnonationalism, a disease or disability) often find themselves as single niche protest groups. People basically know one another; there is a shared history and shared understandings about the reality they are addressing (e.g. farmers driving their tractors to Parliament Hill or truckers massing their trucks on a given highway). On broad issues like globalization or a protest against a war, there may be multiple niche communities involved. Trade unionists, pacifists, development Non-Governmental Organizations, environmentalists, 'Third World' solidarity groups, and anarchists may all join in a single protest (Barlow, 2001). Each of these has its own web-sites and e-mail distribution lists. Each is connected to an international web of similar groups. There may be an intersecting of relationships, since there are shared values between different groups. Just as a word of mouth rumour about a protest spread from household to household in the 1700s, e-mail messages, facebook entries and twitter quickly spread from one group to another with great speed (Deibert, 2002).

In the case of a major protest planned around a specific event involving thousands of people, logistics are extremely important. Organizations with paid staff assign professional crowd organizers to deal with many aspects of protest events. Unions and other groups have marshals whose job it is to keep order within a protest. Food, medical support, transportation and contingency planning are all important. Non violent training sessions may be organized in advance.

In a composite protest, a unique form of organization has evolved that introduces the institution of the spokescouncil. Protesters are organized according to affinity groups, which may be clustered together or may have within them clusters (Barlow, 2001; Epstein, 1993). Each affinity group has what they refer to as a 'spokes,' a person designated to speak for the group. Decisions to be made about a large crowd protest are made by a spokescouncil which is comprised of 'spokes' from the different affinity groups. Decisions are made by consensus. Some affinity groups constantly rotate their 'spokes' in the interest of keeping the organization non-hierarchical. However, social movements that provide continuity for on-going protest efforts will nurture the development of, and connection to high-profile leaders who can give credibility to their effort.

Eli Sopow shows the importance of organizational factors in generating an effective protest movement. The seven organizational factors Sopow identified are 1) news media exposure, 2) group unity, 3) protest experience,

4) high-profile spokesperson, 5) flexibility and willingness to compromise, 6) good funding, and 7) effective use of e-mail and web (Sopow, 2003). These factors represent a current reality in which large scale protests are organizationally sophisticated. Given the organizational sophistication of many protest crowd organizations, it is clear that much of the true management of crowds is done by the organizers. No matter how they are organized and managed, they are perceived in ways that calls up certain designations which, in turn, impact on the relations with those that they interact.

Designation of Protest Crowds

When it comes to the protest crowd–police relational system, many of the dynamics revolve around the question of the legitimacy of the protest crowd. This in turn depends on the language that is used to designate temporary gatherings of those voicing dissent. Language is important in shaping paradigms, establishing stereotypes, and influencing attitudes and emotions. It is also instructive that the designation of protest crowds has its own history, as does the analysis of such designations. For all these reasons, we think it necessary to present the following analysis. (Note that we have recalled details from previous sections to illustrate the power and significance of the rhetorical devices involved.)

How are protest crowds enframed; that is, how do we determine who is included within a temporary gathering? What language is used to describe what constitutes mass protest activity? And how are the actions interpreted? The latter half of the nineteenth century and early twentieth century saw the beginning of theoretical work being done on crowds, generating ideas that were to impact the thought and action of such people as Hitler and Mussolini. The scholarship on crowds and protest has grown significantly in recent decades. Throughout history, language used for groups of protesters has included the following: mob, crowd, unorganized aggregation, public, masses, protesters, the people, dissidents, extra-parliamentary political actors, political militants, or those giving expression to an oppositional consciousness.

Peter Hayes argues that crowd designations have been ideologically driven with people from different polarities of the political spectrum using value-driven language to either deprecate dissenting demonstrators or give legitimacy to the 'voice of the people.' The tendency to use value laden language goes back at least to the 1700s when

> the mob was typically depicted not as a wicked, unproductive minority but rather as the majority of the population. This depiction drew on the classical picture of the mob as the *mobile vulgus*, the unstable common people. (Hayes, 1992)

Rudé, in the same vein distinguishes between two stereotypes: the actors are the 'people' in the discourse of liberals, the 'mob' or 'rabble' in the rhetoric of conservatives. Both 'present the crowd as a disembodied abstraction and not as an aggregate of men and women of bless and blood.' (Rudé, 1999)

The contrast between the 'wicked unproductive minority' in the mob and the 'virtue and productivity of the majority' throughout most of the nineteenth century, argues Hayes, even though the identification of the actors is largely false, shows the ideological importance of the designation. (Hayes 16–17) It was in this context that Gustaf Le Bon did his psychological analyses on crowd action, taking up the assumptions of the conservative side of the ideological split.

Le Bon argued that crowds diminished the rational capacity of its members making each a primitive, emotional being.

> Among the special characteristics of crowds there are several—such as impulsiveness, irrationality, incapacity to reason, the absence of judgement and of the critical spirit, the exaggeration of the sentiments ... —which are almost always in beings belonging to inferior forms of evolution—in women ... for instance (Le Bon, [1986]1930).

The perspectives of Le Bon, expressed in a context of preserving an establishment against those pushing for change, were appropriated by Hitler and used to rally the masses—first against the Weimar Republic and then in support of the Third Reich. Hayes, who reveals Hitler's dependence on Le Bon, gives the following example:

> The masses, Hitler argued, were like women: 'so feminine by nature and attitude that sober reasoning determined their thoughts and

actions far less than emotion and feeling.' ... Hitler added that just as a woman 'would rather bow to a strong man than dominate a weakling, ... the masses would love a commander more than a petitioner and feel inwardly more satisfied by a doctrine, tolerating no other beside itself, than by the granting of liberalistic freedom.' (Hayes, 1992)

In this case the crowd is designated as 'the masses' and the root metaphor of 'woman' is attached to it. In that era in which Freudian stereotypes abounded, the use of 'woman' in relation to a crowd as collective, made it something to be controlled and manipulated—not in the contemporary sense of crowd control from the outside but rather controlled through emotional language of solidarity. Hitler deliberately presented himself as a strong figure who would woo the crowds with his authoritative rhetoric.

Continuing in the German context, a half century later, crowds played a crucial role in bringing down the Communist regime of East Germany. Here again, the discursive structures around crowd designation played a key role. As the government responded with force against the demonstrators the confrontations

> were described by the communists as the confrontation between the mob and the people. Thus, the state press agency said of the demonstrations of October 7–8, 1989: 'The violence caused by hooligans who were provoked by the international media was stopped by the People's Police and order was restored ...'

> The response of the protesters was to reject their designation as the mob by affirming the opposite. Thus, the protestors in East Germany chanted, 'We are the people! We are the people!' at the police. Similarly in Romania, where Ceausescu had branded the protesters as 'hooligans,' they sang: 'We're the people. Down with the dictator.' (Hayes, 137–8)

In this case, the designation of the crowd became the fulcrum on which rested the legitimacy of protesters or police, particularly in a context in which 'people' as a root metaphor carried a positive, legitimating, moral valence.

Peter Joyce locates protesters within a broader field of extra-parliamentary political activity that includes action by individuals or groups who 'feel that reliance on conventional activity will not secure for them the changes they seek.' (Joyce, 1) Extra parliamentary protest activity includes demonstrations, direct action—economic sanctions, civil disobedience, physical obstruction—and counter-cultural forms of protest, including occupation of what is perceived to be common land. (Joyce, 16–21) Related is Jane Mansbridge's placement of protest activities in the field of oppositional consciousness (Mansbridge & Morris, 2001).

What becomes clear is that the designation of 'crowd' phenomena is not only a psychological and political issue, it is very much a matter of identity. For example, Abby Peterson's research on political militancy shows that for certain groups of young people in Europe—on both left and right ends of the political spectrum—militant action-resistance becomes the centre of their identity and focal point of everyday existence (Peterson, 2001). One unifying theme is that emotion and rationality are woven together within individual participants in protest actions and at the collective level of group dynamics. Given the developmental nature of identity, within one crowd the relationship between crowd participation and the identity of each person can vary considerably.

Much of the theorizing on crowds was based on a stereotypic notion of who might be involved. Hipppolyte Taine used the following words to describe those in the mob of the French Revolution: 'idlers, libertines, professional gamblers, parasites, veterans of vice and crime, the rabble of the town.' (Hayes, 1992, 4, quoting Taine, 125–26) Karl Marx described the same mob as

> decayed roués with dubious means of subsistence and of dubious origin, … ruined and adventurous offshoots of the bourgeoisie, … vagabonds, discharged souiers, discharged jailbirds, escaped galley slaves, rogues, mountebanks, lazzaroni, pickpockets, tricksters, gamblers, maquereaus, brothel keepers, porters, literati, organ-grinders, rag pickers knifegrinders, tinkers, beggars. (Hayes, 1992, 5, quoting Marx, 149)

Similar uncomplimentary descriptions can be found of crowds in eighteenth and nineteenth century Britain. Rudé, as was pointed out above, based his research on the occupations of those arrested and those who ended up in the hospital, resulting in a profile of those in the crowd substantially different than the generally accepted stereotypes. They tended to be craftspeople, workers, and small business owners—those with a stake in society (1964).

A contemporary comparison of the language used to talk about large protest groups comes from Naomi Klein:

But what are reported as menacing confrontations are often joyous events, as much experiments in alternative ways of organizing societies as criticisms of existing models ... These protests—which are actually week-long marathons of intense education on global politics, late-night strategy sessions in six-way simultaneous translation, festivals of music and street theatre—are like stepping into a parallel universe. Overnight, the site is transformed into a kind of alternative global city where urgency replaces resignation, corporate logos need armed guards, people usurp cars, art is everywhere, strangers talk to each other, and the prospect of a radical change in political course does not seem like an odd and anachronistic idea but the most logical thought in the world. (2002, xxiv–xxv)

Klein's description is in contrast to the coverage of the broken window at McDonald's that was central to television coverage. The 'riff-raff' versus 'respectable citizen' contrast in how protest is framed continues on.

Regardless of who is in a protest crowd, how it has been organized and what it is called, by its very nature and the unpredictability of its dynamics, it is a complex system, which contains within itself the potential for chaos, the final aspect of crowds to be considered.

Protest Crowds as Complex Systems

Deborah Sword has done pioneer work linking complexity science with protest crowds (Sword, 2003). Here is how she introduces the concept:

Complexity science, which is the study of nonlinear, complex and dynamic systems, includes group interactions, such as public policy protests. Nonlinear systems are identifiable by their complex characteristics. Nonlinearity means that a cause and an effect are not necessarily traceable in a direct line. For example, small inputs into a complex system can amplify, causing the system to move in surprising and unexpected directions. The ways complex systems develop over time, called the property of emergence, depend on earlier events, called initial conditions. Complex systems also accept positive and negative feedback from which they adapt and learn. (Sword, 2003)

Within systems thinking, she argues, it is interdependencies that work together to bring about a particular event. There is not a single cause, *per se* but there are cascades 'where, once one thing happens, more things are likely to happen.' (Sword, 2003) As she applies systems theory to protest crowds in public policy situations, she distinguishes between agents who inhabit the dominant system—including politicians, bureaucrats, most news media and police/security forces—and protesters who inhabit the shadow system. Sword did an analysis of three public protest scenarios in Toronto. Her research demonstrated that protest crowds are complex systems following the simple rules of complexity science.

There are a number of key concepts coming out of complexity theory that are important in the understanding of the dynamics of protest crowds, according to Sword. These include edge of chaos, adaptation, uncertainty, phase transition, bifurcation, and amplification. Let us examine each of these.

Edge of chaos is a point between rigidity and stability that applies to complex adaptive systems (Kauffman, 1995). If the system descends into chaos or closes into rigid positions, the result is death. However, if the agents within the complex systems adapt, the result can be new creative orders of being (Sword, 2003). *Adaptation*, a feature of which is resilience, involves learning and the development of a new level of consciousness (McGuigan, 2006). It is an evolutionary dynamic that provides a capacity for sustained existence.

At the edge of chaos within complex systems, there is always *uncertainty* about the consequences of any particular action. There are tipping points (Gladwell, 2000) that enable the possibility of creative changes from old to new; however, what constitutes the new cannot be pre-determined, but can involve changes in norms, knowledge or behaviour. The change, which can appear suddenly when it occurs, is called a *phase transition*. As Sword explains, 'Phase transitions occur at the edge of chaos, when almost any future is possible and what the future will be is unpredictable.' (Sword, 2003, 22; see also Gell-Mann, 1994; Holland, 1995;)

Bifurcation points are defined by the irreversibility of the results of a choice. They involve a qualitative change in a place of 'maximum instability and maximum possibilities for the future.' (Sword, 2003) In the case of crowed dynamics, the new possibilities could involve an escalation in the intensity and breadth of activity, a lateral shift to a new direction, or a de-escalation of intensity.

Finally, Sword argues that the dynamics of *amplification* are important in an understanding of crowds:

> Nonlinear systems have amplification that creates disproportionate changes, thus cause and effect may not be directly traceable. How a nonlinear system unfolds depends upon how it began and what inputs it experienced. Complex systems have sensitive dependence on initial conditions. Two identical communities might, for example, react very differently to the same policy because their unique community contexts had different initial conditions for receiving inputs. (Sword, 2003)

Besides depending on the context, amplification can be seen as having cascading effects in which a given incident will prompt a number of different actions and events. The particular cascade effects of a given action will depend on the timing, including what has happened just before, what is happening concurrently and what happens immediately after. The effects are surprising because there are unlimited possibilities.

> An input into a nonlinear system, whether it is the initial announcement of a new policy or the protesters' objections, may have surprising, often unforeseeable consequences, with larger effects than one might have predicted. The two concepts of sensitive dependence on initial conditions and amplification came to be known as the 'Butterfly Effect' (Lorenz, 1993). The analogy Lorenz used to explain sensitive dependence on initial conditions and amplification, is a butterfly flapping its wings in Mexico that can cause a tidal wave in Japan, or a storm in Chicago. The Butterfly Effect means that where a nonlinear system ends up depends on where it started and what happened to it along the way. Small perturbations unbalance a complex system from where it looked like it was going, and what

its potential future might have predicted when it was first observed. Inputs into a nonlinear system, whether intentional or otherwise, can increase throughout the system. (Sword, 2003)

If we look at the protest crowd through the lens of complexity science, it becomes clear that prior attitudes and stereotypes of police, politicians, public and media to the protesters are an important part of the context and, as such, will play a role, however unpredictable, in how events unfold. It follows that the designation of the protest crowd and the paradigm used to interpret the protest crowd–police relational system will be factors in determining cascading effects. As well, they could be the locus of learning and the emergence of new possibilities leading to the sustainability and survival of the stakeholders involved.

This look at protest crowds from the perspectives of protest, crowd dynamics, language used to designate protest crowds and their participants, individual and collective dynamics, and complexity science has shown multiple aspects of this phenomenon. What should be clear, as a sub-text, is that emotions play a significant role in motivating people to participate in protest crowd activity as well as in what happens in the course of a protest. In the next chapter we will examine the nature and role of emotions in greater detail, anticipating that they are also an important factor for police, politicians, bystanders and the media.

3. Emotions: The Fuel of Violence

In their book, *Dealing with an Angry Public,* authors Larry Susskind and Patrick Field point out that often groups who gather for angry protest do so for very good reasons (Susskind & Field, 1996). Through stories such as the oil spill of the Exxon Valdez off the coast of Alaska, the Three Mile Island nuclear power plant crisis, the breast implant class action lawsuits and the Hydro Quebec clash with the Cree, Susskind and Field show that people and the environment have been deeply hurt through various actions of government and business. In each case there was a very angry public reaction. In this chapter we hope to provide a framework to understand better how deep emotions are generated within the various stakeholder groups.

In recent years the role of emotions in determining behaviour has come to the fore with the growth of literature that highlights the physiological effect of emotional part of the brain on the mind–body as well as the importance of emotional intelligence in contributing to good communication and healthy relationships. We will outline some recent discoveries of how emotions work physiologically and then show the various ways in which emotions play a role in protest crowds. We will link emotions first, to deep-rooted conflict via human identity needs; second, to levels of moral consciousness; and third, to mimetic (imitation) theory. We will conclude the chapter with a comparative analysis of Sopow's emotional factors in crowd action with human identity needs, and, finally, provide a link to emotional intelligence.

What is experienced as an emotion can be seen in the body as the release of large numbers of particular neurotransmitters that send messages to various cells (Pert, 1997). One of the messages is for glands to release certain hormones which in turn have the effect of shutting down the work of some organs and pumping up the activity in others. In the event of a profound emotional stimulation, like a severe threat to one's survival, the release of neurotransmitters and the subsequent effects are extreme. Blood pressure rises, the digestive system shuts down, hands turn clammy, one's throat become dry, etc. Concomitantly, the body registers memories of all of the activities associated with the fear stimulus—like a computer software program saved on a hard drive that can be activated by a code. That way, if there is another event that stirs up a similar fear, the body is prepared to replicate the physiological reaction. Though the emotional memories are stored in many parts of the body, the amygdala, a small part of the brain, plays a particularly strong role in storing and activating such memories (Niehoff, 1999). When it receives a stimulus that resembles the initial emotion, it can, without any conscious thought, immediately send messages throughout the mind and body to re-activate all of the physical effects in a manner similar to the original experience. There is no time consciousness to the emotional part of the brain so emotional memories of say twenty years ago are experienced as though they are present realities.

This general and simplified neurobiological description maps on to phenomena described by social psychologists. They speak of reservoirs of recollection—emotional memories—that can be triggered by smells, words, objects or symbols associated with what caused the emotional reaction in the first place (Volkan, 1990). They also distinguish between public truth and table truth; the former what one speaks in public among those one does not know and the latter being truth shared with close intimates. Table truth often is linked with reservoirs of recollection. Where an identity group such as one of the distinct groups associated with a protest crowd has gone through similar experiences there may be similar reservoirs of recollection and similar table truths. A crowd of people who share emotionally laden table truths can be aroused emotionally by a leader who uses words and symbols that recall those 'truths.' Those with a capacity to reflect on their experience, to observe themselves, or in psychological terms to develop a distal self, can consciously make the connection between the stimulus and their emotional response. This capacity increases emotional intelligence.

A third aspect of emotions has to do with the interplay between emotion and cognition. What occurs within a deep-rooted conflict is that the emotion associated with a threat to one's identity needs can commandeer the mind. The mind then works in a way that is very logical and deliberate but at a deeper level is propelled by emotion. Examples of this are well-organized lynchings or meticulously planned terrorist attacks. In both cases, there is a strong cognitive component to the activity as indicated by the preparations involved and there are strong passions motivating the commitment to kill. These emotions are linked to a perception of injustice, another way that the cognitive-emotional link is manifest.

On the positive side of emotions, Michael Polanyi has argued persuasively that scientists are guided by what he calls intellectual passions (Polanyi, 1964). They have emotional drives to pursue certain research questions and as they develop theoretical positions they are emotionally driven to maintain and strengthen their paradigms, hence the strong rivalries within scientific communities. Similarly anti-globalization protesters are passionately devoted to doing research on the environment, on practices of multi-national corporations, on government policies and a host of other topics to find evidence to support their positions. As they do this, their passions for activism increase and they enter a public protest highly motivated. Likewise, the police develop strong passions around crowd management—more on this later.

Human Identity Needs

Inspired by the writings of Abraham Maslow, a generation of needs theorists emerged in the 1970s and 1980s. Among them they identified well over twenty needs closely tied to human identity. John W. Burton, a primary theorist in conflict studies, identified human needs as the key to understanding the passions evoked in deep-rooted conflict. Primary emotions can be mapped on to human identity needs (Sites, 1990). Hence when need satisfiers are threatened the emotion can be very strong. The following diagram (Figure 3.1) shows how needs and emotions can be linked together.[11]

Figure 3.1 Human Identity Needs and Emotions

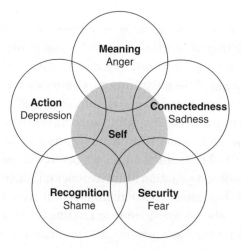

---

11   The concept of human identity needs is more fully developed in Vern Neufeld Redekop, *From Vio-lence to Blessing—How an Understanding of Deep-Rooted Conflict Can Open Paths to Reconciliation* (Ottawa: Novalis, 2002).

The need categories are universal but the satisfiers are unique to cultures, to individuals, to historical circumstances and to personal experiences. Each need category gets at an essential aspect of life. The need for *meaning* is around making sense of the world as we experience it. For some, this need is met through a particular philosophical or religious system; for others, it is through family life; and increasingly, people look to work for meaning. The need for *meaning* includes a sense of justice and firmly held values about what is right and wrong. When the satisfiers to the need for meaning are threatened, the emotional reaction is one of anger. Next, the need for *connectedness* includes a need to belong to a community, to be with people who talk the same language, who share the same experiences. When this is threatened through death or conflict one feels a profound sense of sadness at the loss of friend or family. The need for *action*, third, is the need to be an agent of action, someone who can make things happen. A threat to this involves depression. Fourth, the need for *security* includes welfare needs of food, shelter and clothing as well as security of the person from injury or assault and emotional security. A threat to security invokes fear. *Recognition*, the fifth need, is an acknowledgement of the other need satisfier as well as recognition of the being, or presence of the person as a significant entity. Its threat stirs up a sense of self-doubt and even shame.

For many activists, their identity needs are satisfied through the issues over which they are active. For example, an environmentalist gets *meaning* out of care for the environment and justice is defined in terms of care or destruction of the environment. *Connectedness* includes being connected to the natural world as well as to others who share a passion for preserving the natural order. Significant *action* is that which prevents destruction of the environment and enhances its well being. *Security* of the person is tied to keeping the environment free of significant toxins. *Recognition* includes a validation of environmental concerns and support for actions taken. For some environmentalists the whole self is oriented toward environmental concerns. In terms of developmental psychology, they are 'subject to' their environmental concerns and may have many identity needs met, whereas if they take their environmental concerns as an object, they will be less inclined to have their identity needs met this way. However, most people tend not to be so single-minded; the illustration is used to show that for some people issue areas become very central to their identity and to perpetrate an injustice in their area of interest amounts to an attack on their identity.

Targets of crowd protests, security personnel and bystanders likewise have need satisfiers that give definition to their identities. Police, for instance, have a mandate to maintain public order. When they take *action* to effect *security* of the public at large, their identity need for *meaning* is fulfilled. They may have a heightened need for *security* of themselves by virtue of the fact that they are more aware than many of the threats to public order that exist in society. They get *recognition* when public order is maintained—they also get negative *recognition* when the public doesn't agree with or understand the reasons for their actions or if they experience 'troubles.' If they fail in their task, the negative recognition is great. Their need for *connectedness* is reflected in their close affinity for others like themselves who understand the pressures of their work. With their colleagues they can speak of the many things they know and cannot take action on or share with the public. In these times, the police community fulfills their need for *connectedness*. When we witness huge demonstrations by police in support of their fallen comrades, we see how deeply they are moved when one of their own is killed in active duty.

Politicians and government officials are frustrated when their ability to take *action* and even their personal *security* is thwarted by protesters. There is *meaning* in the election process that gives them a mandate to take *action* on behalf of society. Their work and the power vested in them as individuals supports their need for *recognition*.

Bystanders feel that their need for *security* is compromised when windows are broken and goods looted. When they join in a demonstration (they are no longer bystanders), they feel satisfied in their needs for *action* and *connectedness* by virtue of their contribution to the protest and their association with likeminded people. When they remain bystanders their need for meaning can be met vicariously through the action of others, if they are sympathetic to the cause. If not, they may cheer the actions of police. Sometimes a complex system arises in which bystanders protest the way in which their lives are disrupted by protest activities. This was the case during the Oka/Kanehsata:ke Crisis of 1990 in Canada, during which the Mercier Bridge was blocked by a Mohawk protest. People from Chateauguay and Montreal formed protest crowds in response.

Here are some other examples from seminars on crowd dynamics that illustrated how the affirmation of or threat to need categories affects crowd dynamics:

- One protester from the Quebec City demonstration said that the recognition that Prime Minister Chrétien gave to the protesters was constructive and had the effect of calming angry feelings.
- For another participant, *connectedness* is the most significant of the needs in the protest context. What remains most important for people who demonstrated in the 1960's is the human connections and not the issues.
- Some people who formed crowds were there for *meaning*, that is, political purpose. There was something wrong with the world and they wanted to fix it.
- For street youth, the crowd can be seen as their family—*connectedness* and *security* are important.
- For another participant, the need for *action* was important. Bad things come when access to a venue is cut off. They (activists) protest to be active about an issue and not to stay on the sidelines.

Likewise, security personnel may get very angry with protesters whom they see to be acting violently and threatening public order and their own security. When they see the same person throwing rocks or Molotov cocktails or perhaps bullying other non-violent protesters, they can have strong feelings around the injustice. And when a huge angry crowd comes charging at them, their job, linked with their identity, is to protect those behind them; they may feel afraid and also have a heightened sense of determination to stop the crowd at all costs. On the other hand as they think about their children and others they are connected with being part of the crowd they may have conflicting emotions. Security personnel, activists and media all have significant emotional memories—especially fear remembered from 'the big ones.'

When one incident threatens a number of need categories concurrently, there can be powerful compound emotions. In *Dealing with an Angry Public*, the authors associate anger with hurt, risk, belief, weakness and lies (Susskind & Field, 1996). Using the above diagram to look at multiple threats, we can see that if there is an injustice (meaning) producing anger and if it involves a loss of life (connectedness), the anger is compounded and intensified by the sorrow. If there is a perceived injustice accompanied by impediments to action, the frustration intensifies the anger. A threat to security with injustice produces another type of anger. If a crowd gathers to protest, it may be driven by a sense of injustice or a need for recognition of their cause. If the response of security forces to their protest is considered unjust, their anger intensifies. If there is a threat to their personal security or well being, the emotions soar.

There are also identity needs related to the temporal dimension of life. Related to the past we have needs for memories, stories and a sense of coherence. Projecting into the future are needs for imagination, stimulation and continuity (Redekop, 2002). The importance of the temporal dimension means that protest crowd members carry forward memories of past encounters. The more these are coloured by violence, the harder it is to trust and the better the chance that violence will be introduced on future occasions. When looking at the time series of the protest crowd from a complexity science view, some of their actions come at bifurcation points—what they do sets off a series of events the effects of which are much greater than could be predicted. The actions may be based on strategies decided on the basis of their memories of other actions that were effective or ineffective to achieve their goals or on emotional memories of past violence.

Police like individual protesters are motivated in their work with a passion to do their job well. In addition, they may have strong feelings about the issues involved. Like protesters they too have emotional memories based on past experiences. In this case, memories may include having eggs, feces or bricks thrown at them, being called deprecating names by protesters, being insulted, having a fear that the thin line of police might not hold against a massive unruly crowd wanting to get to a foreign visitor. They too may take actions that function as bifurcation points, unleashing new levels of violence. On the other hand, they may have memories of positive exchanges with activists just as some protesters have good memories of helpful exchanges with police. These positive experiences could influence decisions and actions in the direction of tension reduction.

Emotions and Moral Consciousness

We are now in a position to make some links between emotional phenomena and the moral consciousness that motivates protest crowds. In Jasper's first level of moral consciousness, described in the previous chapter, people are driven to protest by an immediate threat to their basic needs. There is an immediate threat to a need for meaning (justice) and to security and these prompt emotions of anger and fear. In the case of higher levels, there is an awareness of injustice that prompts an anger that suggests that something has to change. As one moves through different stages of consciousness, the sense of justice becomes more complex and highly nuanced but the emotions attached to a threat to this sense of justice remain the same. Someone who really sees the systemic implications of a given policy, for instance, can become quite passionate about trying to make a change in that policy.

For some people, their stage of consciousness development means that their identities will be completely oriented toward seeking some combination of distributive justice, situational justice or systemic change. This passion may be expressed in militancy (Peterson, 2001), volatility (Sopow, 2003) or determination to organize protest as strategically effectively as possible (Barlow, 2001).

Knowledge of emotional dynamics may help to explain various dynamics operative within a crowd and integrate some of the different paradigmatic observations. Certainly some people will be motivated to join a protest crowd out of a feeling of connectedness with other protesters and solidarity with those 'oppressed.' McPhail develops the idea that conviviality is an important emotional dimension of crowds (McPhail, 1991). Once a protest crowd has formed, there is a symbiotic relationship between a crowd leader and the crowd itself. Each feeds off of the other's emotion.

Expression of Emotions

McPhail proposes a useful taxonomy of action words to describe what exactly people in crowds do. These include

> collective orientation (gazing, facing, vigiling), vocalization (booing, yeahing, ohhing), verbalization (chanting, singing), vertical locomotion (sitting, standing), horizontal locomotion (surging, marching, clustering), gesticulation (Roman salute, Digitus obscenus, peace sign) and manipulation (applauding, synchro clapping). (McPhail, 1991, 164)

The various actions—gesticulations and locutions—McPhail has in his taxonomy can all be seen as means for emotional expression. In the course of a demonstration various actions could potentially clearly indicate anger, indignation, support, determination, hate, satisfaction, solidarity, alienation, sorrow or joy.

If a crowd leader is effective in naming shared table truths, releasing reservoirs of recollection, and skilled in accessing the collective consciousness of the crowd, crowd passions can be ignited that can lead to determination to persevere or to take dramatic action. This occurred in East Germany as the New Forum gathered people in churches to consider what was happening. People in their niche groups had developed a table truth that acknowledged the corruption and deficiencies of the system (Grix, 2000). As they came together this became a shared and public truth; the passion associated with the table truths could be channelled by leaders into change. The use of churches and the commitment to non violence meant that the action taken was often limited to lighting candles. The power, truth and passion of the protest crowds were so strong that increasingly members of the ruling communist party renounced their party membership and joined the crowds.

In the course of a temporary gathering of protesters, something may happen that either is a threat to their need for justice or is a trigger to reservoirs of recollection, releasing powerful and immediate emotions. It may be what is perceived as the unjust arrest of a fellow protester, police action that is deemed violent or unjustified, destructive action on the part of fringe protesters or the brandishing of a provocative symbol. When this happens there may be an incident which, viewed from a camera could be deemed out of control. One such example occurred at Oka/Kanehsata:ke on July 11, 1990. A protest crowd had been occupying a small road to prevent development of a golf course. The police arrived and after a standoff for a few hours there was an exchange of gunfire, a police officer was killed, and the police left in a hurry. At this point there was an emotional reaction, which protest organizers were unable to subdue. Immediately groups of protesters destroyed police cruisers and started piles of tires on fire. Some of the protest leaders tried unsuccessfully to stop them since they wanted to obtain the radios and other items of value from cruisers (Redekop, 2002).

Emotions and Imitation

Emotions are subject to mimesis or imitation. 'Mimesis' is the Greek word for imitation; the concept of mimesis as it is used in this book has been developed by René Girard, whose thought will be explored further in chapter seven. Back in the 1700s Adam Smith observed that when one person displays an emotion, another is stimulated to experience similar emotions. In recent years it has become clear that our faces are neurologically connected to our emotional physiology (Dalai Lama; Goleman, 2004). From infancy we learn how to 'read' the emotions of others based on their facial features. Emotional clues are also given through body language and vocal tones. As we perceive emotions of those around us they mimetically arouse similar emotions within us. This process is not straightforward; the degree of this phenomenon varies and increases as we identify with the mimetic models. (This observation is an adaptation of René Girard's development of mimetic desire.) Emotional mimesis helps to explain the concept of emotional contagion whereby a group of people quickly adopts a similar emotional state.

Let us turn now to the question of what motivates activists to place their physical wellbeing in jeopardy as they participate in a passionate protest. We will use the framework of Eli Sopow. This question will, of course, raise the issue of what are the identity and emotional dynamics present among other stakeholder groups present at the crowd event. As one police officer put it, the actions of security personnel are motivated by strong emotions. They share a fear of being hurt in an uncontrolled and violent crowd.

Sopow's Analysis of Emotional Factors

Combining fifteen years experience within protest movements with work as an RCMP protest policing strategist, Eli Sopow reviewed the literature on emotional motivators to protest and synthesized five key factors which he then tested in a quantitative research project in New York City. The two strongest factors emerging from his research are 'fairness and the perception that an issue has a negative impact on a person or their family ... [These] can create strong emotions of anger, fear, and moral outrage.' (Sopow, 2003, 141) The other three factors were that an issue creates uncertainty about the future, the issue is of interest to friends or family, and the issue affects rights as a citizen. Of these, the role of friends and families emerged as significant but least among the five factors. His conclusions resonate with Jasper's assertion that

'Moral shocks' are often the first step toward recruitment into social movements: when an unexpected event or piece of information raises such a sense of outrage in a person that she becomes inclined toward political action, with or without the network of personal contacts emphasized in mobilization and process theories (Jasper, 1997, 106).

Sopow's list of emotional factors can be seen in terms of a threat to identity needs of people.

Sopow's Emotional Factors	Redekop's Identity Needs	Emotion
Fairness	Meaning (sense of justice)	Anger
Impacts you or your family	Security, connectedness	Fear, sadness
Uncertainty about the future	Continuity, action, security	Depression, fear
Friends or family interested.	Connectedness, stimulation	Excitement, intensified other emotions
Affects rights as citizen	Recognition, security, possibly story and coherence if one has come from a history of human rights abuse.	Shame, pride, entitlement, fear

These factors certainly have links to emotions as understood in terms of human identity needs. *Fairness* appeals to the sense of justice embedded within one's meaning system. *Personal impact* could take the form of a threat to security need satisfiers be they physical, financial or emotional. If there is a threat to the wellbeing of people whom we know, it would affect the need for connectedness. *Uncertainty* can be mapped onto a need for security but also a need for continuity into the future. Personal rights affect one's security, meaning (sense of justice) and ability to take action. *Influence of friends* is related to the need for connectedness. James Jasper, likewise attaches great importance to the role of a range of emotions in motivating protest actions.

Invoking these emotional factors involves 'framing' issues in such a way that they will spark emotional reactions. Referring to the literature on the subject, Sopow shows that effective framing provides 'a sense of collective identity to individuals and a sense of shared values and injustice' (Sopow, 2003, 141). Framing is the task of people organizing protest movements and events; thus the organization of protest becomes significant. Whether conscious or not, 'framing' always resonates with some stage of consciousness more than others—i.e. if one is aware of what the consciousness of the crowd is, then they can strategically frame the issues to strongly resonate with the crowd. As previously mentioned this can be a highly manipulative process, as the crowd, then, can be strategically orientated toward peace or violence.

Emotional Intelligence

In recent years, the concept of emotional intelligence has been developed to indicate one's awareness of one's own emotions, awareness of the emotional dynamics that others might experience, and what might be effective strategies for thought and behaviour in light of this awareness. Having high emotional intelligence allows a person to harness emotional energy to work at optimum performance, flowing with the demands of a given situation (Goleman, 1997). Low emotional intelligence means that one is driven or inhibited by emotions that take control of mind and body.

When emotional intelligence is combined with crowd mobilization, the results can be dramatically different from what happens in angry protests. Sharon Welsh describes a situation in which a group of Buddhist monks were present at a protest. Instead of the angry demeanor of most of the protesters, they exemplified in their personal bearing the kind of peace the others were advocating:

> Among the hundreds of demonstrators angrily shouting, fiercely denouncing the design of first strike nuclear weapons at Draper Labs in Cambridge, Massachusetts was small group of robed Buddhist monks, smiling, chanting, beating their drums in the graceful, calming cadences of the human heart. As I participated in demonstrations in Boston and New England in the mid-1980s, I was captivated by the energy of the monks. Their very presence was a gift of healing and beauty, a sharp contrast to the voices of rage and despair. Many of my students and colleagues were equally moved, and we tried to find ways of being present in demonstrations that were both denunciations of what we saw as military and economic aggression, and, at the same time, actions that

in themselves were also expressions of beauty, joy, wonder and peace. We were rarely successful.

In fact, it was not until writing this essay, twenty years after demonstrations in Boston and Cambridge, that I realized that the Buddhist monks were as much an evocative, albeit non-judgmental, 'protest' against us, as they were a protest of the making of nuclear weapons and the support of military action throughout the world. The presence of those gracious, calm, joyous monks was as much a challenge and gift to us angry peace demonstrators as they were to those who created and supported the creation of nuclear weapons. The Buddhist monks could easily have been as focused on demonstrating a different way of being to us, the demonstrators, as they were on showing another way of being to those who supported war. It is surprising that it has taken me so long to recognize this challenge, and this gift. The power of righteous indignation is a remarkable thing. (Welch, 2004)

This example raises the questions, what would happen to protest crowd–police relational systems if there was an increase in emotional intelligence all around? How would it change the nature of protest? What would be the impact on society? We will return to these when we introduce the paradigm of mutual respect; but first it is important to introduce the police as primary agents in the dynamics of public protest, then to look at the structures that systematically increase the rift between police and protesters and then introduce the other stakeholders.

4. Introducing Police

Police are agents of the State who come into direct contact with protest crowds as they place themselves between the targets of the protest and the protesters themselves. As such, their strategic objectives are to maintain public order, protect the target (along with public institutions); uphold the right to protest; ensure the safety of bystanders and crowd participants; and enforce the laws. In the process, they wish to avoid at all costs what noted British police scholar P.A.J. Waddington refers to as 'trouble.' In democratic countries, it is the police, and not the military, who are charged with keeping the peace in the face of public protest.

A distinct role for the police is not to be taken for granted; the first modern police force was established in France in 1664 (Sopow, 2003) with a paramilitary organizational style, centralized command structure with direct accountability to the State (Rigacos, 2005). However, it was in Britain in 1829 that the London Metropolitan Police Force was established by Robert Peel with a mandate to develop a style of policing that was not based on force and weaponry but was to be based on moral authority and relationships with citizens. Furthermore, considerable discretion was vested with constables who did most of their work independently. European police looked at the British model as being based on a policing paradigm to be distinguished from paramilitary policing (della Porta, 1998) and set the model for modern day policing paradigms.

It is significant that the community-based policing movement in the 1980s in Canada, United States and Europe was an attempt to establish a new paradigm of policing based in large measure on Peel's principles. It was during this time that an emphasis on negotiation emerged in protest policing circles. Given its paradigmatic role, our first section will provide an overview of protest policing as it has evolved in Britain in the 1800s. This section may be of particular interest to political and civil society leaders in currently emerging democracies since England of the early 1800s shared many of the challenges they are facing today.

A second major section will deal with public order policing in Western democracies from 1960 to the present. Starting in the 1960s, new waves of protest emerged and the technology, organization and tactics of police started to change. During this time period the differences between British approaches to public order policing and that of other countries narrowed significantly (della Porta, 1998; P.A.J. Waddington, 1991). We will look at how police capacity to control crowds was enhanced through paramilitary organization and training, technological tools, and tactical options. All of these add up to a greater capacity for repressive policing; however, we will show that an early trend toward *escalated force* (or hard) approaches in the 1960s and 1970s was reversed in favour of the use of bureaucratic and discursive control techniques through the 1980s and 1990s, which in policing language are put under the rubric of *negotiated management* (or soft) approaches (della Porta, 1998; McPhail, Schweingruber, & McCarthy, 1998). Concomitantly, there has been a growing body of laws and court decisions that has put limits on police powers in some cases and provided them with greater discretion in others; in addition, we will refer to comparative studies on the impact of different legal frameworks (Björk, 2005). We will also highlight P.A.J. Waddington's notions of 'trouble on the job' and 'trouble in the job,' David Waddington's concept of 'flashpoints,' and Tony Jefferson's 'case against paramilitary policing.' We will describe Public Order Management Systems (POMS) that combine organizational structures, principles, regulations and standard practices in many major police forces/services. We will end this section with a presentation of developments in public order policing in Canada.

In a final section, we will examine some of the ethical aspects of public order policing. Within this section we will first examine the dynamics of public order police in the abstract. Second, we will present some of the ethical issues and questions. These will serve as preparation for an ethical vision for policing that will be presented in chapter nine in the context of a mutual respect paradigm for protest crowd–police relationships.

The Evolution of Protest Policing in Nineteenth Century Britain

Starting with the creation of the London Metropolitan Police by Robert Peel in 1829 and proceeding well into the next century a paradigm of protest policing emerged that was based on moral authority rather than physical control. This manner of dealing with crowds evolved as a function of values and trends within British society (Cerrah, 1998), police leadership (Smith, 1985), the nature and characteristics of 'bobbies,' and the relationship between the police and the public (P.A.J. Waddington, 1991). Metropolitan Police also constituted a force to maintain the kind of order in society that would allow industries to flourish (Jefferson, 1990); in other words, it empowered the industrial revolution and the kind of economic development that followed.

From the mid-eighteenth century on, British society was becoming increasingly urbanized and complex. The industrial revolution was in full swing; there was a growing middle class and a significant lower class made up of workers and those in poverty. Crime, disease, and poverty were all seen as threats to society. Utilitarianism, led by Jeremy Bentham, with its corollary pragmatism was in the air, as was the growth of democracy with an ever growing suffrage and increasing expectation of rights and freedoms. Evangelical Christianity was sufficiently on the rise that it was having an impact on the public sense of morality (Hochschild, 2005; Smith, 1985). All the while, drinking, disorderly conduct and riots (Townshend, [1993]2002) were rampant. Riots occurred based on real or perceived privations caused by increases in food prices or threats to one's livelihood (Smith, 1985). Through the nineteenth century, public dissent would morph into Chartism, a broadly based movement advocating radical political change, and the increased demand for political rights (as discussed in chapter two, eventually most of the Chartist demands were accepted). As industrial capitalism evolved into the modern age, the economy became more complex and 'increasingly vulnerable to disruption in its many parts' (Smith, 1985). Adam Smith[12] himself made the connection between policing and achieving 'wealth and abundance' (Brown & Waters, 1996).

As the English cast an observant glance over the Channel, they saw two trends that they wished to avoid at all costs. The first was violent revolution; the second, repressive policing. Within this context Robert Peel brought forth legislation to establish the London Metropolitan Police. The police were guided in their formation by what came to be known as Peel's principles and by a set of values modeled and inculcated by commissioners Rowan and Mayne (Townshend, [1993]2002). Peel's principles included the following:

To maintain at all times a relationship with the public that gives reality to the historic tradition that the police are the public and that the public

---

12   Adam Smith was a Scottish political economist and philosopher. He has become famous by his influential book *The Wealth of Nations* (1776). Smith was the son of the comptroller of the customs at Kirkcaldy, Fife, Scotland. *The Wealth of Nations* was the first and remains the most important book on the subject of political ecomomy until this present day. (Faber, 2003)

are the police; the police being only members of the public who are paid to give full-time attention to duties which are incumbent on every citizen, in the interest of community welfare and existence.

To seek and to preserve public favour not by pandering to public opinion but by constantly demonstrating absolutely impartial service to Law ... by ready offering of individual service and friendship to all members of the public without regard to their wealth or social standing ...

To use physical force only when the exercise of persuasion, advice and warning is found to be insufficient to obtain public co-operation to an extent necessary to secure observance of law or to restore order; and to use only the minimum degree of force which is necessary on any particular occasion for achieving a police objective. (Eng, 2005)

These principles were 'owned' by the first commissioners, Rowan and Mayne, who worked tirelessly to weave them into the policing culture of the Metropolitan Police. Over time the Metropolitan Police of London became the model for the country. For over a century the police in Great Britain had the respect and support of a healthy majority of the population. This was not only a result of police action but a certain measured responsiveness by the ruling elite who made timely concessions in response to public demands. Not only that, this period saw the expansion of the British Empire and a global network of colonies provided an outlet for people uncomfortable with the status quo. Prisoners were sent to places like Australia. Resources from the colonies and monopoly markets made for a growing economy. During this time there were significant wars that united the population against a shared enemy. Politically, limits were placed on public expression of ideas promoting Fascism or Communism; however, in 1871, the right to speak about anything was extended to those presenting their opinions at Speakers Corner in Hyde Park. The policing model reflected a subliminal hegemony that resonated with the 'hidden' social factors that contributed to social peace.

The hidden baton became a metaphor for a popular mythology that emerged regarding the police. The police appeared to be unarmed and benign; as such they cultivated moral authority and the image of sometimes bumbling, friendly, not too effective, and very human 'bobbies' contributed to public support. The baton was there in the pocket and it could be more lethal than most people thought. Though constables did not carry side arms, guns were available for special occasions. In other words, what passed in the public mind as a police service was, in reality, more of a police *force* than was the popular image.

Repressive Policing

Continuing with the British example, during the period from 1829 to 1960, the British Empire reached and passed its zenith. British hegemony over its colonies was neither established nor maintained without violence. Whenever a minority wishes to assert itself and control a much larger population, it resorts to a certain level of repressive policing, which at its extreme includes the regular use of lethal violence to keep protest in check (P.A.J. Waddington, 1998). It is a significant study in contrasts that while the British were developing a relatively humane style of policing at home, where they enjoyed much support from the general population, they used a policing style much more dependent on force within colonies. Meanwhile back in Britain, the 1960s saw an increase in the use of force at home. This example typifies the observation that policing style results from a relationship among the population, political leaders, cultural values and the police (Cerrah, 1998), an observation that is at the foundation of our work.

In the case of repressive policing, political masters appoint and reward police for maintaining their hegemonic structure, regardless of how much force is required (P.A.J. Waddington, 1998). Referring to conflict theories discussed in chapter three, security of the dominant group is the primary identity need, trumping meaning, connectedness, recognition and action. Police in this context are empowered to use lethal force with impunity on a regular basis and can very easily become agents of injustice. Colonial policing was just one example (Kratcoski et al., 2001) of repressive policing; more extreme forms evolved under dictatorships, totalitarian regimes and/ or weak states (Sheptycki, 2005). It is ironic that in the British public order policing manual of 1982, many of the tactics described to deal with crowds were borrowed from those used in British colonies (P.A.J. Waddington, 1998). Also (bitterly) ironic, repressive policing has been the rule in many post-colonial African countries. A preoccupation with security following terrorist attacks in the USA on September 11, 2001 and the London bombings of July 7, 2005, has prompted a more repressive style of policing in a number of countries.

Reflection on the Early Evolution of the London Metropolitan Police

What can we learn from the experience of the Metropolitan Police? The question and its answer pertain to the process of introducing a new paradigm of public order policing. Even though critics with the benefit of hindsight suggest that perhaps Peel's police were not as devoid of paramilitarism as the myth might suggest, nonetheless, it is clear that Peel, Rowan and Mayne introduced a radical new approach to policing (Europeans generally recognized that something different was happening across the Channel). They consciously attempted to shape policing in a way that made corruption, political influence and reliance on force to be minimized. How they did this could be instructive to any police leaders who might wish to introduce a new paradigm. We will look at five lessons that emerge: have principled leadership; be sensitive to culture; emphasize relationships; learn from mistakes, and focus on legitimacy.

Have Principled Leadership

By making each constable responsible ultimately to Commissioners who were independent of parish politics, Peel could make certain (as much as possible) that they would act impartially, focusing on a combination of pragmatism and rule of law. Mayne, one of the first commissioners, was unequivocally committed to an impartial police force that was free of corruption and political interference and that required of constables that they not let their emotions take control regardless of the taunts and threats to which they might be subjected. He was in control long enough to establish a new policing culture.

Be Sensitive to Culture

London of the 1820s was very unruly with a strong tendency for people to assert their independence and for groups to protest whatever they didn't like in society. The English had little stomach for repression. It has been observed that the policing style that emerged did not work because of the tendency to conform on the part of the British but, on the contrary, because of contempt at having order imposed on them in a heavy handed way. It was a chaotic situation that demanded order but being on the edge of chaos as it was, the wrong approach could have easily resulted in significantly more violence than was the case.

Emphasize Relationships

Much of the effectiveness of the police was derived from the good relationships that they had with the local population. By being present and being friendly, treating the population with dignity and respect, respect was returned to the police. This was not universally the case. People at the bottom of society in terms of social standing were more likely to be discriminated against (Jefferson, 1990).

Learn from Mistakes

The pragmatic approach to public order policing meant that when something didn't work well there was a return to the drawing boards within the framework of a set of principles.

Focus on Legitimacy

The policing paradigm emphasized in the Metropolitan Police of London emphasized retaining a sense of legitimacy in the eyes of the public. This is why restraint in the use of violence became a watchword.

However

Even though British society was better off between 1829 and 1960 through the institution of Peel's police, the actions of the police were not uniformly positive. There were abuses of police powers and not all levels of society experienced the police in the same way. Within British society there was a clear hegemonic structure and the police played a significant role in keeping this structure in place (Jefferson, 1990). Any judgment of this reality must be based on an understanding of the complexity of society, the competing demands of order and change, the relative rigidity and impermeability of class structure and a definition of distributive justice that acknowledges relative responsibilities and contributions.

Since the 1960s, public order policing as it evolved in Britain increasingly came to resemble police practice in other established democracies. We will turn now to an examination of contemporary trends, each of which provides a basis for comparison among police services/forces.

Protest Policing since 1960

The 1960s saw a significant growth in the size, significance and sophistication of protest crowds in Western democracies. Concomitantly, public order policing grew as a specialized aspect of police work. Dedicated public order policing units were organized; national networks of mutual support among police forces and other public service bureaucracies were put into place; legislation and legal decisions created a better articulated framework for public order policing; new equipment and training courses provided new options for controlling crowds; strategic and operational decision making were differentiated and coordinated; new tactics were developed; and finally, Public Order Management Systems were put in place. All the while police worked proactively to avoid surprises and 'troubles' as they moved back and forth along an axis with 'repression' at one end and 'negotiation' at the other.

Paramilitary Organization

Since the 1960s, paramilitary policing has been woven into public order policing as an effective, efficient use of force. Tony Jefferson defines it as 'the application of (quasi-)military training, equipment, philosophy and organization to questions of policing (whether under centralized control or not)' (1990, 16). There are two different aspects to this phenomenon and it is important to differentiate between aspects of the term. On the one hand, 'paramilitary' refers to the manner in which police are organized with specialized squads, unit and incident commanders, and the use of strategies and tactics modeled on the military; on the other hand, the same term refers to an orientation or mindset that is oriented toward control of crowds through the use of force. These two aspects may reinforce one another, but ought to be considered separately for purposes of analysis.

According to P.A.J. Waddington, what distinguishes this organizational style is the distinction and distance from civil society, the hierarchical structure and the tendency to be organized and work in squads. When the Metropolitan Police was established in London, the emphasis was on strong identification with the community. Clothing was more civilian than military and the constable was considered a 'civilian in uniform.' A 1929 police commission painted the police in Britain as never a 'force distinct from the body of citizens' (P.A.J. Waddington, 1991). Waddington maintains that this was the myth and as such it played an important function in the thinking of the public; however over a period of 150 years this increasingly was not the reality. In fact, Jefferson maintains that there was more 'paramilitarism' evident throughout the history of the Metropolitan police than has normally been acknowledged. In any case, there is agreement that new aspects of paramilitarism were introduced to public order policing particularly in the late 60s and early 70s.

In the 1980s and early 1990s there was a strong movement among police in North America to establish 'community-based policing' which was to remove the distance between police and community—getting police out of squad cars was literally and metaphorically the goal. However, as police have donned increasingly more protective clothing and have positioned themselves behind shields, walls and barriers when doing public order policing, they have identified less and less with the community. Police who have little identification with the community have less compunction about using force for several reasons. First, they are anonymous to the protesters—they are not recognizable by community members because they are behind shields and wearing helmets. Second, they do not have personal relationships with protesters so are less likely to see the full humanity of those in front of them; protesters become 'things' to deal with rather than people like those they know and love. Third, they are well protected and able to use more force than they can without good protection; they have more power to get people to do what they want them to do. All of this contributes to the ability to behave in a more effective, forceful, coercive manner. When destructive violence threatens lives, this may have some immediate benefit; when relationships are relied upon to control a crowd this coercive capacity may be counterproductive.

Regarding authority, P.A.J. Waddington points out that legally all police of whatever rank functioned as constables with equal powers before the law. No constable could get off the hook by claiming to act on orders since no other authority stood between him and the law. This distinguished British police from paramilitary police and armed forces around the world. In a paramilitary operation, such as protest policing in contrast to community work, police officers are organized in squads, with each squad having its own function; e.g. a tear gas squad, a front line tactical squad, etc. Senior officers command groups of squads and decisions are made up the chain of command. In a paramilitary environment the first loyalty of the police officer is to his force (P.A.J. Waddington, 1991). There is psychological distance from the people in the crowd.

Thus, it is not simply the paramilitary organization structure per se that is objected to, but what that structure facilitates—the oppressive use of force. Paramilitary police forces blur the line between the police function of using force to arrest suspected offenders and bring them before the courts and the military function of defeating and destroying an enemy. A paramilitary police uses its superior might to suppress. (P.A.J. Waddington, 1991)

This is not to say that every paramilitary organized force will be repressive; however, the more it takes on paramilitary characteristics the greater the capacity—physically and psychologically—to be coercive. The advantages of a paramilitary organization are that it is efficient—all squads operate under consistent commands—extremely important when dealing with crowds at the edge of chaos.

For major protest crowd events there is a division of responsibility: there are detectives, intelligence gatherers, plainclothes police within the crowd, a police psychologist, a media relations specialist to work with the media and make certain that TV cameras are behind police lines, soft hats—police at the edges of the crowd, often on bicycles who maintain a presence and establish boundaries; there are the tear gas specialists and the water cannon operators, police with dogs and the hard hats— the tactical armed police with full protective gear and equipped with pepper spray, stun guns, and guns with rubber bullets. The incident commanding officer, like a battle general, directs the different units; however, in violent chaotic situations order and communication can break down leaving the incident commander with only nominal control over what happens on the front lines. All of these people are empowered by technological tools and the tools that come from well-defined tactics that are drilled in advance of the event. We will examine both of these resources in greater detail to bring out the reality on the police side of the protester–police dividing line.

Tools of Technology

Over the past few decades, police have had ever more effective protective gear and a growing arsenal of crowd control 'less than lethal weapons.' Technology has also made possible better communication among police and between front lines and command centres.

Defensive Technologies

There are two types of defensive technology—attire and shields. Protective attire includes bullet proof Kevlar, masks with visors that can deflect projectiles, gas masks and non-flammable outer layers. It is also possible to have anatomically molded protective 'pads' that make it possible to withstand explosives in close proximity. Suppliers of protective clothing work to provide protection against life-threatening injuries faced in riot and crowd management situations. They work to achieve optimal balance between protection and comfort. There are features that facilitate the rescue of a fallen officer, ensure compatibility with other kits and equipment, offer blunt impact protective coverage and shoulder to ankle flame resistance coverage. Included in the total design of such equipment are psychological advantages so officers on duty remain calm through knowledge of their optimal protection. Hence, it is hoped, they are less inclined to strike out and can maintain their position with unified force, rather than acting individually. All the while, they are to present a professional, yet less aggressive, appearance to a crowd. Experience has shown a less aggressive appearance reduces the risk of triggering a violent reaction from the crowd. The comfort aspect, including a two litre optional reservoir of water, anticipates officers wearing protective clothing for long periods of time.[13]

Shields include the long shield and the short shield. Long shields can be hooked together to form a movable protective wall. Short shields allow for greater freedom of movement and can be used by individual officers who hold the shield with one hand allowing one free hand.

Less than Lethal Weapons

Less than lethal weapons are designed to create a physical distance between police and protesters, immobilize individual protesters, and to induce crowds to disperse. Tear gas and water cannons are used to create a physical distance between police or to encourage dispersal. Baton rounds are 4 inch plastic cartridges that can be fired at protesters. They are not lethal but they can induce sufficient injury as to immobilize people. Pepper spray and Taser guns are sufficiently unpleasant as to induce protesters to retreat. They can also

13   Med–Eng Systems was a supplier of protective gear to police around the world. These descriptions are based on its 2005 promotional literature (*Crowd Management: V-Top Ensembles and Helmets*), included to illustrate the kinds of equipment available to public order police.

produce negative bodily reactions. Tasers can also be used to involuntarily relax the hold of protesters who have linked arms so that they can more easily be arrested. While truncheons can be lethal if used on the head, long truncheons (27 inches) are meant to be used on arms and legs—they encourage dispersal but can disable people. Most up-to-date are expandable truncheons. Though these weapons are designated 'less than lethal' there are instances where some have proved to be more lethal than intended.

Tactical Options
The following tactics are designed to first give police the upper hand even before a protest starts and second to deal with particular contingencies as they arise.[14]

Taking the Ground and Early Resolution
'Taking the ground' means that police arrive at the scene of a protest well before the protest begins. They position themselves in such a way that protesters are directed to gather at a place positioned such that the police can more easily control the situation. As protesters arrive they are explained the ground rules; as these are accepted by the first to arrive they are conveyed and accepted by those who come later. If the police arrive at the scene of a spontaneous crowd that is getting out of hand, 'early resolution' means that they break up the crowd early on before it has a chance to grow either in size or violent behaviour. Early resolution can involve forceful means.

Cordons
Cordons are line demarcations that indicate boundaries for crowds. They may be formed with tape or fences or may take the form of a line of police with spaces between who establish the cordon by their presence. A variation may be filter cordons that either allow protesters to pass through a line in a controlled fashion or that separate crowd members from pedestrians who are not part of a protest.

Trudging and Wedging
Trudging is a tactic that is basically a moving cordon that forces crowds to move back. To accomplish this, police form a line with their bodies

---

14   Most of these are from an appendix in *The Strong Arm of the Law* by P.A.J. Waddington who got them from the Tactical Options Manual published by the United Kingdom Association of Chief Police Officers.

perpendicular to the boundary with the crowd. Each grabs the belt of the one in front and the police move toward the crowd through a series of side steps. This is colloquially referred to as a 'Chorus Line.' Wedging is a specialized form of trudging in which the line takes the shape of a chevron with the tip moving into the crowd as a wedge. This is used to either access particularly violent crowd members for the sake of arrest, to divide a crowd in two (in which the chevron eventually opens in the middle) or to systematically move a crowd back (the tip moves into the crowd then remains in place as the wings of the chevron advance to form a straight line at an advanced position.

Shield Cordons
Shield cordons are lines of demarcation formed by shields that form a wall. Up to three long shields can be physically locked together; they are held up by a team of five—three directly behind the shields and two behind who support the others. A wall of shield units can allow for some police to dart through the gaps to arrest individual protesters and then bring them back behind the line. A short shield cordon makes use of shields small enough to be held on the weaker arm. Sometimes a team of four—two with short shields and two with no shields will advance into a crowd to make an arrest.

Vehicle Tactics
Vehicles can be used to either quickly transport additional police to where they are needed or serve as physical barriers.

Animal Tactics
Mounted police or police with dogs can emerge from behind a cordon to help induce a crowd to move back.

Space between a Cordon and a Crowd
If police wish to maintain a distance between a cordon and a crowd they can use tear gas or water cannons to keep a crowd at bay.

Pens, Limited Access, and 'No Broken Windows'
The New York Police Department has added pens, limited access, and 'no broken windows' to control tactics (Vitale, 2005). The 'pens' are made of moveable fence sections that keep groups of protesters separated from one

another. This hampers the distribution of pamphlets, communication and coordinated action. Police also restrict access to the demonstration; that is, there are limited points of entry to the demonstration site. Protesters may have to walk up to a mile to get to an access point. 'No broken windows' is a metaphor derived from crime prevention where it refers to immediately repairing any broken window in a marginalized neighborhood to avoid the appearance of decline that might set in motion a spiral of deterioration. In a public order context, it entails zero tolerance for contravention of laws or directives from police such as no demonstration on a given street. The first person trying to challenge police directives is immediately arrested as an example to the others.

Pre-emptive Exclusion
When police suspect that certain people will cause 'trouble,' they will keep them from joining a demonstration. If these people have to cross national borders, they will simply not let them into the country. In the case of people within a country, they may try to find some reason to arrest and detain these people to keep them out of a protest crowd. This pre-emptive exclusion tactic is based on police intelligence.

Intelligence Gathering
From the early days of public order policing, it has been important to police to gather intelligence about major protests. Some intelligence gathering involves being attentive to what is in the public domain. In the past posters and pamphlets advertising a protest would have been the equivalent of web sites, blogs and twitter sites that now communicate protest events in a manner that is open to the public. Other methods include the use of undercover agents to penetrate planning meetings of protesters, plain clothes officers being present in the crowd as observers, and paying informers to provide information. One example is Mathilda Gifford who was offered money to inform on Plane Stupid, a group protesting airport expansion in Britain (Lewis and Vallée, 2009). She taped recruitment interviews with a detective and his assistant in which they offered her money for information about the internal dynamics of Plane Stupid. They claimed to have 'thousands' giving them information. In another twist, access to information has shown that public servants in Britain from the Department for Transport are collecting information on protest groups and giving it to police (Tayor, 2009).

Electronic intelligence work extends to monitoring electronic communications (in many countries a warrant is required to do this), maintaining data bases on individuals associated with protest movement and sharing information between countries. Information from surveillance and concealed cameras also adds to the intelligence.

New technologies function both ways, as Leonard Stern observes:

> Everyone has a cell phone camera these days, which means that every protester is a kind of 'journalist,' empowered with the ability to record and to document. Take a look at what's happening in Iran. Most of the images and reports have come from participants, not professional news gatherers. This makes it almost impossible for police or security agents to get away with brutality. The shooting of the poor Iranian girl, Neda, captured on amateur video, was within hours viewed by the entire world. Even a totalitarian government like Iran's couldn't stop that.

> Back in 1997 at the APEC demonstrations in Vancouver, it was just dumb luck that TV cameras captured the RCMP's controversial pepper spraying. If that happened today, the scene would be captured from a dozen different angles and instantly uploaded to the Internet, just like the tasering of Robert Dziekanski in 2007.

> In Iran, the student protesters have been using these technologies to great effect. The Iranian government likes to dispatch plainclothes security agents into the crowds but the protesters are able to identify these agents, take their photos with their cellphones, then circulate the photos electronically (on the Internet, cellphone to cellphone) so that everyone knows who the agents are.[15]

Stern's observations are echoed in recommendation 11 in a report of the United Kingdom Home Affairs Parliamentary Committee:

> Policing public protest is an activity under much greater scrutiny than twenty to thirty years ago, Sir Paul Stephenson told us that 'as technology

---

15   This is from an e-mail to Vern Neufeld Redekop dated July 31, 2009 and is used with permission.

changes, there are different ways and many more opportunities for people to be caught behaving badly if they choose to behave badly.' This undoubtedly increases the pressure under which front-line police officers have to work; because of this they have our sympathy. However, this does not excuse behaviour which appears to contravene the norms of democratic protest. The police must be aware that their behaviour will be monitored, recorded and instantly made public via the internet. They must modify their behaviour and briefings accordingly. (Home Affairs Committee, 2009)

Certainly technology is changing the dynamics of protest in many respects by shaping the quality of information that is available and rapidly shared on both sides of the line. How this technology is used depends on the orientation of the parties involved and, in the case of the police, the limits established by law, government and regulatory bodies.

We will now illustrate public order policing techniques through a description of what happened during the large G20[16] protest in London in April 2009.

The Case of the 2009 G20 Protest in London

On April 1 and 2, 2009, there was a Summit of leaders from 20 countries in the center of London. 35,000 protesters attempted to get their messages across to these leaders. While most of what happened was peaceful, minimizing disruption to businesses and bystanders, there were tactics used by the police and particular incidents of violence that raised questions about trends in public order policing (Home Affairs Committee, 2009). We will return to these tactics shortly but first we will put the situation into context.

The Metropolitan Police Service was notified about the Summit on December 18, 2008, allowing just over three months to prepare (Metropolitan Police Authority, 2009). The main event was in the Excel centre, seven miles

---

16   The Group of Twenty (G-20) Finance Ministers and Central Bank Governors was established in 1999 to bring together systemically important industrialized and developing economies to discuss key issues in the global economy. The inaugural meeting of the G-20 took place in Berlin, hosted by German and Canadian finance ministers. The G-20 is made up of the finance ministers and central bank governors of 19 countries plus the European Union. http://www.g20.org/about_what_is_g20. aspx This particular G20 was a Summit that included national leaders; it was the first overseas visit of President Obama.

from the centre of London with only two roads in and out. Multiple police services had to work together on what the police called Operation Glencoe. Police worked long hours of overtime. In anticipating contingencies for planning purposes, the terrorist threat was assessed as Severe, though there never was a specific threat. Police describe their take on what was going on among protesters as follows:

> Open source monitoring of protest group websites made it quite clear that their intention was to bring the City to a halt by whatever means possible. Most groups clearly stated that they would be peaceful but they would take part in direct action, openly breaking the law to achieve their ends. Other groups clearly stated they would use force and violence if required. A leader of one of the groups appeared on national television urging people to break windows and occupy buildings. (Metropolitan Police Authority, 2)

In this situation, there were some techniques and events that drew widespread public criticism.

One example of these tactics is kettling, a containment strategy and tactical measure used by the police in accordance with Section 14 of the Public Order Act 1986. Some applications not required by the Act include:

> Outside the Bank of England, thousands were held for up to eight hours behind a police cordon, in a practice known as 'kettling'. Parents with children and passers-by were told by officers on the cordon that 'no one could leave'.

> According to witnesses, when they were finally allowed to go on Wednesday night, they were ordered to provide names and addresses and have their pictures taken. If they refused, they were sent back behind the cordon.

> John O'Connor, a former Met officer, criticised the tactic. 'They are using this more and more,' he said. 'Instead of sending snatch squads in to remove those in the crowd who are committing criminal offences, they contain everyone for hours. It is a retrograde step ... it is an infringement of civil liberties.' (Laville and Campbell, 2009)

The report of the Home Affairs Committee weighs in on this issue in its recommendations:

The use of containment involves a shift in power and control from the protesters to the police and should be used sparingly and in clearly defined circumstances. These circumstances should be codified ...

There is no excuse for the police preventing peaceful protesters or other people innocently caught up in a protest from leaving a 'contained' area when the police can be sure that they do not pose a violent threat to society. This is doubly true when people are asking to leave for medical (or related) purposes. We are particularly concerned at the evidence we have received suggesting that an explicit order was given to maintain the 'cohesion' of the police lines at the expense of peaceful protesters' right to egress and to access medicine. (Home Affairs Committee, 2009, 28)

They also raise concerns about how crowds were sent from the area:

The most troubling aspect of the 'kettling' was the subsequent 'dispersal' of the crowd at around 11:30pm. This has been described as a 'very intense, very rapid clearance ... very scary'. The use of force to disperse protesters in this situation could have been easily avoided and can be traced back to an incorrect application of the 'kettle'. (Home Affairs Committee, 2009, 16)

The report of the Home Affairs Committee also focuses on a lack of communication between police and the media; and most importantly, between police and protesters. Several things contributed to this. The untrained, inexperienced officers that were employed on the front lines during the G20 had a strong crowd control mentality that relied on force. Many of their actions were not in accordance with the Association of Chief Police Officers Guidelines. Some had an 'us' and 'them' approach from the outset that is dehumanizing to protesters and fails to facilitate the democratic right to protest. To quote the Committee, 'those who protest on Britain's streets are not criminals but citizens motivated by moral principles, exercising their democratic rights.' (Home Affairs Committee, 2009, 25) Police exclusive reliance on force and the perception that they do not want to be held accountable for this, ultimately brings a disrespectful response from protesters that can result in personal harm and death. '... their actions will be filmed whether or not journalists are present.' (Home Affairs Committee, 2009, 27) The disturbing incident of the police attack on Ian Tomlinson, who was not part of the protest but a bystander walking home from work, illustrates that others can easily get caught up in the ensuing violence. Tomlinson died of natural causes shortly after being hit with a baton by a Metropolitan Police Service officer.

Communication is the responsibility of both sides. While the police failed in this respect, so did the protesters. By choosing to form large disparate organizations with no leaders for police to communicate with, protesters are setting themselves up for being uninformed. The Home Affairs Committee was critical of the reticent attitude of some protesters in the containment area and suggested they make more effort to prevent police viewing them as a threat by communicating their peaceful intent. (Home Affair Committee, 2009, 29)

The Committee also emphasized that 35,000 protesters participated in London with minimum disruption to the City.

Repression versus Negotiation

At various times in different countries, the weapons and tactics available to police coupled with a political climate antithetical to protest result in repressive police measures. Repressive policing involves the use of weapons and physical control tactics to limit or shut down the expression of dissent.

In the 80 and 90s repressive tendencies have been displaced by what is known in policing circles as negotiated management, otherwise referred to as 'soft' tactics. The word 'negotiation' has a range of meanings in this context. In its purer form it includes the facilitation of conditions and processes that address the needs and interests of protesters. One example comes from Jean-Marc Collin, an RCMP officer who was confronted in the Maritimes with fishers who were angry about government decisions that affected their livelihood. They occupied a Department of Fisheries and Oceans (DFO) office. After several days of listening to their concerns and generating ideas, Collins was able to arrange a meeting with DFO officials and the conflict was peacefully settled. However, others with firsthand experience of police–protester relations, show that some of what passes for 'negotiation' is a series of procedural and discursive processes whereby protesters end up doing things the way the police want them to do it. (Sopow, 2003; P.A.J. Waddington, 1998). They maintain that true negotiations involve each side giving up something to accommodate the interests of the other. In interest based negotiation there is a clear identification of each other's interests and a shared effort to come up with solutions that accommodate each side. Whether the discursive practices are true negotiation or a form of manipulation depends on the goodwill, open-heartedness and understanding of negotiation on the part of police and protesters involved. The following practices fall under the rubric of 'soft' practices.

1. Permit to Protest

In many jurisdictions it is mandatory for demonstrators to apply for a permit, sometimes a minimum of three days in advance. This allows police time to prepare for the protest, establish who the leaders are and determine a projected size of the demonstration and what activities might be used in conjunction with it.

2. Offer to Help

At the time of filling out an application for the protest, police will offer to help with the planning. They will point out logistical challenges involved in particular routes or sites and make suggestions helping to make the logistics as straightforward as possible.

3. Friendly Smiles

The attitude of police dealing with crowd organizers is deliberately friendly (P.A.J. Waddington, 1991).

4. Indirect Direction

When plans include a venue that is incongruent with police preferences or protest tactics that are unacceptable, rather than confront the ideas head on and say that they are not allowed, police will point out the potential problems and suggest ways to solve the problems.

5. Official Liaison Roles

Police will appoint liaison officers who maintain contact with crowd organizers. Sometimes they will even lead the protest.

6. Collaboration

Police liaison officers will encourage a spirit of collaboration, with police blocking roads and doing other things to facilitate a protest march or gathering.

7. Institutionalization of Procedures

As the same protesters work together with the same police, eventually procedures are formalized. If arrests are called for as part of a protest, these are orchestrated and become a public drama.

One of the dangers of institutionalization of protest, from the perspective of dissent, and hence, society, is that it can make the expression of dissent limpid and ineffective.

Legal and Political Developments

There are two sets of developments on the legal and political front. The first has to do with the rights of protesters to protest and the second has to do with limitations on police powers or the granting of additional powers to police.

Right to Protest

In democratic societies, there is a right to protest expressed in rights of free expression and assembly. In the United Kingdom, this is not formalized in law but is accepted as a right through custom. In United States this right is expressed in the First Amendment to the Constitution. In France it has been expressed in law. In Canada, the Charter of Rights and Freedoms provides for fundamental freedoms of thought, belief, opinion and expression, freedom of peaceful assembly and freedom of association (Mackenzie & Plecas, 2005). The right to protest, besides being developed in law has been extended through court decisions including decisions from Supreme Courts. In United States it is highly controversial, and for many most offensive, to burn the flag; however, legal decisions have upheld flag-burning as being consistent with the right of free expression (McPhail et al., 1998; M. Welch, 2000).

In Europe, the issue of order versus transnational protest rights is in the process of being worked out in practice. As Reiter and Fillieule point out,

(t)he very police powers coming to play in EU protest policing are ill defined and there are few, if any, public fora of debate on these issues. A similar picture emerges if we look at the *transnational* protest rights of the citizens of the EU: protest rights are formalized in the European

Convention on Human Rights and in the EU Charter of Fundamental Rights. However, until recently the concrete forms and boundaries of protest rights were rarely tested beyond the national level. Consequently, the declarations contained in the Convention and the Charter are not supported by a consolidated *practice of transnational protest rights*. (2006, 146)

The complexity of the situation in Europe is compounded by the fact that member states are responsible for security issues, on the one hand, but there is a trend toward transnational police collaboration, particularly with regard to intelligence on the other. Reiter and Fillieule raise concerns about democratic accountability in this context (2006).

In Canada, in tension with the freedom to protest is the Peace, Order and Good Government clause of the Constitution Act of 1867, which mandates against protest groups. This ambiguity, along with controversies such as the U.S. flag-burning issue, reinforces the point that the protest crowd–police dividing line reflects a boundary line that is physical, moral and legal. It is the space (physical and metaphorical) where anything can happen and where the scripts directing each side must remain open-ended. It is the edge of chaos where anything can happen but what does happen is largely shaped by the operative paradigms including the legal structure.

Directives on Public Order Policing
In Canada, the British inspired principle of the independence of police from political control is a well established legally and in practice:

Canadian Courts have upheld the validity of the doctrine of operational independence by confirming the decision of Lord Denning in the leading English case of *R. v. Commissioner of Police of the Metropolis, ex. P. Blackburn*. The doctrine of operational independence holds that police chiefs are independent from political interference when making decisions regarding deployment of personnel, identifying which offenses to investigate and what charges to lay, or determining how best to handle matters such as public disturbances or disorder. Police chiefs, the commissioner of the RCMP, and provincial police force commissioners cannot be directed in operational matters by politicians, police governing authorities, or even the attorney general or solicitor general. (Mackenzie & Plecas, 2005)

Despite this operational independence, there are strong accountability provisions in legislation; as well, there are external complaints commissions and those harmed by overzealous police can sue for damages (Mackenzie & Plecas, 2005). Within a framework of accountability, it is up to police forces/services to design their own policies and procedures when it comes to protest policing.

In United States, protest policing has been shaped in large measure by the Kerner, in 1968, Eisenhower, in 1969, and Scranton, in 1970, Commissions that were established in response to problematic instances of civil disorder. The Eisenhower Commission saw excessive force as something that would 'magnify turmoil' and advocated that 'the respect for protest, the willingness to negotiate its time, place, and manner, and the granting of permits for protest are the best means of avoiding the necessity of policing, not to mention the use of unnecessary levels of force' (McPhail et al., 1998). The recommendations of these Commissions had an impact on the development of a Civil Disturbance Orientation Course (CDOC which became SEADOC), the second version of which from 1972 on was instrumental in prompting police across United States to develop Public Order Management Systems (POMS). These are now the norm in established democracies.

In the United Kingdom, there is no special framework for public order policing; it is simply part of the job of policing for which the police are responsible (P.A.J. Waddington, 1998).

Micael Björk compares the legal framework for protest between Denmark and Sweden using justice and order as two possible emphases (Björk, 2005). The Swedish legal framework emphasizes justice and takes a more legalistic approach to managing protest. This increases frustration on the part of police, leading, he argues, to a greater tendency toward aggression. Denmark's legal framework is based on order, is simple, and leads to 'opportunistic' policing. The latitude and discretion afforded Danish police leads to less frustration and, hence, less aggression.

Enforcement of Laws
Insofar as there is the potential for laws to be broken in the course of crowd action, police have a mandate to enforce laws. There is considerable ambiguity in this strategic goal in that it is sometimes unclear which laws are being broken. The protest itself may be about perceived breaking of laws on the part of Government. At times the act of enforcing certain laws

could lead to crowd violence. Sometimes in the case of widespread civil disobedience it would be literally impossible to enforce the law. Also, in some circumstances, the 'law is a ass' to quote Charles Dickens (Ciacccia, 2000). In other words, the application of law in some contexts is pragmatically counterproductive at best and morally wrong at worst. Examples of the latter are discriminatory laws that restrict civil rights based on race or gender. Given these ambiguities, police have considerable discretion as to how they approach law enforcement. There is always the tension between maintaining a sense that society is under the rule of law and enforcing the law with such vigour that society loses respect for the law and those standing behind it. Furthermore, these ambiguities reinforce the analysis of the protest crowd–police encounter as being on the edge of chaos.

Avoiding 'Troubles'

Public order police wish to avoid 'troubles' at all costs. Waddington distinguishes between troubles *on* the job and troubles *in* the job (P.A.J. Waddington, 1998). In the former, things get out of hand such that coercive tactics need to be used, potentially generating an inquiry or special forms to fill out. The latter 'troubles in the job' involve doing things that get the police in trouble internally. This can take the form of subjecting police to internal reprimand or the police force/service[17] being criticized by those whom they ignore at their (political) peril—cabinet members, elite business leaders, popular 'stars,' heads of state or, in the United Kingdom, members of the Royal Family. This latter point needs some clarification. In democratic societies, police are to be free of political meddling in how they do their jobs. They are often responsible to boards that are at arm's length from the political process. The reality is, according Waddington, that when people in positions of power or authority complain, it makes for 'trouble.' Police are willing to give protesters considerable latitude in doing things that are strictly illegal in order to avoid troubles. One example in Ottawa was a crowd organized by the Marijuana Party. Those in the crowd were smoking up—as long as they did this only within the boundaries of the demonstration, police looked the other way. To try to arrest the large number involved would have certainly meant 'troubles.'

---

17   Police refer to themselves as police 'forces' or police 'services' indicating which aspects of their role is emphasized (Brown & Waters, 1996).

In situations of dictatorship or weak states, the potential for troubles for the police on account of over aggressive policing are negligible; on the other hand, failure to protect the state's (dictator's) interest gives rise to troubles.

Specialized Roles

Police and other security personnel play various roles. These include intelligence units that provide information on the size and kind of crowd anticipated, front line tactical police, troop commanders and officers in charge of overall strategy. There are also units that specialize in the use of specific less-than-lethal technologies such as tear gas, dogs or horses, or in the use of special transportation such as helicopters, and so on. Others are responsible for logistics and emergency preparations, while another group is closer to foreign dignitaries, briefing their body guards and ensuring smooth collaboration among diverse security groups.

In the case of large international events there may be several police services, some international, involved in collaboration with one another. In these international gatherings, security personnel from other countries are sent for advance briefings, and foreign leaders are sometimes accompanied by their own bodyguards.

In some countries such as Canada, the military is available to assist the civil authority (Lerhe, 2004; Paré, 2002)[18]. In non democratic situations, the distinctions between police and military are not as clear (Vejnovic & Lalic, 2005). In post-conflict situations, peacekeepers are often put in a role not unlike public order police with similar challenges. The Canadian Forces are usually considered the heavy hand and their influence is mostly reserved for security service outside Canada. However, the Canadian Forces can be called out in 'aid of the civil power' at the request of the federal or a provincial government. For example, the 1970 October Crisis kidnappings and murder by the Front de Liberation du Québec led to a massive security operation by police services and the Canadian Armed Forces. Similarly, the 1976 Olympics saw police services and the Canadian Forces cooperating once again to protect Olympic sites, athletes and others against a possible recurrence of the terrorist attack at the 1972 Olympics in Munich. During

---

18   In the United States the Posse Comitatus Act restricts the use of the regular army in domestic situations; rather the National Guard (reserve soldiers normally under the control of the State governor but who could also respond to the President) is called upon for back-up; however, the President can call upon the army in extreme circumstances (Kratcoski, Verma, & Das, 2001).

the Oka/Kanehsatà:ke Crisis of 1990 the Canadian Forces were called out to assist the Sûreté du Québec as a result of blockades by First Nations protesters at Oka and on the Mercier Bridge. Protecting the site of the 2002 G8 International Summit in Kananaskis involved unique military skills and consequently required the Forces to be called out once again to assist the civil power.

Public Order Management Systems (POMS)

Negotiation techniques, intelligence gathering, strategic planning using available tactics, media coordination and social psychological review are combined in Public Order Management Systems (POMS) that allow all the different aspects of protest policing to be coordinated. POMS try to achieve predictability in advance and lines of communication to help things get on track if something unexpected happens (Sopow, 2003). The potential for violence is reduced through a balance of

> negotiation and consultation, providing a visible 'soft hat' police presence (police officers in standard, everyday uniforms) at the protest, but also ensuring that protesters know that police are ready to within seconds to (sic) deploy battle-ready tactical team member equipped with pepper spray and batons who are standing by in the background. (Sopow, 2003)

Citing documents from the New York Police Department, the Royal Canadian Mounted Police and the US Department of Homeland Security, Sopow goes on to show that within a management system police are framed as trusted facilitators. POMS contribute to the institutionalizing of both protest and protest policing, with shared interests between police and professional protest organizers in 'predictability, non-violence, and orderly behavior.' (Sopow, 2003)

Public order management brings together police training, policies, practice and technologies into an organized system (P.A.J. Waddington, 1998) that includes pre-event planning, tactics and command structure during a protest event and post-event de-briefs. POMS have emerged in an environment that values negotiation and non-confrontation approaches with protesters while being prepared for more repressive control measures. However, policing systems may end up being anywhere on a continuum with negotiated management at one end and command and control on the other. As has been pointed out above, recent policies of the New York Police Department have emphasized command and control tactics (Björk, 2005) and other jurisdictions have used apparently soft approaches while maintaining a strong coercive capacity (King and D. Waddington, 2006). POMS provide for both ends of the spectrum and everything in between.

Dynamics of Public Order Policing

So far we have looked at the complex array of factors that influence how protest police do their job. At the first level we find a range of the philosophical orientations, strategies, and tactics. Influencing these at a second level are the legal framework, technology and techniques. All of these come together at a third level, the moment when a protesting crowd is on the verge of starting a destructive riot. David Waddington has developed a flashpoint model to analyze and describe this third level that influences how police work (King & Waddington, 2005; Waddington, Jones, & Critcher, 1989). Waddington sees flashpoints occurring with the convergence of the following six factors: structural, ideological, cultural, contextual, situational, and interactional. These are presented as concentric circles with structural at the outside and interactional nested at the centre (Waddington et al., 1989). We will show how King and Waddington used this framework to analyze the protester–police dynamics at the 2001 Québec City Summit of the Americas. This will provide context for the Strategic Leaders Seminar described in Part Two.

In their overview, King and Waddington point out that 7000 police and 680 army personnel were involved in providing security to the government leaders who met in Québec 20–22 April, 2001 (King & Waddington, 2005). Police put up a 6.1 kilometer three-meter high fence around the conference sight. It was able to withstand 20,000 pounds of pressure. The day the Summit was to begin a group of protesters marched to the 'wall of shame' where some of them succeeded in penetrating the fence. The tear gas and ensuing confrontation delayed the start of the proceedings by 90 minutes. The next day 60,000 protesters were involved. Most of these were self-disciplined but 7,000 had direct clashes with police. In addition to water cannon, plastic bullet rounds, police discharged 5,000 tear gas canisters (King & Waddington, 2005).

King and Waddington analyze the situation using the flashpoints model as follows:

Structural—within the protest organizations was the concern that implementation of free trade policies in the hemisphere would be heartless, without conscience, harming the environment and the most vulnerable. Furthermore, youth participants did not feel represented by political institutions.

Ideological—in the wake of the Seattle protests that halted WTO talks, there was a 'political imperative' to make certain the Québec talks went off without disruptions; hence a 'die in the ditch' resolve to be uncompromising (King & Waddington, 2005).

Cultural—labour staged a peaceful march but the Black Bloc proved to be more disruptive. As King and Waddington observe, "Police knowledge' played a pivotal role in framing their strategy for Quebec City. Culturally mediated perceptions of the threat posed by 'bad demonstrators' (primarily the Black Bloc), combined with their political obligation to protect the Summit and its attending dignitaries, inclined them toward a particular strategic response available within their existing repertoire' (2005).

Contextual—in the weeks before the event, feelings started to run high about the summit and the perimeter wall. New Democratic Party Member of Parliament Sven Robinson arranged for civil disobedience training on Parliament Hill; 450 people demonstrated at Foreign Affairs; and leading artists and political activists made a public statement against the perimeter barricade. Police had negotiations with protest organizers, trusting labour but fearing that anti-global protesters would not be restrained (King & Waddington, 2005).

Situational—'soft hats' were used to police the labour march but a siege mentality was evident when it came to policing the fence which became a symbol of what protesters found most troublesome. There were a 'wide range of situational objectives, including varying commitment to the use of violence as a means to an end' (King & Waddington, 2005). These included trying to reach the fence, breach the fence, or perform various symbolic actions on the fence (e.g. tying bras on the fence to protest the plight of poor women). For the police the wall was a good diversion from anything that would threaten foreign visitors or businesses in the area.

Interactional—the flashpoint came when some protesters climbed the fence and through a rocking motion brought it down. Rounds of tear gas followed and for two hours protesters charged the fence only to rebuffed by tear gas, short shield units of police and dogs (King & Waddington, 2005). Thereafter the use of tear gas and plastic bullets went up as did the determination of protesters. There were several incidents of violent confrontation. In one instance a group of 500 singing protesters were trapped by police who threw tear gas into the group to disperse them. However, in another instance a sit-down protest resulted in a standoff, which ended with an RCMP commander giving instructions that shields and batons be lowered, this was interpreted as a sign of respect to the protesters (King & Waddington, 2005).

The range of issues involved with public order policing, from legal and strategic framework to the use of technology to organization and tactics raises a number of ethical considerations which we will look at in the next section.

Ethical Aspects of Public Order Policing

We will begin by looking at public order policing as a function of various relational configurations involving protest crowds, targets, police and bystanders. This abstract presentation will provide the context for the issues and questions which follow.

Figure 4.1 Security Orientation vis-à-vis Crowds

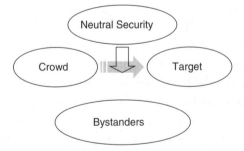

Public Order Policing in the Abstract

On occasions when protest crowds express dissatisfaction with a target, security forces/services are called upon to come between the crowds and targets. There can be different relationships between crowds, targets and security or at least different perceived inter-relationships. Security can be perceived as neutral, pro-target or pro-crowd. The first of these is as depicted above (Figure 4.1).

In this situation security is neutral in relation to both crowds and targets. 'Neutral' is always a relative term; in this case it is used to designate a situation in which there is a sufficient perception of neutrality on the part of both the crowd and target that neither would think that the security intervention was favouring the other side. As individuals, we are seldom truly neutral in a specific situation; however, with a neutral mindset, intention and practice we can behave neutrally. Examples of neutral security might be when two opposing groups of citizens clash (e.g. pro-life versus pro-choice demonstrators), or conflicting ethnic groups demonstrate on different sides of an issue, or a strike where police are called upon to protect each side from violence exerted by the other. The role of security is to make certain that no one is hurt on either side. Police can impose order or they can facilitate order. Police as security personnel do not have a particular position on what is going on and their role is neutral. Neutrality can exist on two levels—neutrality with regards to the issue and neutrality in a role. If police are personally neutral about the issue then it is easier and more natural for them to be neutral when dealing with the crowd—to play a facilitative role. Similarly, neutrality can shift.

Figure 4.2 Security Orientation vis-à-vis Crowds

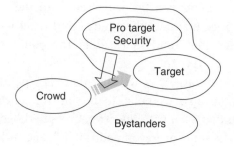

It is relatively easy for police to behave neutrally in the planning stages; however, during the operation one incident can push them towards the primary mission of protecting the target and keeping the peace. What is significant is how people perceive themselves and how others perceive them. Within a democracy, there are many situations in which police see themselves as being neutral; however, those who have experienced police repression and abuse, even in other countries, feel the presence of police as being provocative.

In many instances, security has a particular role to play with regard to the target. They basically have to protect the target (political representatives, industry representatives or the managers of a company) from any violence perpetrated by the crowd (Figure 4.2). This is the case when activists are protesting against the government. The fact that some police may share the opinion of the protesters is of no consequence. The police in this scenario must behave neutrally with regards to the issue; however, their role is associated with protection of the target and keeping the peace. Nonetheless, it has been observed that their behaviour toward protesters changes if they agree with the issues (Kratcoski et al., 2001). The operational objective is to keep the crowd at bay so that those whom the crowd targets can proceed with the job at hand unimpeded by the actions of the crowd. This kind of scenario raises some questions. Since police within a democracy see their role as keeping the peace and protecting the public from harm, does the fact that they are put into this kind of position in a particular instance, compromise their calling? In other words, in this situation what is their role in relation to the well-being of the crowd? And what role would the crowd let them play?

Also, if protesters see the police as representatives of the government, the target of their protest, then the frustrations and anger generated by government policies can be projected onto the police. When this happens, 'the police may feel threatened and react with heavy-handed aggressive tactics that tend to escalate the conflict on both sides.' (Kratcoski et al., 2001)

Whether police are targets or whether there is a political agenda in the protest, the relationship of the police to the state is important. Brewer, et al., take the position that even with the best efforts to de-politicize the police, there will always be some degree of political influence—the question is how much. They use six axes along which there can be strong or weak relations between police and the state (Brewer, Guelke, Hume, Moxon-Browne, & Wilford, 1996):

1. Political beliefs—in a strong relation 'police conduct is structured by [state sympathetic] beliefs.'
2. Policing as an issue—in the strong form, police identify with a particular party.
3. Police resources—at the strong end of the axis, police manipulate government priorities through security threats to get additional resources.
4. Government policies—the strong manifestation includes a positive bias toward policies and denial of 'legitimate opposition to them or in the expression of alternative values.'
5. Government values and ideology—police may actively support values and ideology.
6. Police conduct as a reflection on state institutions—the strong form indicates that police 'deliberately manufacture positive images by careful presentation of its conduct.'

These authors also suggest that police strategies in relation to public disorder include criminalization, accommodation and repression. Both the politicization of police and the strategies they use become part of a framework for ethical questioning.

There is another trend linking security to the target. In this case, corporations that could become targets hire security services that will

Figure 4.3 Security Orientation vis-à-vis Crowds

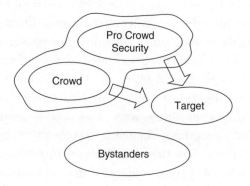

protect them from protesters. One example, Wackenhut Services, offers paramilitary security to protect the Savannah nuclear facility run by the U.S. Department of Energy. The private police force (accredited by the Commission on Accreditation of Law Enforcement Agencies) operates special response teams and a helicopter. The officers are equipped with military rifles and uniforms. They are prepared for anti nuclear protests (Rigakos, 2005). Other specialized private security firms will protect companies from labour protests, even supplying temporary labour to keep companies going (Rigakos, 2005).

In some cases security personnel may side with the crowd (Figure 4.3). Sometimes the personal beliefs of members of security overcome their role of protecting the target. This was the case during the Winnipeg General Strike of 1919 when 'local police resolved to join rather than fight the workers.' (Rigakos, 2005) Similarly, individual security members may simply be following the orders of their superiors who have switched allegiance from the target to a new leader who is supported by the crowd. This was the scenario following the Serbian elections in which Slobodan Milosevic was defeated. Milosevic would not accept the results and was determined to stay in power. Had the security forces accepted his claim to be in control, they might have enforced it in the face of an angry crowd. However, they chose to side with the crowd against Milosevic. It should be noted that this is an unusual circumstance with regard to protest crowds, and it is usually associated with the dying days of a repressive regime such as Milosevic's. The last days of Ceausescu in Romania is another example.

Ethical Issues and Questions
Ethics involves a thoughtful reflection on practical knowledge and wisdom which by definition is a reflection on action. Ethics probes the nature, orientation and moral valence that can be attributed to different actions. Where there is a consensus on values related to generic types of action, a code of conduct is articulated as a set of rules or laws. This represents the deontological moment—the moment when there is an ethical duty or obligation to take a particular action. 'Deontological' comes from *deons* meaning duty and *logos* meaning a rational discourse about something; hence a statement of moral principles. Ethics is much more than this. It examines intentions, proportionality and consequences of actions—intended and unintended. It also looks

at the teleological dimensions of ethical reflection—broad implications, goals and ends of an action. Ethics also is concerned with the origins of beliefs, values and customs and how these are brought to bear on a determination of the ethical valence of a given culture. Given the complexity of human action, there is often ambiguity: certain actions that are intended to do good end up doing the opposite; or there are multiple consequences of a given action such that some are good and some are bad; or there is a choice to be made between two courses each of which involves a different but compelling good; or one must choose between two evils.

Actions can involve basic actions, chains of related actions or ongoing action practices. Sometimes the outcome of an ethical reflection changes as actions are looked at in temporal and circumstantial context or if a basic action is considered as a precedent for ongoing practices.

Within established democracies, there is a consensus on a number of points that could constitute a protest policing deontology: respect the rights of freedom of expression and of assembly; use a minimum of force (though this would be debated by those devoted to command and control approaches (Vitale, 2005)); avoid confrontation; put public order and good relations above rigorous enforcement of the law; in no way let crowds have any access to Internationally Protected Persons and so on. Even with agreement on basic principles, there are a number of areas that are deserving of ethical reflection. The discussion of the issue areas below is intended to highlight what is at stake from an ethical perspective.

Police Judgment of Crowds and Issues

As was pointed out in the section on Protest Crowds, there are different levels of ethical consciousness reflected in the different issues about which crowds might be gathered to protest. Some crowds are clearly gathered for the sake of the public good and formulate their goals in a way that transcends narrow self interest. Some crowds are drawn from one identity group, are motivated by hatred and communicate a desire to work against the interests and well-being of different groups. At times this hatred is based on historic injustices and at other times it is based on stereotypes, fear or hyperthumia—a manic desire for superior recognition. A crowd may have a centre of gravity that reflects both an orientation and a level of consciousness.

This difference in protest crowds raises the question for policing, should a crowd be treated differently based on the level of moral discourse or level of consciousness? If so, who is to judge? Is it at all legitimate for police to be making such judgments? Is it their role? If not the police, then who? Police, as human beings, do have values and they do make judgments. We remember one senior officer, reflecting on the protest at the Summit of the Americas in 2001, who mentioned that he agreed with most of the positions of the protesters and went on to say that 'Our wives and children are part of the protest crowd.' Other judgments are not that generous. It is not uncommon for police to characterize crowds as 'the enemy' or to develop negative stereotypes of various types of protesters, particularly those dressed in black.

This raises the questions, Are crowds treated differently on the basis of the issues they espouse and who might be in the crowds? ... and Should they be?

An open question, then, is how should we handle the phenomenon of police and judgment of protest crowds?

Police as Shapers of Society

Police are leaders in society; their conduct can have a profound impact, for good or ill, on the evolution of societal customs and values. They function as one of several groups in the dynamic changes that take place in a given community. In the case of the Metropolitan Police of London, it is clear that the style of policing was reflective of and at the same time was a shaper of British society. If this is the case, who is to evaluate the longitudinal impact of protest policing styles? For example, there is in the public media significant emphasis on gratuitous violence, in which violent 'good guys' suppress the threat and impact of the 'bad guys' (Wink, 1992). If the police buy into this mentality, it is easy for them to relish physical confrontation with disruptive protesters and thus frame themselves as heroes. However, they have the option of deliberately working to raise the public level of moral consciousness by concentration on other means of 'crowd management.'

The questions then become

- How might the police be involved in influencing culture and public consciousness?
- Who monitors this aspect of police work?
- Which values are paramount as a basis for police action?

Crowd Control and Management

The very concept of crowd control, and even the substitution of 'crowd management' as a term used in protest policing raises a number of issues. First this kind of discourse is a throw-back to Le Bon's concept of a crowd as a collective entity and even suggests that such an entity is irrational and needs to be controlled. We have shown that it often makes more sense to think of a crowd as a temporary gathering of well-informed thoughtful individuals who are engaged in extra-parliamentary democratic action. Isn't it paternalistic to think of 'controlling' such a temporary gathering? Yet the reality is that there are times when riotous behaviour is evident, lives are threatened and property is damaged. Is there a kind of discourse that would include placing limits on the protesters' actions without recourse to a mentality of 'control.' When it comes to 'management' are not protest crowds really managed by their organizers?

Discourse points to a consciousness which has values embedded within it. If change is made only in the words used, the change is often diminished to the level of 'political correctness.' If there is to be a change made in how protest crowds are conceptualized, valued and designated, who will determine this and how will it be communicated throughout the police force/service?

Ultimate Loyalty

To whom or to what are police ultimately loyal at both the individual and collective level? The answer is entwined with some of their strongest values. Possible answers include groups of people, institutions or abstraction concepts like 'the law.' They could be loyal to the community, the government, the police force/service, or to tradition (it is simply not done), rule of law, keeping the peace. How this question is answered, is also a function of level of consciousness. Those functioning at a more complex level will integrate a number of these. Some scholars maintain that ultimate loyalty is to the political masters of the police who form the government. Yet the police do not represent the government and in the context of democratic development, police are to be independent of government in their operations. In fact, one reason for the establishment of the Metropolitan Police of London was to get away from direct local political interference. Mayne and Rowan as strong police commissioners in their own right created a policing culture that had a fair measure of independence from government. In the more abstract presentation of security as being that which stands between protest crowds and targets, three scenarios were presented: security as neutral, security as aligned with the target, and security as aligned with the crowd. These are not absolute categories but they raise the question of the degree to which police have aligned themselves. It is important that there be transparency about the loyalty of police for it will affect their effectiveness and the kinds of relationship they might have with the parties involved.

'Dying in the Ditch' and a Hermeneutics of Suspicion
Within protest policing circles there is an understanding that certain lines constitute such absolute prohibitions that they are prepared to 'die in the ditch' to make certain that they are not crossed. These lines may be geographical or behavioural. It is for maintenance of these ultimate restrictive lines that tactical troops are kept on standby and all sorts of less-than-lethal weapons are procured.

In the case of large crowds organized or self-organized to protest actions of governments or international agencies there is a duty on the part of police to protect government officials. If there are Internationally Protected Persons (IPPs), the pressure on the part of police to avoid mishap is absolute. Should something happen to a foreign head of state or government minister, it would cause an international incident, loss of face for the government that employs the police and serious sanctions for any police officer held responsible. Likewise for domestic leaders.

Many of the tactics, and the negotiation approaches are in place to prevent a situation evolving to the point where police might be called upon to enforce the ultimate restrictions. The parameters of what constitutes a die in the ditch situation point to what really constitutes the primary values of police. There is, however, little public discourse around these absolute prohibitions, which raises the possibility of exercising a hermeneutics of suspicion— raising basic questions—around what they are, where did they come from, and who is responsible for changing them. This kind of discourse does not imply that they will be rejected but it might have the effect of modifying them slightly, and, more importantly, extending the degree to which they are respected as legitimate boundaries by the protesting community. Some creative scenario development involving police and protesters outside the moment of actual decision might help to determine the circumstances under which, for example, the tactical troops need to be called in or less than lethal weapons should be used in the interest of keeping the peace. This might help in the development of new, yet unimagined alternatives to the use of coercive force. It would also clarify who has what authority at each step along the way to make decisions about the use of weapons and forceful tactics.

Intelligence, Interpretation and Transparency

Arising out of the passionate desire on the part of police to neither lose control, be caught off guard, nor be faced with enforcing the ultimate restrictions, the need for preparedness calls for police intelligence. Early on in the history of public order policing, plain clothed officers would mingle with the crowd and report back what was going on and signal potential trouble if they sensed it was in the works. Later detectives worked at gathering information about the organization of protest crowd activities. On the one hand, this is understandable—it makes sense that police wish to be prepared—on the other hand, it raises questions about the lengths police should be allowed to go in the interests of intelligence gathering. It is one thing to talk to organizers in advance to get information about what is planned; it is quite another for police to pose as protesters and go to organizational meetings. It is one thing for police to visit web-sites of protesting organizations; it is another to intercept e-mails or listen in on phone conversations. (Police can only intercept emails and phone conversations with approval of a judge. This approval is given with hard evidence that there is a reasonable surety that something illegal is being communicated.) Once raw information is gathered; it must be interpreted and interpretation is subject to bias. There should also be analysis of mindset orientation and level of consciousness. Sometimes people speak in metaphors or use hyperbole, particularly when there is a good deal of emotion involved. Someone listening in might take words literally when they were never so intended. This raises the question of reality checks on how information taken in by the police is interpreted. Misinterpretation of information can result in people being wrongly arrested and possibly even incarcerated or deported. Who is responsible for checks and balances in this aspect of police work, which may be conducted in a secretive way? A distinction needs to be made between tactics that are used to gather information after a crime for the sake of conviction and tactics that can be used for the sake of prevention.

This chapter has provided an historical overview of the rise and fall of protest policing that has been both supportive and repressive of democratic protest. We have provided some reflection on the issues of the policing organization, then given information on state of the art technological tools and current strategies and tactical options used by police services in Canada and elsewhere. The last section raised many more questions than answers and will provide fertile ground for discussion in the future.

Behind many of these issues is the question of what paradigms are used as the basic lenses through which the phenomena of temporary gatherings of protesters are viewed and information and events interpreted. We are working toward a discussion of paradigmatic options in chapter nine, but before we get to that we have to introduce more theoretical concepts and introduce the other stakeholders. With that in mind we turn now to understandings of how people can be construed as radically other, so much so, that violence against them can be justified.

5. The Violence of 'Otherness': Scapegoating and Hegemonic Structures

We have now introduced protest crowds and given an account of how they have evolved historically to the point they are today. We have shown, through the use of human identity needs theory, that for some protesters, a significant part of their identity is tied up with the cause for which they demonstrate and the injustice against which they protest. In the course of major organized protests they encounter the police. This encounter means that protesters and police become part of a relational system. Each group has to deal with the other in a significant way. Sometimes the encounter lasts for only a single event that includes planning, assembling, crowd activity, dispersal and post event follow-up. In other cases a protest can last a long time—up to several months, years or decades. Other protest activities form action chains or even practices in which one protest crowd after another assembles temporarily over the same issue. This means that the police–protester relational system can be sustained over a long period of time.

Any relational system takes on unique characteristics. If the relational system is mutually hurtful and antagonistic, we can say it has taken on the character of a mimetic structure of violence. Mimetic means that the structure is imitative of both behaviour and intent and so both parties reciprocate ill-will toward one another. If the relationship is mutually beneficial, we say that the character is that of a mimetic structure of blessing. In chapter eight we will develop the concept of mimetic structures of blessing more fully. This chapter introduces mimetic structures of violence; and uses specific theoretical examples of violent relationships where the 'Other' side of the relationship is viewed and treated stereotypically.

Violence can take many forms. Overt physical violence is the most easy to identify. If people are hitting, pounding, throwing stones, shooting, using tear gas, throwing Molotov cocktails, setting fires, or breaking windows, it is easy to say that this looks and feels like violence. Violent actions can be camouflaged, indirect, emotional, or psychological. Threats, or even implied threats, can be forms of violence. Violence forces people to do what they do not wish to do; it hurts them; it diminishes their self-worth and dignity; it keeps them from taking meaningful action; it destroys or steals their property.

The long term effect of violence is that it establishes a rift in the relationship—a profound sense of 'Otherness.' This rift, as it grows in depth, results in dehumanization—the Other is not seen as a dignified human being. It can morph into demonization where the Other is blamed for all that is wrong, or threatens the life of oneself and one's group.

Violence is itself a complex phenomenon with many different aspects to it. In this chapter we will examine in greater detail two dimensions of violence that can play a role in the protest crowd–police relational system; namely, scapegoating and hegemonic, or dominating, structures where stereotypical views of the 'Other' contribute to violence. In the section on scapegoating, the first dimension discussed, we will provide a theoretical base for understanding the violence phenomenon based on the work of French thinker René Girard. Girard makes the observation that scapegoating is a violence of differentiation in which the scapegoat victim becomes completely 'Other.'

Any violence of differentiation can be sustained over time through the second dimension that we will discuss, namely, structures of domination, or hegemonic structures. Those who have the power to subdue others put these hegemonic structures into place. In time, those who are subjected internalize feelings of inferiority. In this way, hegemonic structures are sustained with a minimum of effort or even a minimum of awareness especially on the dominant side. In some instances, police are called upon to maintain hegemonic structures; on the other hand, some social movements are all about breaking free of these structures. In still other instances the protest crowd–police relational system can exemplify characteristics of a hegemonic structure with the police taking on the dominant role. As we look at the different aspects of hegemonic structures, the nature of these dynamics will become clearer. Before that, we will look at the process of scapegoating to clarify by example one way we dehumanize and differentiate 'Others' in our lives.

Scapegoating

Scapegoating involves a frustrated, chaotic community being united in blaming a victim for their troubles and taking out their resentments and violent sentiments on that victim. This phenomenon is often seen emerging within crowds (e.g. burning effigies, chanting against a personality or event), and can also be observed among police (e.g. arresting a token 'trouble-maker'). In a situation where a crowd is angry about an injustice they are facing and frustrated that their message is not getting through to the public, politicians or media (this is important because protest groups will escalate to get publicity), they could make scapegoats of security or even journalists. One example happened during the Oka/Kanehsatà:ke crisis of 1990, Mohawks had blocked the Mercier Bridge turning a 15 minute commute into Montreal into over an hour trip as commuters were forced to take the long way to the city. Protesting crowds in opposition to the blockade were angry about the inconvenience that they thought was unjust, upset with the Mohawks and frustrated with the Government for not resolving the crisis. The scapegoat impulse was like lightening looking for a place to strike. Sometimes members of the crowd turned on journalists or individuals who wore a Canadian flag. They burned in effigy both Premier Bourassa and a Mohawk warrior, examples of symbolic scapegoating. A second example was during the Quebec Summit of the Americas in April 2001, when a Global TV vehicle was trashed by demonstrators. During the Strategic Leaders' Seminar on Crowd Management and Conflict Resolution that May, participants reflected on the fence at Quebec City becoming the symbolic scapegoat for activists. They felt the fence was illegitimate. One participant commented that once scapegoating catches on it is very powerful and difficult to define. Another suggested that it was better to have a fence as a scapegoat than a political target.

The scapegoat is one who threatens the security of the group causing fear of losing their group identity. They become a threat to the sense of justice of the group resulting in anger and a threat to the connectedness creating a sense of sadness. The action is distorted, differences are not recognized, the group is seen as incoherent and the continuity is threatened. In other words, the human identity needs of the community are threatened. As a result, the community turns against those they can blame. In the case of the fence, the mere existence of the fence thwarted the needs of the protest community and this became very personal for those fenced-out.

It is also possible that security becomes the scapegoat for the crowd and perhaps for the target and the bystanders (Figure 5.1). Returning to the Oka/Kanehsatà:ke crisis of 1990, the crowd in Chateauguay, at one point, turned on the Quebec police who had to lock themselves in a detachment for their own protection. The Royal Canadian Mounted Police intervened to help protect the provincial police.

Figure 5.1 Security Orientation vis-à-vis Crowds

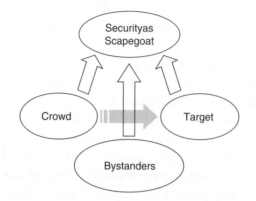

Knowledge of the dynamics of scapegoating will help police and protest leaders work strategically to prevent scapegoat victimization. Hence, we will look first at the characteristics of the scapegoat and the process of scapegoating itself. We will then look at some of the cultural permutations of scapegoating as it takes the form of sacrificial rituals and is embedded in community mythology.

Drawing on Girard's careful analysis, it becomes evident that scapegoats are different (Girard, 1989), but not too different; are powerful, but not too powerful (Girard, 2000); and are illegitimate. Historically scapegoats have been physically different. Sometimes the difference is based on class—either those at the bottom or those on top are singled out in a special way (Girard, 1989). The ideal scapegoat identifies with the community in some ways but is distinguished from it in other ways (Girard, 1988). Scapegoats are powerful enough to be responsible for the frustrations of the community yet they must be sufficiently vulnerable that the scapegoat action can work without backfiring. The sense of illegitimacy can be a result of real or perceived injustices, remembrance of past violence, suspicions of a potential threat to the well-being of the group, someone having broken the law or done something that violates established custom. The scapegoat may be an individual or group that shows up the defects of a community, causing it to lose face, thus bringing negative recognition to the group. In scapegoat action people are united in projecting their frustrations onto the scapegoat. Scapegoating as a phenomenon is always hidden to the participants; that is, people are not conscious of the scapegoating dimensions of their actions.

Many crowds work in a scapegoating manner. The Seattle protesters who shut down the World Trade Organization talks were convinced that the participants in these talks were about to reach agreements that would have given more power to multi-national corporations, resulting in reduced rights of workers and a threat to the environment. The talks were illegitimate in their eyes. The world leaders taking part in the talks were clearly powerful enough to cause these perceived threats. They were different from the participants in that they were government representatives. A wide variety of groups with various identities and agendas were united in a common purpose and their resolve revealed a passionate commitment to achieve their goals. Indeed, they were powerful enough to unseat the representatives from their agendas and shut down the meeting.

Most crowds are not assembled with an intense sense of scapegoating present. As observers of crowds have noted, most people come in small groups of friends and they maintain a sense of their own individuality. Hence, 90 per cent of protests occur without incident. However, sometimes in the course of a protest, something may happen that galvanizes a group of protesters and there is a violent contagion as they pour out their frustration on a particular scapegoat victim. In a highly volatile crowd situation where frustration is rampant, the tendency to scapegoat can galvanize a sub-group within a crowd to destroy property belonging to the target or turn on someone who does something at the moment that triggers their anger. Identifying a scapegoat can also create the crowd in the first place. Someone takes a soapbox to a public space and starts to talk about the perceived wrongdoing of a potential target. The crowd forms, gets inflamed, and marches to wherever. The crowd might have been individual shoppers with no intention of joining a protest when they left home that day.

The process of scapegoating starts with the frustration of the community (Girard, 1988). This frustration may be caused by interpersonal jealousies and rivalries; it may be an external threat or reverses in the fortunes of the community as a whole or it may be a feeling of powerlessness in the face of perceived injustices. It can be a diversionary tactic to deflect examination from the wrong doings or deficiencies of some by focusing blame on others. The internal build-up of latent violence can bring a community to the edge of chaos where anything can happen.

The second step in the scapegoat process is the selection of a scapegoat or, as Girard would say, sacrificial victim. In some instances, where this happens with some regularity, the victim is clear. The same victim group might appear again and again. In other instances, a victim emerges spontaneously. A police dog may be accidentally let loose on a crowd and threaten innocent protesters. The police then are perceived to be unjustly violent toward the crowd; the crowd then turns on the police in a scapegoat action. On the other side of the divide, police may be frustrated at having to wear uncomfortable protective clothing for hours on end. One protester may be particularly provocative, hurling insults at the police. When this person hurls a Molotov cocktail and one police officer is burned, even slightly; it tips the balance and the police go after this protester, arrest and constrain the person sometimes with far more force than is necessary. The situation reaches a flashpoint.

Without drawing on scapegoat theory, Abby Peterson observes that in Denmark, the undercover police, whom protesters recognize, are viewed as the 'toughest and baddest', making them 'the scapegoats for activist discontent with Danish public order policing' (2006, 57).

A third step is the scapegoat action itself which is a combination of isolating and identifying the scapegoat and perpetrating some form of violence that has the effect of hurting, killing, banishing or otherwise disempowering the victim. In some cultures, particularly in former times, it could take the form of stoning someone or pushing the victim off a cliff. In more modern times, a scapegoat action also is often symbolic. A scapegoat may be removed from a situation or emotionally isolated or shunned. There is a rapid, almost simultaneous contagion as a number of people together are united in a violent action against the differentiated Other. The violent action includes the release of violent emotions that have nothing directly to do with the victim but are the result of an accumulation of frustrated desires, injustices and thwarted actions. Various over-aggressive baton charges of police can be understood in this way. The recipients of the baton blows can be completely innocent of any violent acts or gestures but they are vulnerable because they are at the front line, they are perceived as powerful because the crowd is powerful and they are illegitimate by association since members of the crowd may have been threatening the security of the police or of political targets whom the police are duty bound to protect. In one example, during a protest a bystander was walking in the vicinity and the police attacked him with batons; he fell down and the attack precipitated his death.

A fourth part of the process is that the scapegoating group is united in its action. Differences dissolve as they work together toward the same objective—stopping the ill effects of the scapegoat.

Throughout, the scapegoat dimension remains hidden to those caught up in the action. At a primal level they are caught up in the passions of addressing the injustices they perceive in the situation.

Finally, if the victim is killed or extracted from the community in some other way, the victim becomes a hero for having brought peace to the community (Girard, 1988). The mythology that evolves has the double action of concealing the illegitimacy of the victim and the scapegoat action and communicating some form of banishment or victimization. Eventually an initial scapegoat action can lead to sacrificial rituals in which the effects of group unity are achieved regularly through the sacrifice of someone or some animal from a victim group. In contemporary society, blood sacrifice has been replaced with symbolic acts, although some terrorist actions can be understood in sacrificial terms.

In classical scapegoating, where there are no accountability structures outside the community, scapegoating results in a new peace that is established among formerly antagonistic community members. In the context of the protest crowd–police relational system, a number of things might happen, exemplifying aspects of this phenomenon. One scapegoat action on one side may prompt a scapegoat phenomenon on the other side. Recognizing the potential for this, police overlook many actions that could be in and of themselves transgressions of the law with the realization that strict enforcement could cause 'troubles' which could be interpreted as scapegoat actions. Sometimes the zeal of a scapegoat action means that accountability structures will hold protagonists accountable. On one occasion one girl in a crowd was killed by a police projectile, the image of her in the coffin became a rallying point against the police as she became a hero for the crowd and the cause of additional protests. In 1833, there was a major protest in London. It was only a few years after Peel's principles had been introduced along with a new Metropolitan Police Force, which was put to the test. At the end of the protest–police encounter, the only fatality was a police constable. The dead police officer consolidated public opinion in favour of the police and the crowd strategies they had employed; had the victim been from the crowd, things might have evolved very differently.

In recent years, there has been a significant emphasis in policing circles on maintaining a sense of legitimacy in the eyes of the public. This has found expression in negotiated management procedures, avoiding confrontation, keeping tactical troops hidden until they are absolutely necessary, and not enforcing the law strictly. We can see that in the light of scapegoat theory, this is a wise approach on the part of police, since one of the qualities of a scapegoat is that they are perceived as illegitimate. Not only does it reduce troubles (some of which could be scapegoat related), keep the public on side, and avoid violence, it also is good from the point of view of scapegoat prevention. In jurisdictions in which repressive policing is the norm, police avoid being scapegoated in the short term by being too powerful for the crowd; strategically, in other words, they avoid the quality that the scapegoat is vulnerable. Hence police have a choice: are they to avoid be scapegoated on the grounds of being perceived as legitimate or on the grounds of appearing too powerful for it to work?

Where police negotiators or liaison officers build relationships with protesters, scapegoat action against the police is reduced because it is harder for protesters to put police in the category of the differentiated Other who might become a scapegoat victim. The same holds true on the other side. As police see the human side of protesters and understand why they are doing what they are doing, it is less likely that police will resort to repressive measures that can take the form of scapegoating a protester.

We turn our attention now to a second structured way of expressing both otherness and power, that of hegemonic structures.

Hegemonic Structures

Hegemonic structures are patterns of social and political relationships whereby some groups are consistently dominated by others (Cummings, 1993; Gramsci, 1968; Linger, 1993; Redekop, 2002). One extreme form of a hegemonic structure was the institution of slavery in which the slaves' lives were totally controlled by the slave owners. They were treated as property and all of their skills and energies were harnessed in the service of the physical and economic benefits to their owners. More subtle forms of hegemonic structures involve societal racism and class distinction in which certain races or classes have system wide barriers to their advancement within society.

The dominant controllers may exert control *physically, politically* through curtailment of rights, *economically* by making rules that benefit their own interests, and *discursively* by thwarting full expression of what is key to the identity of those subjected, favouring a particular language, accent or affectation, and by designating identity groups with language that implies inferiority (Linger). Also there is a controlling kind of *energy* or spirit that keeps people in their place. They can also control the flow of *information* and access to education. These different aspects of dominating structures are depicted in Figure 5.2.

If hegemonic structures are accepted and interiorized, there is superficial social peace as was the case when slavery, fascism and communism, as controlling structures, were accepted by the populations they controlled. (Typically, these practices were not universally accepted so the 'social peace' was an illusion existing in some places some of the time.) When people become aware of these controlling structures and want to change them, there is conflict, passion and social unrest.

Hegemonic structures are a significant part of the protest crowd–police relational system for two reasons. First, police often are put into a position of having to protect political and business leaders and institutions that are in a dominant position within society. For example, preceding the Oka/ Kanehsatà:ke Crisis, Mohawks were blocking a tiny road in order to prevent the development of a golf course on land they claimed to be rightfully theirs. The claims to the land were complex and John Ciaccia, the Quebec Minister of Native Affairs believed these should be settled before any trees were cut down. The interests in the golf course included both the golfing community and the Mayor and council of Oka who saw many economic advantages to the development. Ultimately, they had the power to set in motion a raid by the SQ, the Quebec Provincial Police. Police responded to requests for help from democratically elected community leaders enforcing the hegemony of the local political structure. In that case, the Mohawks feelings of subjugation were compounded by what they saw as unfair suppression of their right to protest in a situation in which they could make a case for historic rights to the land (Gabriel-Doxtater & Hende, 1995; Redekop, 2002). Second, within the police–protester relational system police play a dominant role. They have the resources of the state behind them and can procure powerful weapons of many types that can be used to force crowds to disperse, weapons that are illegal for ordinary citizens to carry.

Figure 5.2 Hegemonic Structures

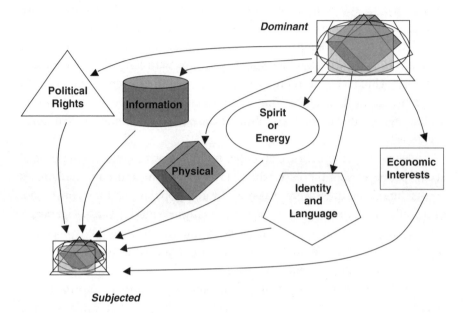

Crowd anger is intensified if participants become conscious of being controlled and overpowered by dominating groups. Currently, many activists feel the force of dominating structures at two different levels. First, they believe the evidence that trends in corporate globalization are setting up grand controlling political structures that they object to but feel powerless to change. Second, when they protest they understand that the security actions are meant to control them. In crowd dynamics the demonstrators consider the police to be the dominators. They have the power. One activist said, 'it isn't realistic to talk about equal adversaries in this situation—the police have all the power and are using it against demonstrators in an abusive way'.

The position of police in relation to society wide hegemonic structures is not without its ironies and ambiguities. Lower ranking officers and some senior officers are part of police unions and, as such, have certain sympathies for labour unions who feel dominated by management. Furthermore, as thoughtful individuals they can understand the plight of people who are alarmed that concerns for the environment, social justice, distributive justice and other issues that may not be addressed or considered by dominating institutions. However, the police as a body have a special responsibility to keep communities safe and peaceful, protect the lives of Internationally Protected People, protect public institutions, and create a context in which events like international summit gatherings, like the annual G-8, can take place without disruption. Police are in a position to sense the frustration of protesters for situations the police have no power to change. That is, police have no responsibilities with regard to the issues that are at the heart of the protest crowd–target relational system and consequently, must behave neutrally with regard to those issues notwithstanding their personal convictions. Similarly, governments in responsible democracies keep themselves at arm's length from the day to day functioning of the security forces. In instances where the injustices of government personalities and/or institutions are significant enough and sufficiently known, police may stand by as crowds effect a dramatic change in hegemonic structures. Examples of Milosevic and Ceausescu have already been given.

The concept of hegemonic structures helps us to understand how police can be effective in controlling crowds. In repressive styles of protest policing, it is the physical power of police that puts them in a dominant position. Police fire-power can easily be used to get crowds to disperse. However, dominance is established and evident in other aspects of policing. The use of soft tactics to get protesters to do what the police want is an example of discursive hegemonic structures. Many people within society have a tendency to do what police tell them to do, based on a combination of respect and fear. Police demonstrate that they know how to plan a demonstration better, which routes work best, etc. By smiling and using language that is both helpful and authoritative they can shape behaviours so the outcome is to their liking. We must qualify this by saying that some police negotiators forego the subtle forms of dominance that accrue to them and go out of their way to facilitate a situation so that the interests of protesters are addressed. Some police also have an authoritative dominating spirit making it difficult for less experienced protesters to stand up to them. Economically they have an advantage in that they can hire full time professionals to work on controlling a protest crowd. Politically they have an advantage in that they have lines of communication to political and bureaucratic leaders. Regarding information, they have the ability to collect information about the protest whereas protesters cannot have similar information about the strategy of police. Often police have dedicated media experts that can work strategically to get television cameras positioned to highlight crowd violence and minimize coverage of any police violence.

In this chapter we have shown how both the protest crowd and the police contribute to relationships of violence that dehumanize the 'Other' by the process of scapegoating. The scapegoating process effectively expels the 'Other' from the relational structure or community. Those doing the scapegoating don't recognize the humanity of their victims and, typically, they don't want to know them. They may even go so far as to fear getting to know the 'Other' and will come up with many reasons for maintaining their distance.

The stereotype of the 'Other' is maintained by a perceived or real hegemonic structure maintained by both sides. Protesters sometimes feel they must overcome the power imbalance inherent in the hegemonic structure and, consequently, feel justified in resorting to violence in order to do so. This is the only power they feel they have; they are determined to use it. Police similarly, recognize the legitimacy of their own dominance and are willing to exercise this power if they feel they have to. The hegemony reinforces the feelings of conflict and, typically, perpetuates the spiral of reciprocating violence.

So far, the emphasis has been on the protest crowd–police relational system. The targets of protest have been standing in the shadows, we have been aware of their presence but they have not been formally introduced. In the next chapter we will rectify this as we talk about different types of targets and introduce various bystanders who impact and are impacted by the protest crowd. Through the media, the bystander population can grow to global proportions; often protest crowds assemble primarily for media coverage, hence the media will demand a formal introduction as well.

6. Introducing Targets, Bystanders, and Media

Protesters are out to change a situation by having an impact on decision makers directly and indirectly by mobilizing bystanders and the general public. Media coverage can have an impact on public opinion, which in turn can influence policy. In most cases protest crowds direct their dissenting voices and actions toward a target in the belief that this will change a situation to benefit the public good (or their interests, depending on the level of moral consciousness). In the first section we will examine the protest crowd–target relational system.

In the process of demonstrating, marching or engaging in other protest actions, the crowd has an impact on the bystanders. Bystanders can include those physically present but not part of the crowd itself, those living in the vicinity, businesses and commuters who are affected, and others who hear about or see what is happening by means of the media. They may be watching; their property may be jeopardized; they may have relationships with people in any of the other groups. The second section will elaborate on the protest crowd–bystander relationship.

When a crowd event makes it into the news, the general public gets drawn into the bystander group. Part of the bystander group, the media, facilitates the growth of the bystander group and deserves special consideration in the third section. Once our introductions are complete, we will focus on the significance of crowds as complex systems.

Targets

The protester–target relational system is central within a web of inter-related relational systems. After all, protesters wish to have an impact on the organization and people that they see as having the ability to effect those actions and decisions they have identified need to be taken. The target may be government, business, an international organization or an identity group that is doing something perceived by the protesters to be unjust, unwise, or ill-conceived. For example, the Global Justice Movement (GJM) has concerns about what is happening within the 'global economy' (Reiter and Fillieule, 2006, 145–173) They perceive a web of interconnecting issues including: environmental degradation, global warming, concentration of economic power among wealthy nations and corporations, labour exploitation, and the use of health related products and processes for corporate profit. This makes for a very diffuse target that includes governments and corporations and those people associated with both. Summit gatherings, especially those involving the most powerful economic nations, are natural targets for anti-corporate globalization demonstrations as are institutions like the World Bank, the International Monetary fund and organizational gatherings of the World Trade Association, the Multilateral Agreement on Investment (MAI) or anything that symbolizes the web of interconnected issue areas that concern activists. Related may be more specific issues of concern: a company that pollutes, a logging industry that cuts down old growth forest, a pharmaceutical company that dumps drugs banned in North America in southern markets, or a company that has rendered local drinking water toxic because of industrial waste. Each can become a target. Especially in the last instance, local people may protest both against the company and against a government that did not sufficiently regulate the industry.

Targets may be separated into two broad categories: institutions and individuals. Institutions may be governmental, non-governmental or corporate. Individuals may be leaders who have committed atrocities— remember all the protests against Pinochet who led a repressive regime in Chile. Criminals who have committed the worst of crimes are the focus of protest if they become eligible for parole. Canadian criminals whose parole has been protested include serial child killer Clifford Olsen and Karla Homolka, who, together with her husband Paul Bernardo, was responsible for a number of rape-murders. At times, both institutions and individuals are combined; for example, during protests against the pending Iraq war in 2002, a placard talked of eliminating 'Colin cancer' referring to United States Secretary of State at the time, Colin Powell. Likewise, in the case of criminals eligible for parole, the protest may be directed toward the criminal justice system.

Often there is a strong symbolic dimension to the target of protests. Embassies both represent and are symbols of particular governments. Likewise, statues and memorials are symbolic sites for protest. During the Israeli–Hezbollah violent conflict, a Jewish and Muslim joint peace march went from the human rights monument in Ottawa to the War Memorial.

In most instances, the individuals against whom the protest is organized or the leaders to whom it is directed are not present at the protest. However, it is possible that they send messages or that crowd organizers meet with their representatives. During the Quebec City Summit of the Americas, Prime Minister Jean Chrétien sent a message to the protesters that acknowledged the legitimacy of their concerns; the result was a calming effect on the crowd.

If there is a great psychological or physical distance between crowds and their targets, the communication between them is very indirect, often played out in press coverage that will provide quotes from people on each side of the relational system.

If the goal of the protest crowd is to communicate a truth that they feel passionately needs to be communicated and work for change, we can discern a more nuanced differentiation of targets:

- Primary Targets—those perceived as responsible for the injustice
- Authority Targets—those with the authority and capacity to make changes
- Public Opinion Secondary Targets—the point of the protest is often to impact public opinion so the strategy is to protest the Primary and Authority Targets in a manner that will capture the support of bystanders and the broader public through media coverage.

Targets of the protest crowd activities are vital to the success of the protesters' objective whether this objective is to make change, stop change or to influence public opinion. Although protesters usually want to communicate directly with targets most often they have to be content with passing their message through bystanders, the next relational system we will examine.

Bystanders

There are three ways of having an impact on the target: through direct impact, public opinion and media coverage. The latter two involve media and bystanders in relational systems with the protesters and with the police. The bystanders can be separated into immediate bystanders—those physically present who can either watch the protest or who might be affected by it because they live, have businesses or work in the vicinity—and public bystanders—those who become aware of the protest through the media, internet or word of mouth. One can imagine concentric circles of bystanders going from those directly affected because of their close proximity—such as shop owners who may be the victims of the breaking windows and looting—to those inconvenienced—commuters whose road is blocked temporarily—to those who are indirectly affected.

Political psychologist Ervin Staub has done extensive research on the role of bystanders in influencing social dynamics (Staub, 1992). Initially he did clinical experiments that demonstrated how the actions of individuals were subject to the influence of those around them. Later he applied his theoretical conclusions to group actions, showing how the encouragement or silence of bystanders can strengthen the impulse to be violent. As people not directly involved in a crowd action, especially if it is long standing, bystanders can influence the course of events. By either disapproving or encouraging they can diminish or exacerbate crowd violence. Staub extends the bystander circle to include the global community, suggesting, for example that if the global community had expressed unequivocal disapproval of the initial repressive actions of the Nazis in the 1930s, things might have turned out very differently.

There are four groups of bystanders who are particularly significant for protest crowds and police: property owners, moral and opinion leaders, civil society observers, and the media. The media play a distinct role and will be treated separately in the next section.

Property owners and citizens living near the protest area may be drawn into the action in a number of ways. They may need permits and have to

Figure 6.1 Bystander Groups

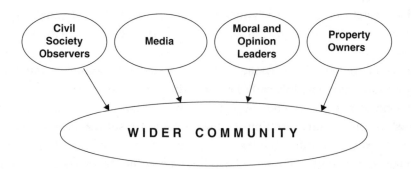

pass through security checks to get to their homes or businesses. They may be asked to provide help to those injured. Their property may be damaged or looted. They may choke on tear gas that the wind blows in their direction. Their free movement through the streets may be blocked during a demonstration and the resulting anger can create more conflict as they are called to join in the escalating violence of the crowd. They may inadvertently encounter angry interactions between police and protesters. Whatever their experience, they communicate it to friends in the wider community. How the information is interpreted has an impact on the overall sense of security, justice and hope or despair for the future.

Some civil society institutions have a concern not only for the issues raised by activists, but also for the dynamics of actions taking place at a demonstration. They may have concerns about violence, human rights and the impact of the protest itself on the viability of civil society. Moral and religious leaders who communicate with significant numbers of people may observe and reflect on what is happening and communicate their thoughts to people in the wider community. Through the intermediate efforts of these groups, people within a country and internationally are made aware of what is happening as a result of a protesting crowd.

Given all of these diverse players within the total picture of a crowd action and the response of the various parties, there are many choices that people can make. A basic choice is to a) work from a paradigm of trying to control the situation from one's own frame of reference or b) accept a paradigm that emphasizes communication and creative options that enhance the well-being of everyone.

Through the media the circle of bystanders is widened; it is the next focus of attention.

The Media

Media have the power to satisfy certain identity needs of protagonists in a demonstration. What journalists choose to cover can either satisfy or threaten needs for recognition and action, since some demonstrators have the goal of attracting media coverage. How a story is covered has an impact on the meaning systems of those involved. If coverage is perceived to be unfair, it provokes anger. If the frightening dimensions of either side are exaggerated it diminishes a sense of security and increases fear. If a story enhances mutual understanding, it makes people feel connected. Given the power of the media to impact identity need satisfiers, it is easy to see how the media prompt a strong emotional reaction—people love and want the media for the exposure and information offered and hate the media for perceptions of bias, incompleteness, or sensationalism to 'sell papers' and increase ratings. An indication of the power of the media is that Seattle, Quebec City and Genoa have become code words for violent protest, largely because through the media they have become part of global consciousness.

As people not directly implicated in the crowd action, media play a number of roles. They are key members of the bystander group. Through media coverage, all of society can get drawn into the bystander role. As commentators, they help the public interpret what goes on and this interpretation may be either critical or encouraging of one group over the other. Their coverage helps to shape the overall impression people have of each group. Consequently, police now engage media consultants and arrange for cameras to be set up behind police lines. Each stakeholder group tries to put their own spin on the story. Stories are told of protesters who launch a violent action when the television cameras are rolling and stop as soon as the media leave. Protest becomes performance. In the end, media coverage does not always reflect the true nature of the demonstration. However, given the power of the media to influence public opinion, media access and attention become objects of mimetic desire for activists and politicians as well as the police.

Media have a tendency to focus on the conflictual dynamics of life—conflict makes a better story; they can get diverted from the substance of the meeting by a violent side show. Television media looks for gripping visual footage that is easiest to get in a violent situation. As such, there is a built-in media bias toward the more violent confrontations between crowds and security or crowds and targets. Furthermore, covering violent confrontations requires less research and feeds the demand of pressing deadlines. Taking stereotypical positions such as 'police are aggressive,' or 'free-trade is bad' means they don't have to think about the issue in a deeper way.

Journalists are not objects to be manipulated; they are people and they are actors within the whole situation. They have their own values that find expression in the work they do. During the Quebec Summit, one reporter attempted to experience what it was like to be on the security side of the fence and he became the target of projectiles from the activists' side. He felt this happened because he was the only one without protective gear.

Various media imitate one another in covering the same stories and highlighting the same details. Images of the APEC (Asia-Pacific Economic Cooperation) Conference and the pepper spray incident[19] in Vancouver have been aired again and again and again. This makes for some anomalies. One police officer told of a situation in Atlantic Canada at the same time as the APEC meeting where police actions to suppress a demonstration were far more violent but because the Atlantic situation was a local event, it received hardly any coverage. At the time of APEC, police relied on the use of pepper spray; it was used with less objection from the public than has been the case after the APEC incident. The officer who sprayed the APEC pepper has been subject to endless ridicule (e.g. 'Sergeant Pepper' jokes); his family and his career have both suffered. This police officer became a scapegoat in the policing community, in part because of the repeated playing of a few seconds of footage where he was spraying people with pepper.

Pressure from editors and publishers sometimes controls what journalists are allowed to write, either by virtue of the time given or the material that will be accepted. Individuals within the media from front line journalists to editors, publishers and producers are affected by events and filter their actions through the so called 'good story' filter, the 'balanced reporting' filter and through other media cultural values that operate on a tacit (unexpressed) level. They have their own identity needs which find expression in the way in which they do their work.

As significant relational systems are multiplied vis-à-vis a protest event the interconnections increase exponentially to the point where the whole becomes a complex system. It then becomes important to include complexity theory in the composite framework used to understand what is happening during major protest crowd events.

---

19   At the 1997 APEC Conference in Vancouver, B.C., UBC students carrying protest signs were angry that the issue of human rights was not on the APEC agenda. The RCMP tried to clear the area but chaos erupted. Protestors tore down a fence and pepper spray was sprayed into the crowds. Later, an un-apologetic Prime Minister Chrétien brushed away the pepper spray incident, saying 'For me, pepper, I put it on my plate.'

Complexity

What happens in any of these relational systems has an impact on all of the others. We can now revisit the concept of complexity in relation to protest crowds as developed by Deborah Sword:

> Complex systems are dynamic, nonlinear, unpredictable and self-organizing. In complex systems, an infinite number of parts make the whole but the whole cannot be known by summing the individual parts. The parts are interdependent, meaning they influence each other in a feedback loop, not in simple action and reaction. (2003, 29)

Sword applied chaos-complexity theory to an analysis of three protest movements, focusing primarily on the protester–government relational system. In her research, she looked at the dominant and shadow systems that formed into a complex conflict system. Depending on the protest, the dominant system was comprised of those agents that had the ability to influence the conflict system in a direction supporting the policy that the protest group objected to, such as government, police, mainstream news media and industry. Protest movements and those agents generating knowledge that influenced the conflict system against the policy being protested were designated the shadow system. She demonstrated through these case studies, the non-linear, mutual dynamics in relational systems and surprising outcomes along the way.

One of the unpredictable dynamics Sword develops as part of her complexity framework is that of mimetic contagion:

> Agents in complex systems are influenced by what networks they are in and what people they know are doing. If a public policy protest has already begun to attract a crowd, it will attract more of a crowd. As Gell-Mann (1994) quipped: them that has, gets. Gladwell's (2000) research into tipping points demonstrated, that in complex systems, things do not necessarily become popular by building acceptance slowly and steadily. Instead, popular things have contagiousness and unpopular things do not. If something is going to become popular, it will do so suddenly and dramatically, although the popularity may only seem sudden because the observer has not noticed the small inputs that have been accumulating to create that dramatic moment. (Sword, 2003, 32)

Mutatis mutandis, the mimetic contagion effect could happen at any point in the interactions within and between relational systems. For example, a generally peaceful law-respecting crowd that witnesses what is perceived as unjustified violence on the part of the police may, in an instance become highly agitated, mimetically mirroring and amplifying the violence they have witnessed. Likewise, police are impacted emotionally by what they see going on in a crowd.

It is clear from the introductions of protest crowds, police, targets, bystanders and media that each of these groups can represent a complex system. Bringing them all together in the context of a major protest multiplies the complexity of factors at play. At any moment, actions coming out of any of these groups can have an enormous impact on all of the other systems at play, particularly if that action comes at a bifurcation point. In the next chapter we will examine the concept of mimesis as developed by René Girard. This will provide some insight on the dynamics by which actions take on an amplified importance within complex systems.

This chapter has extended the structure of demonstrations to include the relationship of the protest crowd with the target and the bystanders including the media. Protest has a primal and a dramatic component to it. The key objective of the crowd is to get the message to the target that has the power to do something about the perceived problem and to engage the help of bystanders including the media along the way. Through the process of mimetic contagion and with a basic introduction to complexity theory we are able to project the unpredictability of crowd actions and appreciate the significance of having a framework with which to analyze crowds. The next chapter introduces mimetic theory, which will ground our understanding of mimetic contagion and reciprocal violence.

7. Reciprocal Violence

So far, we have introduced protest crowds and have shown how the passion that they bring to dissent is linked to their human identity needs. The police were introduced with the recognition that their work is similarly intertwined with their identity. We showed that the protest crowd–police relational system may involve a radical 'Othering' whereby each group is dehumanized. This Othering process may take the form of scapegoating in which the frustrations each side is struggling with are projected onto the Other side resulting in a violence of differentiation. Another form of a violence of differentiation is a hegemonic structure where one side dominates the other. Scapegoating and hegemonic structures are different forms of mimetic structures of violence—structures we examine in greater depth in this chapter.

In the last chapter we introduced targets of protest, bystanders and the media. We also showed that the protest crowd phenomenon with all its attendant relational systems and unpredictability is a complex system that can very well end up at the edge of chaos at which point any small thing can make a big difference and anything can happen. This 'anything' that suddenly results in a moment could be interpreted as either a bifurcation point in complexity theory or a flashpoint in the police literature, the point when it becomes imperative that decisive action be taken.

In this chapter, we will use the mimetic theory of René Girard to illuminate the dynamics within a relational system. In the process we will develop the concepts of mimetic desire, reciprocal violence, mimetic contagion, and mimetic structure of violence.

Mimetic Desire

Mimetic desire is a helpful concept at this point for two reasons: first, the concept helps to explain some of the actions of protesters, police and others involved in the crowd process; second, mimetic desire points to the mimetic nature of humanity and this helps to explain why people join crowds in the first place.

We have already made the basic link between *mimesis*, the Greek word, and *imitation* the more popular English word derived from it. What Girard has done, through academic research spanning more than half a century, is to show how deeply our lives are permeated with mimetic impulses. It is clear that knowledge of language and culture is learned by mimesis—we watch, we listen, and we imitate. Girard's key insight is that what we desire, what motivates to extend our reach to do, become, or acquire something is arrived at mimetically. That is we watch one another and when someone else has something, does something or becomes something that appears to be satisfying to them we want the same for ourselves. If other people give recognition to this other person for possessions, actions or prestige, the value of the object becomes so much greater and our desire, arrived at mimetically, becomes much greater. However, as Girard points out, as soon as we have acquired something, it loses its value to us because the game was to get what the other wanted; so we find something else to desire.

The person or group whose desires we imitate, Girard calls the Model (Girard, [1965] 1990). If the Model stands in the way of us getting the object of mimetic desire, the Model becomes an Obstacle. If we succeed in getting what the Model/Obstacle has prompted us to desire, we look for a more challenging Model/Obstacle.

Mimetic desire increases when the Model is someone we can identify with (Girard, [1965] 1990; Redekop, 2002). If there is a hegemonic structure in place, those who are subjected cannot identify with people from the dominant group, rather they have intense mimetic desire for those who, like them, are subjected. In instances where a crowd looks up to the police as a dominant group, they will not desire control of the situation. In this instance they are simply happy to have the police help them with their protest. In instances where a protest is organized by professional, sophisticated organizers, control becomes a matter of mimetic desire which operates in a reciprocal fashion. The more the police try to control the situation the more the demonstrators want to take control. The bigger the obstacle the police put in place, the more determined the protesters to find a way around it. Hence, the police need back up plans with lots of force whether they be in the form of troops, forceful tactics or weapons. Mimetic effects can also be seen in regard to clothing and tactics. As police have donned protective clothing that covers their faces, protesters have covered their faces. As fences have gone up, the desire on the part of protesters to penetrate fences has grown. With tear gas have come cloths soaked in vinegar to protect against its effects; at times tear gas canisters have been hurled back toward the police.

With escalation of violence, intelligence gathering plays an increased role, becoming increasingly intrusive; on the other side, protesters take concrete steps to keep police infiltrators out of their meetings. The same mimetic dynamics take place between protesters and those they target. Suppose the object of desire is an old growth forest. A forestry company makes plans to cut it down for lumber. Environmentalists are convinced that it needs to be preserved intact. Each side does its research to corroborate its position. When the time comes for the cutting to begin, protesters live in the trees, chain themselves to trees, blockade logging roads—they do anything they can to keep the forest. The more they try to preserve the forest, the more the logging company is determined to go ahead. They file court injunctions, call on the police, and take advantage of any opening they can. Each side has its own interests behind their position but the mimetic desire effect increases the commitment and the passions on both sides.

In this era of globalization, the objects of desire can become abstract and symbolic. They can include the terms of international treaties and agreements that make it possible for multinational corporations to extract resources with minimum compensation to local populations, keep moving production to places with few rights for workers, and so on.

Mimetic Contagion

While mimetic desire is operative in situations where two parties develop a rivalry for the same things, mimetic contagion is a phenomenon in which people get onto the same band wagon. It is a matter of people imitating the movement, action and ideas of those around them. This is clear to see in the stock market where if there appears to be a strong movement to buy a certain stock, everyone wants a part of the action and the price goes up dramatically. Similarly if word gets out to sell, everybody sells and the price goes down fast. This has three dimensions as is illustrated by the saying 'them that has gets.' First, 'them that has' always want more; they compare themselves to 'them others that has.' Second, 'them that has not' desire 'what them that has' have. Third, because 'them that has' are mimetic models, people follow their lead; hence, if they invest in a given corporation, others follow them and it becomes self fulfilling since share prices in that company go up.

Similarly, crowds assemble and grow through a mimetic contagion whereby word gets out that something is happening; some people assemble and others who see or hear about what's going on think that because some people are there, it must be the thing to do and the crowd grows. Within the crowd there may be a mimetic contagion around a certain action. Some people start chanting a slogan and before you know it, many are doing the same thing.

Not everything that is initiated catches on. It is one of those complex dynamics of crowd behaviour. If the right people start it at the right time when the circumstances are right, it can take off. The fact that many people are gathered together and are close enough to see, hear and touch each other increases the chances of a mimetic contagion happening.

Among crowd theorists there is some debate about the concept of contagion, which we are now in a position to address. Gustaf LeBon and other theorists of the nineteenth and early twentieth century developed the notion of contagion within a crowd suggesting that people lost their individuality and with the anonymity of the crowd surrendered their rationality and became totally subject to the power of contagion so as to act unanimously. Empirical researchers who have carefully observed many crowds have clearly shown that people go to crowds with groups of friends and tend to keep their independence and their rationality.

Mimesis means that somehow or other we are always picking up on things going on around us and to some degree or another imitate that. If crowds are highly diverse, there are so many things to imitate at any given moment that it is unlikely that anything will take off in a mimetic contagion that involves everyone. Girard says we will choose to imitate those who are within the closest relational system to us—those who we admire most. It is the size of the commonality that determines the extent of the contagion. If frustrations increase and if everyone starts feeling the same level of frustration and some action, which is perceived unjust and is a shared experience of a group, is perpetrated by an actor that can be blamed for this frustration, a scapegoat emerges and everyone has a cathartic experience as they express passionately and perhaps violently their anger at the scapegoat. Scapegoating is one strong form of mimetic contagion.

In a large crowd like the demonstrations at summit gatherings, there can be limited versions of a mimetic contagion as a small portion of a crowd gets involved in attacking a vehicle or in trying to dislodge a fence that is used to limit access to the venue where leaders are gathered.

We can now see how both sides of the argument can come together. LeBon and others witnessed examples of what we describe as mimetic contagion where a crowd got carried away in collective action. They interpreted what they saw as a propensity for people to lose their minds and individuality in the crowd. Empirical students of crowds saw that people tend to keep their faculties and individual identities. With the concept of mimetic contagion we can nuance the discussion. People see themselves as individuals but at the same time are subject to influence in crowds no less than in any other area of life. Mimetic contagion will take off where there is mimetic resonance; that is people will identify with the passions, concerns, frustrations and behaviours of certain mimetic models. In certain cases, like 'hooligans' after a sports game there is a sense that a certain type of rioting is 'the thing to do.' Many will have seen or participated in such rioting in the past. Where the circumstances are right, a flashpoint around a wrong call, a win or a loss, they will get involved in the rioting activity. Some will have wanted to do this in the first place. Those that start the rioting will have a mimetic resonance with those who have a similar sub-cultural mentality and the mimetic contagion will happen. In protest crowds, there is a more likely potential for mimetic resonance than in a random group from the general public because certain shared motivations have brought them together in the first place.

Reciprocal Violence

When people experience violence, they have a strong tendency to return the violence, mimetically, with interest (Girard, 1987). The other side then imitates the violence and again returns it with even greater force. The result is an upward spiral of violence. Violence that is imitated escalates as each side gets even with the other, which in turn gets even again.

Protesters in a crowd may view the actions of the government or of business (e.g. clear-cutting an old-growth forest) as essentially violent. They feel they have no choice but to use violent means to stop what they consider a greater violence. Security is called in to control the violence. As security experiences the violence of the protesters they feel they have no choice but to use violent means to stop what they perceive to be the greater violence. What the crowd experiences as the violence of the police in turn prompts them to become more violent. With a trend toward ever increasing violence associated with major international events, everyone is concerned. Security personnel have been assuming better and stronger physical protection, better and stronger fences and, as one police participant said, 'What next—barbed wire?' One activist commented that when being attacked you have to take action—there is a time when talking is over.

In the case of reciprocal violence, there is a mimetic contagion on both sides as they try to return violence mimetically to one another.

Mimetic Structures of Violence

When the attitudes, actions and orientation of both parties are turned against one another as they attempt to control, hurt, diminish or otherwise do violence to one another, we have a mimetic structure of violence. The mimetic dimension includes mutual mimesis of one another in terms of orientation—mutual hate. It can include reciprocal acts of violence. Also evident are competing interpretive frameworks and public relations strategies in which each party minimizes its own violence and maximizes the unjust violence perpetrated by the other side. There is no desire for mutual understanding. The mimetic effect prompts new ways of diminishing the other side based on an imitation of violence in other relational systems.

Within mimetic structures of violence identity needs are defined in terms of getting power at the expense of the Other. All of the dimensions of hegemonic structures can be part of mimetic structures of violence. Memories of past injustices and victimization are kept alive. There is no way out of the negative energy associated with past traumas.

Mimetic structures of violence can characterize a number of relational structures implicated in protest crowd dynamics. The protest itself may be between parties caught in a mimetic structure of violence. Let us provide a few examples:

Protest Crowd–Target
- Citizens of a repressive dictatorship have moved to another country and the dictator pays a state visit to that country. The expatriates protest.
- An indigenous group is being harmed by multinational corporation resource development perpetrated by a hegemonic entity. Activists in solidarity demonize the supporting hegemonic entity in protesting native's victimization.
- A Government is hosting an international event and protest activity that insults foreign visitors is interpreted as an embarrassment. Government determines that protester crowds need to be repressed.

Protest Crowd–Police

- What is interpreted as a 'diversity of tactics' or civil disobedience by activists is interpreted as illegitimate violence by police. Leaders advocating these tactics are treated as subversive troublemakers and police make pre-emptive arrests.
- Police become angry at individual protesters throwing projectiles at them; when they have a chance to make an arrest they use more force than necessary to subdue the protesters.
- In Los Angeles, in the early 1990s there was a history of tensions between the police and Afro-Americans who felt discriminated against. The video tape of police beating Rodney King invoked feelings of anger on the part of people for whom this was one example of what was happening on a broader basis. When the police seen beating Rodney King were given a not-guilty verdict, rioting ensued (Times, 1992).

Protest Crowd–Bystander

- During the Rodney King riots many businesses were looted; a white truck driver who happened to be in the wrong place was mimetically clubbed in the same manner as was Rodney King.
- Bystanders can take a position contrary to protesters resulting in violent exchanges.

Mimetic structures of violence can easily draw others into their vortex as members of the public end up taking sides on an issue. Family members on one continent can be hostile with one another on the basis of each taking different sides in a violent conflict in another part of the world. Mimetic structures of violence tend to be closed, acquisitive (each trying to get as much as possible at the expense of the other), aggressive and death-oriented (Redekop, 2002).

After having introduced the many different parties implicated in protest crowd activity we have shown that mimetic dynamics crop up all over the place. Some of these have the effect of generating violence, some increase violence, some entrench violence, and some spread violence. When there is an on-going pattern of violence in a relational system we have a mimetic structure of violence. The peacebuilding strategy in this situation is to transform the structure. In the next chapter we will look at mimetic structures of blessing as an alternative to violence.

8. Mutual Blessing

From the framers of constitutions to spiritual leaders, people have created language that provides a vision for human well-being—from 'life, liberty and the pursuit of happiness' and 'peace, order and good government' to 'let justice roll like a river' and 'I have a dream that ... little black children and little white children will walk hand in hand.'[20] These all contribute to a discursive field that can be related to the concept of mimetic structures of blessing. These are structures in which the attitude, actions and orientation of the parties in a relational system are directed toward mutual well-being (Redekop, 2002).

The transformation of mimetic structures of violence to mimetic structures of blessing includes both the reduction of violence and the hold that violent impulses have on people, on the one hand, and the development of a context in which creative new options can emerge that enable all parties to both thrive and contribute to the thriving of one another, on the other. This transformation is the goal and the process of reconciliation.

As noted in the introduction, for some people, 'blessing' can be a problematic word (Redekop, 2007). When we use it to designate mimetic structures of blessing, we mean a pattern within a relational system whereby people contribute to the mutual wellbeing of one another. Blessing includes generosity, care, willingness to understand, and empowerment. Mimetic structures of blessing are joyous, creative and life oriented. In mimetic structures of blessing, people include the Other positively within their identity make-up. The advantage of using the concepts of mimetic structures of violence and mimetic structures of blessing as categories of analysis is that it gets away from the discourse of blame which can be another form of violence and form the basis for scapegoating.

Much of the mandate, vision and orientation of both protest crowds and police is the building and maintaining of mimetic structures of blessing. Protest crowds that speak of injustice are oriented toward trying to reduce the violence that adheres within various relational systems. They have a vision

---

20   These phrases come from the Constitution of the United States of America, the legal mandate for Canadian peace officers, the book of Amos in the Hebrew Bible, and a speech of Martin Luther King, Junior, respectively.

of blessing. Police, as peace officers, are oriented toward protecting people who might be victimized; they are trying to prevent violent outbreaks that destroy property. In a democratic environment, they are trying to uphold the constitution, the rule of law, and the orderly change of government that provide a context for a non-violent approach to governance. These are police and protesters at their best and in response to their respective callings. However, they, like people everywhere, are not immune from mimetic structures of violence.

In this chapter we will develop further the concepts of mimetic structures of blessing and of reconciliation. We will then try to identify where these are present within the protest crowd–police relational system and how they might be extended. This will prepare us for the discussion of paradigms in the following chapter.

Mimetic Structures of Blessing

Parties may create mimetic structures of blessing in one relational system and participate in mimetic structures of violence in other relational systems. Some protesters may use the discourse of care in relation to the environment, for example, but use hostile words and actions in relation to police. Police, for their part may express brotherly and sisterly solidarity with other police, marching in support of 'fallen comrades' on one hand and use violent actions against 'bad apples.'

The concept of mimetic structures of blessing suggests a broad ethical vision that transcends antagonistic polarities. It does not preclude conflict but offers a framework in which conflict is transformed into creativity and ever new options. It suggests an orientation of mutual respect and even care without prescribing how that might be expressed.

In this section we will examine the connections between mimetic structures of blessing and emotions as well as the links with creativity, complexity, and level of consciousness.

Blessing and Emotions

Probably the biggest single obstacles to mimetic structures of blessing are the emotions and the subsequent interpretations and impulses that support violence. We will examine these first, looking at some of the ambiguities associated with them. We will then look at how mimetic structures of blessing can address these emotions and finally talk about the emotional payoff if mimetic structures of blessing are created.

In chapter three we talked about the emotions that are stirred up with a threat to human identity need satisfiers:

security–anger,
action–depression,
connectedness–sadness,
security–fear, and
recognition–shame.

We also said that a large number of emotional combinations can be invoked through a threat to a combination of need satisfiers.

Within a mimetic structure of violence, identity needs are repeatedly, and sometimes continuously, threatened. There is not only a primary emotional reaction to a given threat, but there is an immediate calling up of emotional memories associated with a similar threat in the past such that the emotional impact is intensified. If people are locked into a hegemonic structure in which they are at the mercy of a dominant group, every time they try to advance themselves relative to this group they are put down. Each time, they feel powerless to do something and angry at the injustice of it all. Each time, the feelings grow stronger, resentment deepens and turns to hatred. Hatred is a combination of emotions that prompt an orientation and commitment to do violence to one's Other. At an extreme it wishes the death of one's Other.

Those whose identity is wrapped around their superiority in relation to others are threatened at the identity level when the Other tries to identify with them. They do all they can to keep in their superior position and as tensions and threats escalate they can become imprisoned in their own security systems. They refuse to have any contact with the Other for fear of losing their superiority. When protesters refuse to meet with police or police refuse to meet with protesters there are some elements of fear of sharing strategies and fear of losing their superiority involved. The fear reflects a mimetic structure of violence.

In the face of injustice inspired anger, fear, resentment and hatred, the last thing that people want to hear about is reconciliation and blessing. These emotions function as a firewall against any real consideration of these concepts and the actions that might lead to them. The only things that can overcome this emotional firewall in people locked in a mimetic structure of violence are

- an experience of positive emotion-charged action such as a gesture of generosity or hospitality which then can grow mimetically, or
- a cognitive and volitional transformation whereby they decide to embark on the reconciliation/blessing journey even though it flies in the face of what they are feeling.

In order for the latter to happen, they have to have a conceptual understanding of blessing (in whatever words it might be expressed) and an imagination that is open to its pursuit. In the section on reconciliation we will explore further how this might come about.

It is important that the very process of creating a mimetic structure of blessing be deeply respectful of the emotional realities of the parties involved. At times these are at the level of post-traumatic stress syndrome. There is a complex emotional dance that is involved that demands sensitivity to the emotions that exist without allowing those emotions to dictate future relationships. If people, who are emotionally vulnerable or charged, interpret outside actors as asserting pressure on them to change they will feel re-victimized and the emotional firewall will grow stronger than ever.

Destructive emotions drive mimetic structures of violence. However, because they hijack cognitive, volitional, heuristic and hermeneutic capacities of the mind, they can disguise themselves in the language of logic, justice and objectivity. They may say, 'Reason over passion,' but their behaviour shows how reason is prompted by passion. How they think, what they commit to, what they discover and how they interpret reality are all driven by their emotions. If they hate their adversary, that hatred will captivate their imaginations such that they will not even see gestures of goodwill, nor will they hear conciliatory words, nor will they imagine a positive future together.

If the firewall is penetrated by goodwill and parties proceed in a process of reconciliation, there will be an emotional pay-off. As relationships are built up and trust re-established, fear diminishes. As stories are shared, historical memories are re-framed. Not only are destructive emotions reduced, but positive emotions like self-respect, self-confidence, and joy are increased. Emotional transformations are some of the hardest goals to achieve. There is neither formula nor technique that makes it easy. However, when they occur they provide some of the greatest satisfaction ever.

Protest crowds are driven by emotions—positive and negative—that are inspired by injustice. Some protesters harness their care for third parties by pressing for a message to be heard and change to be implemented at the level of policy and practice. Other protesters are driven by hatred that is nursed by a history of bad experiences. These emotions are operative in the primary relational system that includes the protest crowd and the target. However, if the police are perceived to be in solidarity with the target, are seen to be thwarting effective protest, or are experienced as being violent toward the protest crowd, the destructive emotions can be directed toward the police. Dealing with the emotional side of protest crowds in a way that will enhance mimetic structures of blessing in all relational systems is itself a complex undertaking.

Complexity, Creativity, and Consciousness

Complexity, creativity and level of consciousness are interconnected concepts that can work together to build mimetic structures of blessing even in the most unlikely circumstances. It has already been argued that protest crowd events are themselves complex systems. As such they are beyond linear control, can evolve to the edge of chaos where anything can happen, and are subject to significant change with minor interventions at the right place and time.

Complexity

Numerous aspects of a large protest crowd, such as a G-8 protest, constitute a complex system. The issues combine different intertwined aspects of globalization. The perceived target is multi-faceted—multinational corporations, corrupt governments, multilateral financial institutions— even though the immediate target, the government leaders, is more focused. The protest crowd has an array of affinity groups, many of them concerned about different issues—labour, poverty, environment, human rights. Security involves multiple police forces/services from all of the different countries represented. Military force may be implicated as a back-up plan. Surveillance and intelligence gathering are multi-focused and could involve several agencies. The bystander population reaches out in concentric circles to a global media audience, as media from many countries are present.

The protest crowd–police relational system is complex even in smaller more focused crowd situations. The complexity may be a little less obvious but it is there. First, in terms of discourse about the issue, there is a flurry of communications through the internet. Communications from Government are meant to 'sell' a given policy. Critiques are evident in the media, but also whizzing through internet connections. Organizational information is received by members of affinity groups but police also receive the same information and interpret it differently. There are ethical ambiguities built into the dynamics as well. Protesters may be attuned to a high ethical standard in terms of the issues but may revert to a different standard if they get into a good guy—bad guy mentality towards the police. The police may agree with the issues of the protesters but they 'have a job to do' which may involve limiting the scope and effectiveness of the protest. On one hand, police can differentiate between a protest against human rights abuses and a racial supremacist group that spreads hate; on the other hand, it is not up to police to determine who can protest and about what.

There are legal issues as well. We have already shown that police are not always rigorous about law enforcement in the context of a protest crowd because to do so indiscriminately could cause 'troubles.' However, this raises questions around which laws are enforced, or if the enforcement of some laws could be used to manipulate a crowd, or perhaps if the appearance of enforcing a law might allow police to arrest a protest leader who has broken no law. The cumulative effect of all this complexity is that protest crowd events are positioned on the edge, the border, if you like, of not only chaos, but of cultural norms and limits. As such, they are at the confluence of change.

Creativity

Creativity involves new combinations of things and ideas, re-framing and re-interpreting reality and the emergence of new paradigms and world views. A simple illustration of creativity, that is combining things in new ways, was the placement of a motor, already developed, into a carriage which became a 'horseless carriage' that evolved into an auto-mobile (self-moving) or car. In the realm of ideas and art similar things happen. In the 1930s in Saskatchewan, Tommy Douglas took his concern over poverty and health and combined it with the concept of publicly funded programs to support the common good. His position of Premier in the provincial government enabled him to institutionalize publicly funded hospitals and eventually medical care for everyone in the province. This became the model of Medicare for all Canadians.

Creativity can lead to a change of paradigm, or way of perceiving reality. Charles Darwin took observations about similarities and differences in plants and animals and re-interpreted the data within a unified theory of evolution. Similarly, Copernicus took the intricate measurements of the different positions of planets in the sky and re-interpreted the same data as had previously used to plot complicated circles in the sky to see the planets simply as moving around the same centre—the sun.

In the next chapter we will use the concept of a change of paradigms to look at the protest crowd–police relational system. For the time being, we are looking at a shift of paradigms as one dimension of creativity. As data is reframed and new paradigms are developed creativity pushes us in the direction of new insights and the emergence of new levels of consciousness and worldviews. The very nature of creativity as insight and emergence of new ways of thinking is such that the results can never be pre-determined. Insight happens in an open system and usually through the interaction of diverse perspectives.

Creativity can be oriented toward violence or toward blessing. Command economies of weapons development can create the means to hurt and destroy populations in new ways. On the other hand, research into the prevention and cure of diseases can enhance the lives of many. Similarly the dynamics of protest crowds interacting with government and business leaders could produce new solutions to old problems or they could deteriorate into violent confrontations in which everybody loses except those who have a vested interest in nothing changing or the conflict continuing.

New Levels of Consciousness

Over the last several decades, a great deal of work has been done around the emergence of new levels of consciousness (Wilber, 2001). This has included developmental psychologists measuring cognitive development and moral thinkers looking at stages of moral development, anthropologists examining cultural development, and integrative thinkers combining insights from all of these into integrated models of levels of consciousness. One of the latter, Richard McGuigan, used developmental theories of Robert Kegan and Ken

Wilber to examine the question of levels of consciousness and conflict. He demonstrated that the more complex the conflict, the higher level of consciousness was needed to deal with it effectively—that is, creatively, without letting it deteriorate into violence (McGuigan, 2006). This suggests that if all of the parties involved in protest crowd–police dynamics have an openness to learn from each other and from the complexity of the situation they could deal with it more productively, allow new and creative options to emerge and grow in their own levels of consciousness. Much of this has, in fact, happened within a number of democracies as the interactions between protest crowds, governments and police has moved societies into universal suffrage (from only propertied white males being allowed to vote initially) and to such things as a recognition of the right to collective bargaining on the part of labour unions. These developments can be seen as creative, emergent and transforming.

Since the transformation from mimetic structures of violence to mimetic structures of blessing can be framed as reconciliation, in the next section we will present elements of reconciliation—aspects and processes that need to be present in varying degrees to move destructively conflictual parties closer to a situation where they can co-exist tolerantly and further to where they can enhance the well-being of one another.

Reconciliation

Reconciliation is concerned about long term relationships. As such, it can be understood as both a goal and a process (Bar-Tal & Bennink, 2004). Reconciliation as a *goal* may have spectrum of outcomes, ranging from an agreement to stop all forms of violence, to living with as much distance between the parties as possible, to tolerant co-existence, to mutual respect, to friendship and a desire for mutual well-being (Sluzki, 2003). Reconciliation aims to deal with the aftermath of *past* victimization and prepare parties for a peaceful *future* together.

At times, parties needing reconciliation are separated geographically and psychologically. In other instances such as the populations of such conflicted areas as Northern Ireland, Bosnia-Herzegovina, Rwanda, South Africa and Israel–Palestine, antagonistic parties to a deep-rooted conflict continue to live as neighbours. In these cases the need for reconciliation at levels from political leadership to grass roots is particularly acute (Bar-Tal & Bennink, 2004).

Reconciliation as a *process* may be understood as a complex set of exchanges that include a number of elements. At times, the process is directed through a conscious well-defined effort to achieve reconciliation, in other instances, the process may take place at the tacit level with different actors intuitively taking a variety of initiatives. Invariably, the process will include some or all of the following elements (Redekop, 2002):

1) Vision and mandate: either one of the parties or a third party has a vision and desire for reconciliation and obtains a mandate to work to that end.

2) Safety: the safety of the parties needs to be assured. This means that overt violence must be halted. Sometimes a legal framework needs to be in place to assure the safety of potential victims. Safety also means that the parties do not intimidate each other (Redekop, 2007b).

3) Immediate survival needs: reconciliation processes can be demanding both cognitively and emotionally. Hence it is important that parties are assured of having their immediate physical and emotional needs sufficiently met to function through the process.

4) Teachings: the process of reconciliation is directed by a framework, values, root metaphors and mental models that provide motivation and insight to keep the process going. Teachings may take the form of stories of previous reconciliation processes, traditional proverbs and customs, or analytical insights. Education for reconciliation includes the development of skills (Huyse, 2003) and generation of new beliefs and attitudes about both the conflict and the other party (Bar-Siman-Tov, 2004).

5) Gradual Reciprocated Initiatives in Tension-Reduction (GRIT) (Osgood, 1966): one party may decide to make a low-risk gesture of goodwill; if the other party reciprocates with a similar gesture the first party may take another positive initiative (Osgood, 1966). Gradually the tension dissipates and the parties are prepared to enter into another level of discourse to address the deep-rooted conflict.

6) Dialogue: at some point parties will enter into a dialogue in which they are motivated to truly understand one another. Dialogue means that meaning flows freely between the parties (Bohm, 1997). There is also open disclosure of the emotional dimensions of the conflict.

7) Truth-telling: in addition to the dialogue there may be a need to formally establish the truth of what occurred. Ideally this will lead

to a shared acceptance of the same presentation of the history of the conflict. Analysts, historians and lawyers may play a role in this and it may involve a formal process (Lederach, 1997).

8) Expressions of acknowledgement, remorse, and apology: eventually those who have committed acts of violence will understand the impact of these acts on the other party. As they acknowledge a) what they have done, b) the hurt it has caused, c) feelings of remorse over having caused the harm, and d) a desire to not commit the same acts in the future, they will be able to offer an effective apology (Redekop, 2007a).

9) Expressions of victimization, openness to forgiveness: those victimized will express to the perpetrator and third parties what they have experienced. As they hear an acknowledgement of their hurt from the perpetrator along with apologies and expressions of remorse they may become open to forgive. Forgiveness means to give up an impulse or right to make the perpetrator suffer in response to the suffering caused by the perpetrator, implying moral judgment, the humanity of the perpetrator, and a desire for a renewed relationship (Bole, Drew Christiansen, & Hennemeyer, 2004; Shriver, 2001).

10) Justice and mercy: justice involves making some judgment about what would restore a sense of balance to the relationship. Where violence has involved theft or destruction of possessions, these can be restored. When there is emotional pain, torture, or loss of life, it is impossible to return parties to their previous state. Some things may be done by way of compensation or compensatory actions to alleviate the loss. Strict retributive justice could result only in another round of violence. Some form of mercy or generosity of spirit may be combined with positive balancing measures to craft a profound forgiveness (Lederach, 1999).

11) Re-orientation: at some point the parties will re-orient their relationship. This re-orientation may demand inner changes of identity, attitude and orientation in relation to the other (Bar-Siman-Tov, 2004). Both parties and the relationship itself will be transformed such that both parties will contribute to mutual empowerment.

12) Healing of traumas and memories: in order for the reconciliation process to be sustained and for both parties to flourish, it is important that as much as possible emotional traumas and memories be healed.

Reconciliation rituals may play a role in this process (Schirch, 2005; Redekop, 2007a) as can various forms of therapy (Herman, 1997), cognitive reframing and spiritual disciplines and practices (Hermann, 2004).

13) Re-defining terms of the relationship including transformation of structures: reconciliation is not complete if the structures left in place continue to victimize. For example, hegemonic structures, in which one party systematically dominates another party, involve economic, political, physical, and/or discursive dimensions. Action has to be taken in each of these areas to address systemic imbalances. New laws, customs, economic regulations and institutions may be needed to sustain the reconciliation process (Kriesberg, 2004; Redekop, 2008).

Reconciliation is not a linear process; rather it is cyclical and iterative. Not all of the elements above may be present each time and some may have to be addressed repeatedly. Reconciliation can be understood as a freedom from mimetic (imitative) structures of violence that take on a life of their own and a freedom to create and nurture mimetic structures of blessing or peace, in which new life-enhancing options are systematically generated.

In cases where there has been a history of violent exchanges between police and protesters, like the G-8 Summit in Italy where a protester was killed by police, there may be a need for reconciliation processes. The above elements could be used to design a process to work toward that end.

Protest Crowd–Police Relational Blessing

What would it mean for there to be mimetic structures of blessing in the protest crowd–police relational system? First off, what it would *not* mean would be an absence of conflict; neither would it mean that the relationship would be prescribed. Rather it would mean a dynamic relationship that interacts respectfully with inevitable conflict in creative and transformative ways. The attitude of the players is what is important. The very fact that protest crowds are pushing the edges, often in the interests of extending mimetic structures of blessing to people violently victimized means that there is a tension with the status quo and with peace understood as tranquility. As we showed in chapter two, expression of dissent is an important part of a thriving community, organization or political system. This means that police as a party in the relational system can express dissent at protest activities just as protesters may critique police tactics. In our examination of the meaning of mimetic structures of blessing for protest crowds and police we will first examine the current situation to see if there is evidence of mimetic structures of blessing within this relational system. We will then look at the challenges of blessing and the potential of blessing as a supra-ordinate goal. Finally we will stress the importance of mimetic modeling by all parties.

The Presence of Blessing

Within repressive regimes that see dissent as a threat, the inherent dynamic in the protest crowd–police relational system is a mimetic structure of violence. However, in democracies where temporary assemblies to protest is a right, there has been an evolution in the relational systems such that consistently 90 per cent of protest crowd activity happens without incident. In most of these instances, protesters see the police as playing a helpful role in making the demonstration happen without a problem.

The Challenge of Blessing

While the 90 per cent statistics sound appealing and represent a higher level of consciousness than the situation in countries where all expression of dissent is put down, there still are a number of challenges to be faced if there are to be truly mimetic structures of blessing. First, much of this police helpfulness comes out of a paternalistic, controlling attitude. Police are more sophisticated in getting crowds to do things their way without a show of force. Notwithstanding this, the 'velvet glove hiding an iron fist' approach is not devoid of violence. Second, there may be a different mentality on the part of public order police whose job it is to develop good relationships with protest crowds and front line police officers who might see things differently. For example one of the police officers in our seminars reported about a fellow police officer, lacking in training and sensitivity, who referred to protesters as 'the enemy.' When protests turn chaotic, both protesters and police on the front line make their own decisions on what to do second by second. There is no time to consult with leadership about strategic and logistical options. Yet what happens at the moment of confrontation reflects on each group and may set in motion some significant new developments—oriented either toward violence or blessing. This suggests that as much as possible, as many as possible from all sides should be given the chance to participate in training sessions together (see the final chapter).

Another challenge arises from the very different organizational styles of the two groups and communication and leadership issues that arise. Police are organized in a hierarchical manner; at times policing decisions are made at a level that may not be aware of understandings reached between police liaison officers and protest leaders. This problem is a function of internal communication, leadership and decision making. Similarly the diversity of affinity groups on the protest side and the emphasis on consensus means that negotiations can be complex and with a large number of players with diverse perspectives, miscommunication can happen. The 'spokes' who may be present for the negotiation may not speak for all the affinity groups. Third, the very presence of police tactical troops, their equipment and their training are designed for violent engagement with protest crowds. The visible presence of these officers is a symbolic form of violence; if they are hidden, their presence still works at a tacit level, leading some to refer to a 'superficially soft hat' mode (King & Waddington, 2006, 95).

There is cutting edge thinking taking place around the concept of morphogenic fields that could eventually be helpful in analyzing the influence of unseen troops on the behaviour of protesters. Morphogenic fields are information fields that influence all who have morphic resonance (Shelldrake, 2003). For example, if a group of people think and feel a certain way, they establish a morphogenic field such that those who are sensitive to this field could be affected by it. There is currently scientific research going on regarding these fields. If the early research in this area is correct, it would suggest that preparations for violence by the police or having a violent orientation can influence a situation by increasing the potential for violence. On the other side, there are protesters who are convinced that the use of violence is essential to their effectiveness. This intent can influence the field around them and consequently influence police officers in that field.

A final challenge is that police and protesters have trouble seeing the humanity of one another. This is a result of differences in mentality, physical and psychological distance between the groups, the use of masks to hide faces, and a rhetoric of 'us' versus 'them.' Dehumanization makes it easier for either side to be violent towards the other.

Police are to a greater or lesser extent responsible to the government that ultimately provides their budgets. Some governments have little tolerance for dissent, or little tolerance for protests that might cause them to lose face or control especially in the presence of foreign visitors. If police are directed to either repress protest or keep it so far away as to be benign, they may have to use violence to fulfill operational goals imposed upon them. This raises the paradox that on the one hand it is essential for police to be subject to democratically elected governments; on the other hand, it is essential that police not become instrumental in imposing partisan or capricious policies of a government on a population. (It is noteworthy that Rowan and Mayne, as the first commissioners of the Metropolitan Police of London were able to model an approach to policing that carved out a space at the centre of the paradox.)

Finally, real violence is a fact of protest crowd–police interactions. Police can violently arrest protesters. Even before an event, the detention of leaders is a form of violence. Baton charges, intimidating tactics, and the use of less than lethal weapons—all are forms of violence. On the protester side, throwing stones and Molotov cocktails are forms of violence as is forcibly pushing back a police cordon. On both sides, there is discursive violence through language meant to put-down, intimidate, dehumanize and demonize the other parties.

Blessing as a Supra-Ordinate Goal

What is advocated here is that if the building of mimetic structures of blessing based on justice becomes the overarching goal of all the parties, that, in and of itself, could be transformative. It could form an ethical vision to guide assessments of strategic goals and ultimately operational plans and on the ground tactics. In so far as protesters are visibly working towards mimetic structures of blessing, police would be oriented to helping them achieve their goals. Likewise, governments, multi-lateral organizations and multinational businesses could also be challenged to work for mimetic structures of blessing. If things are framed this way and if the importance of dissent, complexity and creativity were to be affirmed as part of the process of blessing, protest crowds could be embraced as an essential part of collective evolution to higher levels of consciousness.

Mimetic Modeling

It is not likely that the concept of mimetic structures of blessing will be understood and embraced by all parties at the same time. In the mean time, given the power of mimesis, any individuals and groups who are committed to moving in this direction can have an impact by modeling, in a congruent way, their understanding of mutual blessing. Little did the Buddhist monks, peacefully protesting in the 1970s realize the impact they would have on Sharon Welsh, then an angry anti-war protester using a rhetoric of violence to talk about peace (refer to her story at the end of chapter two).

Having developed key concepts of mimetic structures of violence, identity needs, hegemonic structures, destructive emotions, trauma as well as mimetic structures of blessing, reconciliation, complexity and creativity, we are now in a position to see how these translate into paradigms of protest policing. Knowing how government, multinational business, and multi-lateral organizations are implicated as targets of protest and how bystanders and media play important role, we are in a position to explore the implications of these concepts for all the parties involved.

9. Towards a Mutual Respect Paradigm of Protester–Police Dynamics

Police are essentially mandated to establish and maintain geographical and behavioural boundaries for protest crowds. How the boundaries are set and how they are maintained is a function of policies, established practices, strategy, tactics, policing and popular cultures, organization, training, equipment, command structure and the personalities of those involved. These boundaries conform to interpretations of what it means to preserve the peace, protect the property and persons of citizens and government, and obey the law. All of these are determined, in many respects, by the paradigm of protest policing that informs those who make decisions that impinge on police activity at any level. Paradigms function as different lenses that determine how facts and events are interpreted.

Similarly, through experience, protesters repeat successful strategies, practices, and tactics—always pushing the edge of the envelope for something that will make a difference and gain the attention of the targets of their demonstrations. They too interpret what they do through a paradigmatic lens that includes values and expectations around roles and behaviour of police, targets, media and protest itself.

We will develop the concept of paradigms, first, showing how they work, how they change, and what a difference this makes. Then we will develop three different paradigms of protest policing: crowd control, crowd management, and mutual respect. Given significant changes in protest policing over the last several decades, it is clear that not all approaches fit cleanly into one paradigm or another; hence, we will look at the interplay among them. Just as police are essentially reactive in relation to crowds—that is, they only have to take action if their boundaries are threatened—so protesters are reactive in terms of paradigmatic development. That is, protesters orient themselves to the police based on the paradigm of protest policing that they experience. Often governments have a more repressive attitude in dealing with protest crowds than do police. We will examine why this is the case and why it is important that the paradigms of governments in relation to protest crowds are important and how they need to change. Finally we will look at the importance of these paradigms for the public and for the media which reports on protest crowds on the basis of their own paradigmatic lenses.

Paradigms

A paradigm is a way of perceiving a phenomenon as whole; the paradigm determines what the component parts of the phenomenon are, how the different parts are interpreted and what their relationship

is to one another and to the whole. Examples of paradigms are pictures that can be seen in two different ways. For example, the picture at the left could be seen as either two faces or as a chalice. Depending on how it is perceived the different lines take on different meaning.

In the case of a paradigm concerning human relationships, a shift in paradigm can make a huge difference in attitudes, values and actions. A shift in paradigm may depend on the development of a more complex level of consciousness in the same way as some computer software will only run with a more complex operating system. We will give two examples: the shift in policing paradigm from fighting crime to community policing and a shift from a retributive justice paradigm to restorative justice.

In the 1980s there was a movement among police to change the paradigm of policing from a strict law enforcement approach to 'community policing' in which police were to identify with the community as part of the community. This later morphed into problem-solving policing in which police were to look at difficult situations as problems to be solved rather than simply bad people breaking some laws. Careful analysis of the root causes of the problem and creative solutions were rewarded. One Canadian police inspector who took a national lead in community policing used to reward one of his officers monthly on the basis of who had worked with community members to find a creative long-term solution to an intractable problem. This is in stark contrast to police being rewarded for arrests made or cases closed.

Beginning in the 1970s there was a shift in criminal justice from retributive justice to restorative justice. It all started with the Elmira Case in Ontario, Canada. Some boys had vandalized a number of cars and properties in a neighbourhood. Contrary to all expectations, the judge ruled that these boys should visit all the homes they vandalized and offer to make things right. From this emerged a whole new approach to dealing with crime. It starts with the view of crime as harm done to people (in contrast to breaking a law) and the goal of justice being to make restitution for harm done (instead of paying one's debt to society through being punished by spending time in prison). Programmatically, it finds expression in Victim Offender Reconciliation Programs, Community Healing Circles, Alternative Sentencing, Circle Sentencing processes, Face to Face encounters in penitentiaries, and so on. Restorative justice is now an international movement, even informing such institutions as the Truth and Reconciliation Commission of South Africa. As we shall see below, a new paradigm in protest policing has the capacity to change dramatically the strategic planning and operational dynamics of dealing with protest crowds.

Three Paradigms of Protest Policing

The three paradigms of policing that are presented below have evolved in a particular way since the 1960s, even though elements of all three can be seen in different historical settings. The first of these is given the name, Crowd Control Paradigm. It evolved as protest crowds became larger and more sophisticated during the time of the Vietnam War; its roots are evident in colonial policing. Referred to as 'hard' policing, it resurfaced with the development of new protective gear for police and a whole new range of less than lethal weapons. Second is the Conflict Management Paradigm which evolved through the 1980s onward with the realization that police could be more effective through the use of 'soft' tactics sometimes referred to as 'negotiation.' Third is the Mutual Respect Paradigm that recognizes a greater degree of mutuality between protest crowds and police. Its emergence can be traced to a series of seminars described in the Case Study of Part 2.

Each of these paradigms has an impact on the following component parts of protest policing:
- Perception of the crowd and the language used to talk about it
- The nature of the challenge
- Strategy
- Tactics
- Intelligence
- Decision making.

- Organization
- Policies
- Values
- Accountability
- Identity

Within each of these paradigms there is wide latitude as to practices and attitudes of those who operate within them. In order to differentiate the paradigms, they will first be presented with their distinctions clearly defined and contrasted. It may seem to be an over simplification at the outset; however more of the subtleties will be developed later.

The Crowd Control Paradigm

The *language* that is used by police to designate themselves and the protest crowd has both a power and an ethical dimension to it. To designate a unit as responsible for crowd *control* makes the crowd into an object. To say it must be controlled speaks of a hegemonic structure where a powerful body is able to determine what the crowd can do. This language harks back to LeBon's notion of a crowd as hysterical, uncontrolled emotional woman who need a strong 'man' to control her. Crowds are seen as essentially problematic; some would even go so far as to call them the enemy. Even though the language of enemy may not be used, the kind of strategic preparation is akin to facing the enemy with whom police are at 'war.' The designation 'riot squad' speaks to the reality of potential riots.

The *challenge* of crowd control is to make certain the crowd is under control all the time. That means that the crowd is confined into its designated area, is held there, and if its behaviour becomes more rowdy than is allowed it is forcibly dispersed. The *strategy* is to have a strong show of force to be certain the crowd knows who is in control. This may take the form of well armed police forming a cordon, the use of shields, and perhaps fences to form a boundary. Beyond that it is to use specialized squads to keep the crowd at bay or to disperse the crowd. Water cannons and tear gas are readily available as are less than lethal weapons that can immobilize protesters who get out of hand. All contingencies are covered in advance.

Tactics of crowd control are quickly reactive to any violent behaviour within the crowds. Should demonstrators prove menacing, they are quickly forced back. Particularly violent protesters are apprehended with enough force to make examples of them. Any controlling action is in the hands of police. Decision making happens in a hierarchical manner. Emphasis is put on obedience to orders. The organization is paramilitary. Communication with protesters takes the form of directives and orders. Extensive intelligence is used to gauge the threat of a protest crowd and to identify potential troublemakers. Since avoidance of things getting out of hand is of paramount importance, if protest leaders can be isolated from the crowd by denying them entrance into the country or arresting them on spurious charges, so much the better.

Policies

Within a crowd control paradigm, strength is valued. The decisive leader who takes firm action to stop a crowd and the 'tac troops' with the fully protective clothing, who know how to advance on a crowd or dart into a crowd to make an arrest would receive the highest recognition. Accountability and loyalty is primarily to the police force/service that wishes to come out looking good at all costs. The identity of the valuable protest police officer is one who is strong enough to not take anything from protesters; and is a well trained professional who can use all the weapons available when commanded to and with great effectiveness.

The Crowd (or Negotiated) Management Paradigm

Within the Crowd Management paradigm protesters are thought of as citizens exercising their right to protest. There may be problems that develop but good management strategies will keep these to a minimum. Given the fact that a crowd is thought of something that needs to be managed, the discursive structure is still hegemonic. Crowds will be directed and every effort will be made to make certain they do things in line with what the police would desire. The language of negotiation is used to indicate that processes of planning, crowd events, and dispersal are arranged through discussion; however, discursive tactics are used to make certain things go right for the police.

The challenge is to facilitate protesters in organizing their crowd events in a way that does not create incidents. It is important at all costs to avoid troubles. The strategy is to use discursive means if at all possible to control the situation. All the means of crowd control are still available but only as a last resort. Confrontation with the crowd is to be avoided at all cost. Latitude in law enforcement, compromises (real and apparent) and a helpful attitude become part of the strategy of making this paradigm work. The following chart (Figure 9.1), made available by the Royal Canadian Mounted Police, shows the tactical options available. Clockwise from midnight tactics are increasingly heavy handed. The strategy within this paradigm is to continually try to keep on the right side of the diagram and to resist clockwise movement if at all possible.

Primary tactics have to do with creating psychological boundaries and maintaining a non-threatening presence. Helpfulness in planning logistics and diverting traffic are used to establish goodwill and to control the situation. There are meetings with crowd organizers; crowd marshals are briefed. There may even be outright collaboration between crowd marshals and leaders and police. At times marshals will even direct troublesome protesters down a lane into the hands of police who are waiting for them.

Intelligence gathering is done first and foremost through permits that crowd organizers need to fill out before a protest crowd event. In the process

Figure 9.1 Risk Diagnosis and Use of Force Options

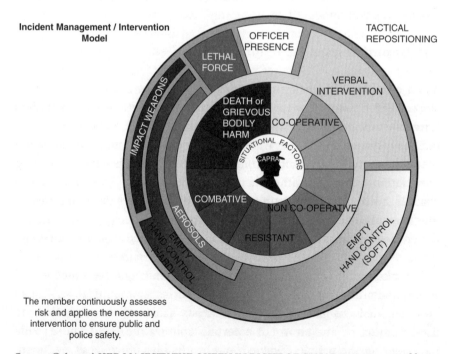

The member continuously assesses risk and applies the necessary intervention to ensure public and police safety.

Source: © (2009) HER MAJESTY THE QUEEN IN RIGHT OF CANADA as represented by the Royal Canadian Mounted Police (RCMP). Reprinted by permission of the RCMP.

of filling out the form, police will go through a check list of questions to be sure that planning is complete. The process both ensures that there is good planning and that police get enough information for them to plan properly. Information that is publicly available such as pamphlets, web sites, advertisements, etc. is a primary source of intelligence. Greater authority is given to crowd liaison officers to make decisions in concert with protest crowd leaders. Public Order Management Systems are put into place with sophisticated information loops and decision making flow charts. Policies and values emphasize the avoidance of confrontation. Training puts greater emphasis on negotiation and other discursive means of management. There is considerable emphasis on the strategic use of the media to convey information in such a way as to show the police as competently managing a situation in conformity with the public good. There is a greater sense of accountability to the public.

Protest police see themselves as being identified more strongly with the community. They see themselves as professional crisis managers, team builders who can collaborate with crowd organizers and even build a relationship with them.

The Mutual Respect Paradigm

In this paradigm, police view crowds as groups of people who do what they do for a reason. This means they think in terms of crowds being one part of a relational system that includes government institutions and businesses (targets), bystanders and security. To think of crowds as being part of a relational system means that what anyone does has an impact on all of the others, hence the relationship is *dynamic*. The emphasis is put on managing the relational dynamic rather than on controlling the crowd *per se*. The heart of this paradigmatic approach is to set up structures through which all the different parties can communicate with one another, explore the identity dimensions of the issues involved and create dynamic situations that can serve the interests and well-being of all the different parties.

First, the Mutual Respect Paradigm is based on language, dialogue and communication. Not only is language used for communication it also becomes the focus of discourse and analysis. The kinds of words that are used to describe an action put a certain spin on the event and a value judgment on the people involved. A word like 'violence' is value laden. Within this paradigm, there would be open dialogue on the meaning of violence in different contexts. What exactly is a violent action? If shown a video of certain actions deemed by some as violent, others might say that these were non-violent. For example, one activist has said that the attempts to take down the fence in Quebec City were justified and not violent in that they had no intent to enter the restricted area, yet security personnel took aggressive, 'violent' action to limit it. From the security perspective, the fence was deemed necessary for them to be successful in their prime mission of protecting the meeting; any destruction was violent and their actions were justified in the circumstances. The seemingly uncontrolled use of tear gas canisters was considered violent by peaceful protesters who were gassed, yet security personnel found the inaccuracy of the tear gas canisters and their limited scope of vision to be at least partially to blame for their gassing peaceful protesters. The same words used differently by different parties can promote misunderstanding and distrust; on the other hand, when people share their mutual understandings of a given phenomenon they may not always agree but they will respect the perceptions of the other. Words are found to express emotions. Using words to talk about emotions is very different than simply acting on them.

Second, the Mutual Respect Paradigm is relational, emphasizing the building of respect and trust. Dennis S. Reina and Michelle L. Reina have said that in high-trust environments, people are more willing to keep agreements, share information, admit and learn from mistakes, and take on greater responsibility (Reina & Reina, 1999). There is a value to relationships and a sense that respectful relationships in and of themselves are a positive factor in managing the interactions in a way that benefits everyone. All parties share a common commitment to explore the development of positive relationships.

Third, the Mutual Respect Paradigm is sensitive to the identity needs and interests of the various parties. One's identity needs are those things which are important to support the person's well-being; the need for meaning in their lives, to be able to take action, to be connected one with another, to be recognized as good and worthy, and to be safe and secure.

Fourth, the Mutual Respect Paradigm values creativity. Creativity involves discovering new, helpful and innovative approaches to meeting the needs of various parties at the same time. It brings together a variety of resources and combines them in a way in which they have not been combined before. Creativity is a result of looking at the same old problem in a new way. It is inspired by insights and in this case the insights are stimulated by dialogue among the parties. To value creativity is to value open-ended processes that allow creative ideas and approaches to emerge. Creativity within a community also involves discernment. Not every new idea is significant and helpful. In brainstorming, for instance, every idea is welcomed and received equally by facilitator and group. Later, in thinking about the ideas and working with them, some will emerge as being truly insightful and helpful and others will be put on the backburner to simmer until such time as they are needed or inspire other useful ideas.

Fifth, the Mutual Respect Paradigm is driven by principles. There is an ethical culture that is developed through the interaction among the parties involved in the collaboration. The principles that underlie this ethical culture can be identified, written down, taught, discussed and explained. Principles need to be developed collaboratively and, at this time, their formulation is in the early stages.

Sixth, the Mutual Respect Paradigm has about it a spirit of generosity, mutual care and joy. The story is told of a joint Israeli–Palestinian working group on water management. They became close personal friends through their collaboration. While they were together at a location far removed from Israel/Palestine, a suicide bomb was detonated a few blocks from the home of one of the Israelis. Immediately one of the Palestinians was on the phone, calling to his contacts to verify that the family of his Israeli friend was unharmed.

Out of recognition of the importance of each for the other should emerge an attitude of respect. Such an attitude is important for the development of authentic relationships and mutual trust. The same action done with a different attitude takes on an entirely different character. The action of police consulting with protesters is very different if the purpose of the consultation is to enhance police intelligence and establish a way of controlling or managing the crowd as opposed to a genuine desire for protesters to do what they have to do in safety and in an atmosphere free of hassles and violence. As Kratcoski, Verma and Das observe:

No country, regardless of how traditional its values and culture are, will remain static. There is constant change, and often protests, demonstration and strikes are the mechanisms used to being about desired changes more quickly. If the police approach such disorder events from the perspective that these are opportunities for peaceful solutions to political or social unrest problems, the outcomes are likely to be productive. (Kratcoski et al., 2001)

Likewise, if protesters respect the mandate given police and the actions taken, they will be able to combine effective protest and maintain the dignity of police and those they are called upon to protect. This reminds me (VNR) of participating in a march to commemorate the Oka/Kanehsatà:ke Crisis of 1990. I was walking with Ellen Gabriel through the golf course. When we got to one of the holes she took the flag marker out of the hole and gently laid it down, remarking that we were not there to hurt anything, just to make a point.

Communication—There are some built-in challenges to effective communication between protest crowds and police. These are a result of their very different characters and organizational systems (and the stages of consciousness of the actors). Complex protest crowds are usually made up of a diversity of groups; these groups work together on the basis of consensus. Police are organized around a hierarchical structure with a command and control leadership style. Nonetheless, given the political will, effective communication can happen. It is important for police to listen carefully to not only the needs and plans of protesters but also to their goals, the issues they espouse and the vision they have for society. Protesters should listen to the challenges facing police. If there are 'die in the ditch' boundaries for the police, these should be talked about openly and various scenarios should be worked through in advance. There should be some openness to re-defining boundaries on certain occasions. Where the absolute boundaries are inviolable, they should be explained to protesters along with the rationale. Every effort should be made to arrive at shared understandings of the meaning of boundaries. Solutions to various other problems could be arranged and joint contingency plans developed. During a major crowd protest event, lines of communication should be open such that if something goes wrong on either side this can be immediately communicated and explained to the other side. After an event, a joint de-brief would contribute to mutual understanding and further planning.

Chaos and Creativity—Given the ambiguity described above regarding laws and peace, and given the passions involved to work toward change, it will likely happen that protest crowds will push legality and public order to its edges. As Deborah Sword points out, protest crowds have a tendency to be at the edge of chaos and members of protest crowds may well have a high level of tolerance for such a situation. Out of chaos may emerge either creative blessing or contagious violence. It is important that police school themselves in chaos theory and even work with protesters on role plays and contingency plans to deal effectively with life at the edge of chaos. It may even be that those assigned to work on public order policing be screened according to their capacity to deal effectively with chaotic and ambiguous situations.

Mimetic Structures of Blessing—In many instances protest crowds and police do play mutually empowering roles. It is important to identify the mimetic structures of blessing where they occur. It is also important for police and protesters to explore together what mimetic structures of blessing might mean to them and to jointly commit to the creation and nurture of such structures.

A mandate may be given to a neutral third party organization to facilitate the operationalization of the above points. Unless someone has a mandate to organize joint action it will not likely happen. In some cases there is a high level of distrust on both sides so an initiative from either side would be held suspect. A third party involvement would diminish the sense that police would use joint sessions to control the situation. (This point is derived from a number of seminars that brought police and protesters together see Part Two.) Such involvement would not preclude bilateral communication and negotiation but would help provide a supportive framework. During one of our seminars there was an evening debrief of the protest crowd activities at the Summit of the Americas in Quebec City in 2001. Protesters and police spoke openly about their respective experiences; along the way one of them commented, 'We usually do our debriefs separately but this is much better!'

With a shared vision of mimetic structures of blessing we can imagine a vibrant dynamic society in which new perspectives are constantly generated and shared in public spaces, where roles of stakeholders are periodically scrutinized, and where different voices of response express divergent views in a spirit of transparency, respect and openness to change.

Paradigms Compared

The following chart offers a concise point of comparison among the different paradigms.

Crowd Control	Crowd Management	Mutual Respect
Crowd thought of as 'enemy' or 'problem' by security	Crowd thought of as citizens exercising their rights; not a problem in itself but causing potential problems	Crowd welcomed as essential component of civil society and generator of creative options for society
Security develops strategy on its own	Crowd leaders consulted by police; joint plan but police strategy and back-up plans are hidden	Crowds, security and possibly targets collaborate on strategy for the event
All the means of antagonistic preparations are used including surveillance and covert intelligence gathering	More emphasis on collecting information through permit forms and publicly accessible information like web sites	Information is shared openly all around; identities and roles are transparent
Security is derived from using the tools of control including less than lethal and lethal means	Security is based on getting agreement on as many points as possible; open lines of communication; clear demarcation of boundaries	Security is derived from trusting relationships based on mutual dignity and respect
Tries to have all contingencies covered before engagement with crowd	Shares responsibilities with crowd marshals and organizers; on occasion collaborate in dealing with instigators of violence	Uses open processes to imagine new and mutually beneficial ways of dealing with conflicts
Security fundamentally responsible to Target	Keeps arms length relationship with target at most; neutral at best	Security responsible for well being of entire population including protesting crowd
Focuses on violent protesters as 'criminals,' 'troublemakers,' etc.	Differentiates among different types of protesters	Tries to understand reasons for extreme emotions and passions
Tries to thwart actions of protesters by closing borders, impeding logistics, harassing and arresting protesters	Expedites movements and organization of protesters	Creates a context for protest effectiveness

Crowd Control	Crowd Management	Mutual Respect
Debriefs a crowd event alone	Communicates informally with crowd organizers	Debriefs a crowd event together; periodic facilitated workshops to reflect on the nature and role of organized protest
Media frames event around conflict between protesters and police	Media portrayal of police violence kept to a minimum	Media frames stories around the creation of mimetic* structures of blessing arising out of mimetic* structures of violence
Targets see crowds as nuisance and threat	Targets reluctantly open to negotiation with crowds; police and/or mediators facilitate the process	Targets see crowds as a sign that some things need to change; as a source of key information about the world
Activists see police and targets as enemy	Police are seen as rendering helpful advice and assistance	Activists see police and leaders playing essential roles
Mimetic* and escalating violence	Violence minimized	Mimetic and expanding blessing
Public gets message that violence is on increase	Low key message to public	Public gets new vision for future possibilities
Public increasingly worried about future		Public re-assured
People are boxed into roles and spaces		People move respectfully into each other's spaces

Relationship among Paradigms

The relationship among paradigms is not straightforward. First, there is considerable *latitude* in the range of actions and attitudes that can be evident within each paradigm. Second, since these paradigms are paradigms of policing, developed from the perspective of the police, it is important to examine *paradigms from a protest crowd perspective*. Third, each paradigm can be seen as reflection of a different level of consciousness; with that realization, insights about relations among levels of consciousness prove instructive. Forth, the development of new paradigms can be seen as creative emergence; looking back one can identify a number of factors that worked together to stimulate paradigmatic change. These four aspects of the relationship will be developed in greater detail.

Latitude within Paradigms

Each of these paradigms allows for considerable latitude in behaviour and attitude. Within the Crowd Control paradigm could be an attitude that is hostile toward protest crowds with repressive behaviour that limits protest crowd activity completely. It would also be possible to have relatively benign and friendly attitudes toward protest crowds as long as they stayed within the behavioural and geographic boundaries with which police would feel comfortable. There are also differences within this paradigm of how police present themselves. This ranges from immediately presenting themselves with protective shields and the 'Darth Vader' look to appearing first on bicycles with soft hats. What distinguishes the paradigm is how police understand their task; in this case it is to control crowds that have the potential to get out of hand or to riot.

The Crowd Management Paradigm likewise can exemplify a broad range of approaches. What passes for 'negotiation' can range from outright manipulation to get protest crowds to comply with police wishes to a genuine interest in accommodating concerns of protest. Intelligence gathering can range from collecting information that is publicly available to intrusive intelligence that has undercover agents posing as crowd participants or organizers. There is also a range of relative weighting of the component parts of a Public Order Management System. In some cases the negotiation side is dominant and in other cases it may be simply window dressing to camouflage what is in effect a crowd control approach. There is also a distinction to be made among the different kinds of relationships between liaison officers and the command structure. In one instance the liaison officer has direct access to the operational commander and ensures that if there is a change from what she or he has told crowd organizers, this is immediately communicated to crowd representatives. Alternately, the liaison person is thought of by police leadership as a means of collecting intelligence and they think nothing of overriding what might have been agreed upon in negotiations with the protest organizers, nor of withholding significant information from them.

The Mutual Respect Paradigm likewise can be expressed in different ways. It is certainly open to subversion on both sides by people who do not communicate in good faith and choose to use the openness of others in the relational system for strategic advantage. On the other hand, it can be used to genuinely improve the situation for all concerned.

Paradigms from a Protest Crowd Perspective

These three paradigms also apply to protesters and how they view police. The corresponding paradigms are as follows:

Crowd Control : Police as Repressive

Crowd Management : Police as Potentially Helpful

Mutual Respect : Police in a Complementary Role in Advancing Public Goods

The paradigm used by crowds may or may not correspond to that of the police in any given protest crowd–police relational system. We will describe the different paradigms.

In the Repressive Police paradigm, police are seen as enemies of dissent. There is a substantial amount of suspicion towards the police who are seen as doing everything in their power to thwart the efforts, interests and goals of protesters. Police are regarded as potentially violent and special training is given to minimize the effects of tear gas and to maximize the difficulty in either breaking up a protest group or arresting members. Special precautions are taken to keep police infiltrators out of meetings. Information about strategy and tactics is kept as secret as possible. One leader within the protest community even came to a joint protest crowd–police training session primarily to make certain that fellow protesters not divulge too much information. Chosen traumas of the protester community include memories of police violence, people hurt (some killed), exposure to many less than lethal weapons, activists being stopped and turned back at the border for no apparent reason, and brutal arrest procedures. Chosen glories include shutting down the WTO talks in Seattle.

In the Helping Police paradigm, a certain rapport and working relationship has been established between protesters and police. There is a sense that people on both sides know the score – they know and understand the limits of their actions. Protest becomes institutionalized and follows a certain routine and rhythm. If there are to be arrests, this is agreed upon in advance; police acknowledge that the arrests are needed for publicity and everyone plays an appropriate role. The venue for protest is agreed upon in advance. Marshals within the crowd work with the police at dealing with troublemakers. Those that are relatively inexperienced at organizing protest crowds are grateful for the advice and information they receive from the police.

The Mutual Respect paradigm from the perspective of protesters includes a recognition that

- police have the necessary function within a democracy to preserve the peace;
- police are human beings with a capacity to understand complex issues;
- it is counter-productive for the side-show (police–crowd dynamics) to become the main show;
- it is likewise counter-productive for protest to be institutionalized.

In the light of these observations, there need to be ever new and creative ways of expressing dissent such that the message will get across. In order for this to happen, protesters need to engage police, government leaders, media, and community members in dialogue sessions or workshops aimed at both mutual understanding and the generation of ideas as to how the common good can be improved through the free flow and expression of ideas. The deep-rooted conflict is brought out into the open: some protesters are prepared to put their lives on the line because they believe so strongly in an issue; police are prepared to 'die in the ditch' to make certain that some lines are not crossed. Protesters are open to being challenged on their perceptions, values and beliefs without immediately reacting. There is openness to reconciliation of past rifts and victimization and a willingness to develop mimetic structures of blessing.

Paradigms and Levels of Consciousness

Each paradigm can be understood as representing a certain level of consciousness. As such it conforms to general understandings about levels of consciousness. These general understandings include the three principles that

1. The individual is usually operating at one stage of consciousness across a wide variety of contexts. All levels of conscious can be accessed in any one context.
2. Those at a higher level of consciousness can understand the levels below them but those at lower levels cannot understand those above them.
3. Higher levels of consciousness can accommodate and work with increasing levels of complexity that may be present in the environment.

With these in mind we can now present in a more nuanced manner the relationships among these different paradigms.

First on the matter of how crowds are perceived. At an extreme the Crowd Control paradigm is still informed by elements of the old Le Bon idea that crowds are wholes in which individuals lose their individuality and respect strong leaders who direct them. Empirical evidence has shown that this is highly misleading and people continue to have a sense of rational individuality even when participating in corporate activities. However there may be instances of rioting in which mimetic violence catches on; even though, as some observers point out, this may be less often the case than is generally thought. At times when protesters damage property, there may be historical and symbolic reasons for doing that. Elements of Crowd Control can be seen as embedded within Crowd Management Systems, the difference is that they are kept at the level of contingency planning for a worst case scenario. The paradigm itself emphasizes the right to protest, the pragmatic approach dictates that it works better to use discourse to manage the dynamics and the training includes the development of interpersonal skills.

The Mutual Respect Paradigm does not preclude offering practical assistance to crowd organizers as is the case in the Crowd Management Paradigm. Nor does it preclude contingency planning for a potential outbreak of violence. However, these elements take on a relatively less significant role. The emphasis is on working with protest crowds in such a way that their message and its urgency are effectively communicated to targets and the general public. There is an openness to flow with the dynamic as a creative process. There is also transparency about contingency plans and about 'die in the ditch' boundaries. However, there is an openness to negotiate boundaries and even to find safe ways in which the boundaries can be symbolically transgressed. Authentic trusting relationships are valued; these preclude manipulation; hence, the way in which Crowd Control and Crowd Management elements are used may be different.

Development of New Paradigms Can Be Seen As Creative Emergence
What does it take for a group to move from one paradigm to another? Such a movement is essentially a creative act. New paradigms generally take place when there is a convergence of factors, including an indication that

old paradigms are not working. In the 1960s there was a marked increase in the size and number of protest crowds. There was a general trend to use paramilitary forceful means to suppress crowds. As police communicated with one another, techniques were shared and a broad based trend emerged along with a discursive field that included the term 'crowd control.' As this became systematized, there was growth in the kinds of equipment, tactics and command structures that would make this more effective. There were also instances where this approach was shown to produce disastrous results. There were investigations into some of these mishaps, recommendations were made, legal and procedural limits were put into place. As a result, it became clear that this paradigm had some basic flaws.

Concomitantly, community policing was emerging as a new paradigm that recovered some of the early principles of the nineteenth century Metropolitan Police of London. As discursive approaches were used with crowds, it was found that these worked much better. Empirical data coming out of crowd research emphasized that crowds were not the product of society riff-raff, rather they were made up of citizens who demanded respect. The idea emerged that there were a few 'bad apples' that caused the problem. If police worked with crowd leaders and marshals these could be controlled in a collaborative fashion. In the 1980s and 1990s the Negotiated Management paradigm became better established. However, since September 11, preoccupations with security has had the effect of moving protest policing in the direction of more coercive methods with significantly more emphasis on the use of information strategies (della Porta & Reiter, 2006). There is now a differentiation being made in policing circles between contained and transgressive groups (Noakes & Gillham, 2006). Contained groups, like labour unions, are well-known to police, have their own marshals and can deliver a protest within the bound of agreed upon criteria. The negotiation paradigm is used with them (Noakes & Gillham, 2006). Transgressive groups are thought of as 'bad' by police, even though they can be further categorized into those committed to non-violence and those who are open to a 'diversity of tactics.' They are not centrally controlled and their actions cannot be predicted. They have a capacity to disrupt the daily life of people living and working in the protest area. They are dealt with by means of an incapacitation paradigm (Noakes & Gillham, 2006) which is a variation on the crowd control paradigm that gained ascendancy in the 1960s but instead of control though confrontation it emphasizes control through over-enforcement of the law, show of strength and through placing limitations on the capacity of protesters to protest. Based on our research and experience, the increased use of a control paradigm coupled with more passionate resolve among protesters concerning justice issues will inevitably lead to more intense conflict between protesters and police. As will be argued in the next chapters, both dissent and non-violent policing are necessary for a thriving democracy. It is in this context that the Mutual Respect paradigm is advanced.

The emergence of the Mutual Respect Paradigm is new and time will tell whether it becomes accepted in the field. It represents the convergence of a number of factors:

1. A series of encounters with police, protesters, journalists and other stakeholders showing the potential of open dialogue. These will be described in detail in Part Two.
2. Research that establishes the link between protest crowds and complex systems.
3. Research on the development of higher levels of consciousness.
4. Comparative research that shows how the protest crowd–police relational system is clearly linked to the local culture and is a function of values, attitudes, governance institutions, and a history of how the relationship has evolved.
5. Groundbreaking work done by creative police officers who exemplify this new paradigm.
6. Dialogue among protest groups particularly those advocating non-violence and those whose diversity of tactics includes violence.
7. Open-ended workshops with representatives of all stakeholder groups (see Part Two for a description of what is possible.)

An Integral Approach

Ken Wilber has developed a four quadrant model (Figure 9.2) that can shed some additional light on how these paradigms function (Wilber, 2001). A horizontal axis forms a division between individual (above) and collective (below). A vertical axis divides an interior approach to reality (left) from an exterior approach (right). Interior approaches stress how events are interpreted by individuals and groups; exterior approaches emphasize what can be observed empirically. He argues for an integral approach that includes the different approaches at both the individual and collective levels. Wilber's model can be represented in the following diagram.

Figure 9.2 Ken Wilber's Integral Model

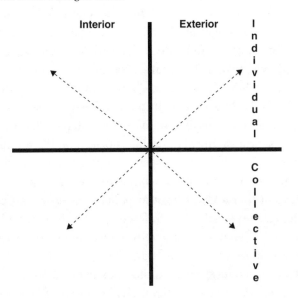

Each quadrant contains a significant dimension of reality as follows:

1. Individual Interior—this pertains to how the individual experiences something at a primal level; it includes how the individual interprets experience based their personal reflections, beliefs and values.
2. Individual Exterior—this pertains to how the behaviour (including verbal expressions) of the individual are observed. Knowledge of our observed experiences are categorized in this quadrant.
3. Collective Interior—pertains to how groups experience a given phenomenon; included in this are the cultural values of the group that give particular meaning to what is happening.
4. Collective Exterior—pertains to how the actions and experiences of groups are observed by others.

The dotted arrows going out from the centre indicate how levels of consciousness evolve; they generally are operative within all quadrants.

When we apply this to the three paradigms, the distinctions among them are startling. The crowd control paradigm emphasizes the collective nature of crowds so it is stronger in the bottom two quadrants. Crowds are basically seen as collectives. The individuals of the crowd as represented in the top two quadrants would be understood to be at a lower level of mentality (riff-raff). The Crowd Management paradigm has been influence by empirical studies and is much stronger on the right hand side. There is also a greater appreciation for specific individuals—especially organizers, marshals, leaders, and troublemakers. The Mutual Respect paradigm emphasizes all the quadrants. In addition to taking note of the empirical studies, it values the subjectivity of crowd protesters and the multi-valenced messages that crowds wish to convey. It also attends to how police understand and experience their role in relation to protest crowds. A value is placed on the interiority of the actors; this results in a desire for respectful dialogue and a commitment to respectful treatment of all parties in relation to one another.

In the bodies of literature on protest policing, protest and crowds, the various studies can be placed within different quadrants. De Bon and Canelli, writing on crowds, tried to understand the collective dynamics from within; they emphasized the lower left quadrant. Rudé and MacPhail worked on the basis of empirical data so their studies took place on the right hand side looking at both the experience of the individuals and the collective nature of the phenomenon. David Waddington's flashpoint model emphasized empirical studies but also paid attention to how people experienced the various phenomena—as such it had potential for an integral approach. Similarly P.A.J. Waddington's work emphasizes how police experience protest policing (the concept of 'troubles' is key to this) and he attends to the empirically verifiable description of tactics and how these tactics play out in the field.

In the diagram, there are diagonal arrows in each quadrant going from the intersection of the axes out toward the four corners. These indicate lines of development. One aspect of development has to do with level of consciousness; the higher the level, the more complex the situation one can deal with comfortably. At earlier levels of development, individuals and groups tend to think in tribalistic terms, seeing reality only in terms of the primary groups to which they belong. Related to protesters and police, those who are at this level will be inclined to adopt an 'us' versus 'them' mentality. It will be hard for them to see how all the actors fit together into a bigger reality with each playing a necessary role. In so far as the Mutual Respect paradigm is demanding the development of authentic relationships between police and protesters, it encourages the development of the level of consciousness among people in each group.

Implications of the Mutual Respect Paradigm for Stakeholders

The Mutual Respect Paradigm functions within an ethical vision of blessing. This means that there is an ethical imagination operative that envisages the mutual well-being of the various parties involved as they remain open to doing what is in the ultimate long term benefit to both humanity and the biosphere. As we examine the implications to each of the key parties involved, we will look at their role, attitude, orientation and behaviour within this paradigm. We will begin with the police since they are a constant in the face of numerous different protest crowds, the second group. Then we will address the implications of this paradigm for governments, multi-national corporations, the media, bystanders and the general public.

Police

Police will begin within an attitude of thanks for those people who care enough to protest. It is acknowledged that the level of care may vary from those who care to express grievances about their own life situation to those who care about collective rights to those who care about the well-being of third parties who might not have a voice to those people who care about systems. The potential contribution of protesters is

- to make certain that there is a general understanding of the different needs and perspectives out in society at a minimum and potentially to halt destructive policies and behaviours of powerful groups,
- to add creative analyses and perspectives to the common marketplace of ideas, and finally
- to be open to the fact that the very phenomenon of a protest crowd could itself generate some new perspectives or directions for society.

With this orientation, planning and operational decisions are made to optimize the effectiveness of the protest endeavour. Eli Sopow has developed a Public Order Integrated Network Team (POINT) approach to public order policing. He suggests that police use the five emotional factors and the seven organizational factors operative in effective protests to systematically work with protesters to maximize their effectiveness (these are presented on pages 34 and 67). Sopow's POINT approach does not necessarily mean working within the Mutual Respect

Paradigm since this could be done with a Crowd Management mentality. However, it does offer clues as to how those wishing to move into the Mutual Respect Paradigm could operationalize their thinking. In order to make protest effective, they may also need to question assumptions about behavioural and geographical boundaries.

This paradigm also suggests that dialogue and the open, transparent and free communication among parties needs to happen around major protest crowd activities (before, during and after) and periodically between such activities when the focus is on the nature of the relational systems involved.

Protesters

Protesters, like police, operate out of different levels of consciousness. We can distinguish among protesters who see things in absolute terms and wish to control the situation in line with their perspective. Other protesters wish to contribute to public discourse on a given issue; they would like their perspective to be communicated, understood and hopefully acted upon. At another level, protesters would like to be a part of a bigger dialogue within which creative options in terms of ideas, policies and actions that transcend individual perspectives already out there. Within each of these broad perspectives are a wide range of attitudes and behaviours.

We have already shown that protesters are highly motivated by something they feel is unjust or illegitimate. Those that are in a control frame of reference can be motivated to the point that they are willing to do anything, to the point of forfeiting their lives, for the cause of their protest. Mark Juergensmeyer has analyzed religious based terrorism, itself a form of protest (Juergensmeyer, 2001). He has found that each group—from Christians who bomb abortion clinics, to Jews who assassinated Rabin, to Muslims who were involved in the 1993 attempted bombing of the World Trade Centre—had a sense that they had a direct link with the Divine that enabled them to determine what was absolutely good and absolutely bad—the latter going against what they believed was the direct will of God. He shows that they view the world in Manichean terms with a clear distinction between good and bad and an absolute certainty that they know which is which. With a certainty that goes beyond any open discourse, they are convinced that they have a binding alternative to stop what they feel is bad with whatever means necessary even if it means the loss of life and the blowing up of property. This is the ultimate of a control oriented protest.

At the beginning of the Oka/Kanehsata:ke Crisis the protesters blocked a road to prevent the cutting of trees for the extension of a golf course. When they were attacked by the police who wanted to force down the barrier and one police officer was shot, another group of protesting Mohawks blocked the Mercier bridge under the conviction that without this act of protest, their fellow Mohawks would be subject to violent attack at Oka. Another very different example includes the protest crowds that were convinced that the World Trade Organization talks aimed at finalizing the MAI would do something in gross contravention of any standards of social justice. They were convinced that the result would be even greater wealth in hands of multinational corporations and greater poverty and oppression of the working poor. Furthermore, they saw the process itself as being illegitimate. For them, it was absolutely essential for the talks not to go ahead. They succeeded at shutting down those talks. They would have much preferred to be party to other discursive structures that would have given their perspective a serious hearing (Barlow, 2001). It should be noted that protesters came from a variety of backgrounds and with a variety of levels of consciousness. (The perspective advanced above represents the more sophisticated among them. Some workers, for example, protested because they feared a loss of jobs in the United States as factories moved to other countries.)

An overwhelming majority of protest in democratic countries is focused on getting a message across. In 2003 there were demonstrations around the world involving many thousands of people protesting against the pending United States invasion of Iraq. They expressed their perspective and the media reported it, but in this case it made no difference to the actions of the world's only superpower. The 90 per cent of demonstrations that occur without incident are of this variety; they want to express their point. Even those protests that involve a dramatic symbolic act are essentially discursive—they want to communicate a perspective.

There are groups of protesters that do sophisticated social analysis and are aware of the discursive control tactics of the police that pass under the rubric of 'negotiation.' They feel strongly about the potential damage to people and the environment if certain policies are carried out. For them, it is a stretch to think about the Mutual Respect Paradigm for it would involve trusting that the police would act in good faith. Some of these have been subject to brutal treatment on the part of police. Some of their leaders have not been allowed free access across borders for protest activities both into countries like Canada where democratic expression is valued. For them, the implications of the Mutual Respect Paradigm would be that they would either have to agree to some limits on the behaviour of protest crowds or respect the position of police who must enforce certain boundaries. If the limits they would agree to transgressed the 'die in the ditch' limits of the police, they would either have to negotiate these or at least let the police know how far they would be prepared to go. They could at a minimum work with police on creative scenarios of what would happen at the edge of chaos so as to avoid anyone literally dying in any ditch. If this paradigm was accepted all around, the way would open for protesters to work with the other stakeholder groups at generating new options that would reflect their values.

Government
Governments, like the police and some of the protesters, can work out paradigms emphasizing control or discourse. In fact, often governments are even more in favour of repressive control than are the police or military. John Ciaccia, Quebec Minister of Native Affairs during the Oka/Kanehsatà:ke Crisis, reports that it was the military generals in the context of a cabinet meeting who talked the Bourassa government out of repressive violent suppression of the Mohawk protests (2000). Often a mimetic structure of violence is created between protesters and governments. In order to get a strong message across, protesters might use highly disruptive tactics. In response, control oriented governments vow to not 'cave in' to their demands. As governments dig in their heels around certain issues, protesters feel they have to take more aggressive action. The spiral of violence continues until the police or the military break up the protest, or public opinion sides with the protesters and the government must find a face-saving way to extricate itself from the situation (during the Oka/Kanehsatà:ke Crisis the Government bought the land in dispute to give to the Mohawks).

Within a Mutual Respect Paradigm, governments would welcome protest as a contribution to public debate on an issue. The concepts and critique offered by the protesters would be received non-defensively by the government and considered on their merit. In certain instances where a well researched protest group has broad based backing and is operating at a high level of concern for either third parties or the public good, representatives of the protest movement could be invited to meet directly with government representatives. The goal would be to use the ideas of protesters creatively to develop better practices and policies.

Governments set broad policy goals for police. It is no accident that the coercive side of protest policing grew during the era of Prime Minister Thatcher who wanted protest activity to be controlled. Likewise, incapacitating actions on the part of U.S. police became more pronounced during the Bush era, which has been marked by a strong desire to use force to control situations. This means that in the coming years, there will be a need for new leaders to set a tone that welcomes dissent and the complexity and creativity that could be derived from divergent public discourse. In the next chapter we will examine the potential for the evolution of new structures of governance.

Multi-National Corporations

Structurally it is almost impossible to hold many multi-national corporations accountable for their actions. By having a strong presence in many countries they can shift capital, personnel and decisions around the globe, finding countries whose laws fit what they want to do such that they can do what they like. Furthermore, those based in Western countries often have enough financial clout that they have significant influence on governments. They operate in a control paradigm, even using the discourse of 'control' as they try to 'control' market share and resist any government 'control' of their enterprises. Within corporations it is all about having 'controlling' interest.

Public protest is one way of holding multi-national corporations accountable for their actions. If a resource company is causing suffering on the ground in a southern country and protesters bring that to light near their power base, this can have a significant impact. It was through widespread persistent protest, including demonstrations, that Talisman Oil Company, based in Alberta, sold off its oil interests in Sudan (subsequently there were some second thoughts about this in Sudan because of all oil companies, Talisman had more of a concern for Sudanese people, a greater openness to moral arguments, and a greater understanding of human rights than some other oil companies.) Protesters have a responsibility to accurately assess the impact of what they are advocating.

Were multinational corporations to accept a paradigm of Mutual Respect with an ethical vision of blessing whereby they would see their role as primarily contributing to the well-being of humanity and the biosphere, they would embrace thoughtful, research based protest as a way of generating what they were there to do even better.

Media

News media can be caught in a control based paradigm as they frame stories as conflicts over control over a situation. If there is outright violence between police and protest crowds it makes for a good story because the images are visually arresting. They too are in competition for control of market share—wanting to get more viewers and readers. What seems to work for news hungry media are stories that emphasize conflict. Conflict is complex and has a capacity to stimulate creativity; hence, media could play an exciting, provocative and constructive role within a Mutual Respect Paradigm. In order to do this they would need to take a step back from the confrontation and analyze the deeper issues at stake.

Bystanders and Public

As immediate bystanders and, in the case of major protests that receive media coverage, the general public become aware of the issues raised through the protest, they can begin to think about the issues. Given the inter-connectedness of complex systems, it may well be that thoughts, ideas and actions generated by people who 'randomly' hear of the protest may make a new contribution to the issue. In a Mutual Respect Paradigm, there is an openness to new ideas wherever they may come from. Some of this is already starting to happen through news networks that solicit ideas and comments from their viewers. With internet communication available, protest organizations and government can open themselves to new ideas. The nature of creativity is such that even what might seem like an 'off-the-wall' idea can function as the spark that gets people to think of things in a new way.

Dialogue

Nothing can take the place of face to face dialogues among people, dialogues that reveal deeply rooted stereotypes of the Other and consequently bring potential surprises to the surface so they can be dealt with before the event and before the edge of chaos is reached. As will become apparent in the case study in part II, it is amazing what can happen in terms of mutual understanding, breaking down of stereotypes and generation of new ideas when people are given the opportunity to communicate openly with one another in a safe, neutral environment. Universities were created in Medieval Europe to provide a context for open, probing and questioning of ideas. They provided a context for the open expression of ideas and critique of what was happening in society. Within a Mutual Respect Paradigm, universities could play a role at hosting dialogues involving protesters, police and whatever other stakeholders could play a role. The purpose of the dialogues would be to communicate openly about the issues involved, clear the air of misperceptions of the Other and allow for the possibility of generating entirely new ways of thinking about potential opportunities. Creation of a safe neutral environment allows for highly charged emotional issues to be discussed without violence. The basic principles would be that participants would treat each other with dignity and respect and that all would be encouraged to develop a distal self capacity—that is to be able to observe themselves and what is happening to them emotionally and cognitively in response to what others are saying.

Three paradigms have been defined for the protest crowd–police relational system. Each was looked at first from the perspective of police who have mandate within society to maintain order. The crowd control paradigm establishes order through force and the threat of force that includes control tactics and weapons. The discursive management model uses language in the form of offers to help, assumptive precluding, and questions to keep order. The Mutual Respect model emphasizes respect, inclusion and an ethical vision that emphasizes the well-being of humankind (especially the most vulnerable) and biosphere. The bounds of the meaning of control are opened to allow comfort at being at the edge of chaos where there is an openness to flow with new possibilities and be open to the emergence of creative new options for thought, values, ideas and action. As the implications of this new paradigm were explored for the various stakeholders, a new vision for society began to emerge. Historically we can now see that a version of the discursive management paradigm emerged in a number of historical contexts. First, the Metropolitan Police of London in the 1800s made a categorical shift in approach from a military, repressive approach to one based on discourse and moral authority. The latitude for protest offered by the police in many old democracies is significantly greater than is the case in authoritarian regimes. Protest has been responsible for many significant reforms—the institutions and presence of democratic governments are largely the result of protest. Likewise, the responsiveness of governments to protest has allowed for the evolution of the right to protest and expanded suffrage to include all adult citizens regardless of race, class or gender. Protest has made governments more accountable to the people. We will examine these themes in greater detail in the next chapter as we go a step further by asking what might be the implications of this emerging new paradigm on the institutions of democratic governance.

10. Protest Crowds and Police in the Context of Democracy

P.A.J. Waddington calls the policing of protest in democracies 'intrinsically morally ambiguous: protesters are not criminals, but citizens participating in the political process; ... and conflict between protesters and the police tends to be a battle of moral equals in which both sides are seeking the approval of bystanders.' (Della Porta, 23)

Within most democracies, there is now consistency around the figure of 90 per cent of protest crowds that take place without incident. There is an acceptance that the right to assemble for protest is essential to the functioning of a democratic government. There tend to be registration systems in place so that police get advance basic information about potential protest crowd activity. Many protesters look to police for advice around protest logistics. In many instances police play a helpful role.

For those whose reality means living and working in a non-democratic environment—totalitarian, dictatorial, fascist, Communist, under occupation, with a religious autocracy, or in a post violent conflict—this chapter puts into perspective the evolution of democracy and the drama of evolving new forms of governance. The significance is brought into sharp relief through the observations of the General in charge of the Police Academy of Sudan in Khartoum in 2003. In a conversation with Vern Neufeld Redekop about the importance of Community-Based Conflict Resolution, Third Party Neutral training and reconciliation, he remarked, 'We have been training our officers to kill for the last few decades; we really need to develop new skills so they can deal with problems in ways that do not involve the use of force.' However, lest Canadians or any others be smug, a priest friend tells the story of wanting to show a poster to President Bush a few years ago. He happens to be Ukrainian and the context was the Orange Revolution. The President was visiting Ottawa and had publicly announced plans to visit Moscow. The poster read, 'Tell Putin to stay out of Ukraine.' Our friend lived a few blocks from the motorcade route. He positioned himself at a spot where there was at least a chance the President might see his message. An Ottawa police came by and, talking in coarse language and with harsh terms, coerced my friend to leave his spot. The experience left him with a bad taste in his mouth regarding the police. Even if for 'security' reasons he might have had to leave, the manner in which it happened revealed a forceful control paradigm attitude.

For those living in a democratic environment, this chapter is meant to show how important protest crowds and police have been in the evolution and maintenance of democratic institutions. It will also provide a vision for roles each might play in taking us to new forms of governance that transcend our current conceptions of democracy.

We will start by looking at the emergence and evolution of democratic institutions as a function of protest and policing. A comparison of protest policing within a number of different democracies will show how policing and democracy as institutions develop in counter point to one other. Finally we will look at protest and protest policing in the development of ever new forms of governance.

Protest and the Emergence and Evolution of Democratic Institutions

The very emergence of democratic institutions can be traced to protest. The American Revolution can be seen as a sustained protest event that turned violent. The protest was against the non-democratic hegemony of Britain over the Thirteen Colonies. Eventually it would take a military victory to decide the question. For several years after their victory, representatives of the Colonies met in Philadelphia to negotiate and write the Constitution of the United States. The protesters became the creative thinkers to design something new. The form of democracy upon which they decided was designed to minimize the possibility of a sustained tyranny. It did this through checks and balances and periodic elections. Later, amendments to the Constitution strengthened the institutions of democracy.

In France, the transfer of power from the king and aristocracy took place with the violence of the French Revolution. Security forces became complicit in the revolutionary movement. It was in part, the negative model of revolution that encouraged the English elites to make timely concessions to avoid something similar in England.

The emergence of democracy in England meant first a transfer of power from the Crown to the aristocratic lords, then a transfer from the lords to parliament and then increasing transfers of power from the upper and middle classes to the people. The transfers were and are not complete but in relative terms, they represent significant changes. Each new reform in the process was preceded by protest. In the 1840s the Charter of the People focused the energy of diverse pockets of protesters around six demands for democratic reform discussed in greater depth in chapter two. Even though the Chartist movement was defeated in the short run, over time five of six of their demands became a reality. The evolution of democracy through the nineteenth century came as a result of a complex interplay among protesters who established a de facto right to protest, a form of protest policing that allowed for effective protest and calculated decisions to give in to some of the demands of protesters by the ruling elite.

In the 1830s there were strong protest movements in both Upper and Lower Canada. These were in reaction, once again, to the non-democratic hegemonic governance of Canada by Britain. These protests prompted the British, who had shown themselves responsive to protest demands back home, to put in motion processes that led to the emergence of Canada as a separate Federal, democratic state in 1867. Subsequently in the 20th century, democracy was strengthened when, in response to protests, women gained the status of persons and the right to vote. Eventually Chinese and other non European groups likewise gained the vote as did First Nations people who, for years were left out of the democratic equation. Many of them continue to feel left out and additional protests by Indigenous peoples in Canada can be foreseen in the years to come.

In Canada, some protest movements have been transformed into political parties which have come to power at the provincial level. During the 1930s, protests by labour over working conditions and the lack of rights for workers combined with protests over the lack of health care for the poor evolved into the Canadian Commonwealth Federation (CCF) which ran candidates for office and took control of the Saskatchewan provincial legislature under the leadership of Premier Tommy Douglas in 1944. The CCF was in the position of a protest group in charge of creating new policies. The result was a comprehensive Medicare system introduced to Saskatchewan in 1964. This became the model for the Canada Health Act which established Medicare across the country.

In the 1960s during which time there were global protests against colonialism, a protest movement against English dominance in Quebec evolved; one organization within this movement was the *Front de Libération du Québec* (FLQ). At its zenith in 1970 it resorted to violence, including kidnapping and murder, and was violently repressed with the help of the Canadian Forces, but not before the death of one Quebec minister and the hostage taking of an international diplomat. Subsequently and in a much less violent mode, those who wished to see French Quebec gain mastery of its own future organized themselves politically and legally as the Parti Québécois which gained power in Québec in 1976. The Québec Province then succeeded in enacting language laws which had the effect of reversing the linguistic hegemonic structure, making French the dominant language. They also organized two referenda calling for Quebec sovereignty and a radically new relationship with Canada. Sovereignty efforts were not realized; however, social and political change in Quebec and with Canada did happen.

In Canada, the Mohawk protest around land rights in 1990 and the Oka/Kanesata:ke Crisis led to the Royal Commission on Aboriginal People. However, most of its recommendations were ignored by the Government and likely will continue to be until there is a significant enough protest on the part of Canada's Aboriginal peoples and those that stand in solidarity with them.

In recently formed democracies, public protests are 'related to deep-seated quality of life issues; employment, housing, education, representation in government political power that cannot be resolved until sweeping social, economic, and political changes occur.' (Kratcoski et al., 2001) In Zambia, for example, full democratic rights were granted in 1991, since then 'the country has seen a proliferation of civic organizations such as political parties, non governmental organizations, religious associations, cultural groups, trade unions and student bodies.' (Kratcoski et al., 2001) The shift from an authoritarian communist country to a war situation then eventually to a fledgling democracy involves the dramatic shift in the identity of the police. In Bosnia and Herzegovina (BiH) in 1996, the 45,000 police had been trained only as soldiers, were not distinguishable from the military and had a history of human rights violations (Vejnovic & Lalic, 2005). An International Police Task Force has been working since 1996 at training personnel in such things as human dignity and community policing, restructuring organizations, building institutions, and strengthening the role of parliament and civil society in the oversight of the police (Vejnovic & Lalic, 2005). The many facets of preparing BiH police to function in a democratic environment highlight what has already been developed over a long period of time in older democracies.

Some countries have particular challenges when it comes to protest crowds. In India, one of these is sanitation facilities and water; the police help by providing some of these services to crowds (Kratcoski et al., 2001). Given religious cleavages in India, it is important to find demonstration routes that do not pass temples or mosques. In most cities there is a demonstration area referred to as 'Dharna Sthan' where protest can happen and violence is avoided (Kratcoski et al., 2001). In Ghana the challenge for both civil protest and democratic development is that police can delude themselves into thinking that they can interpret and shape the law, resulting in the oppression and intimidation of law abiding citizens (Kratcoski et al., 2001).

Protest Policing in the Current Context

Governments are essentially conservative when it comes to forms of governance; they are risk adverse and will tolerate protest within certain limits. This leads to a number of ambiguities in the role of protest police within a democracy. There was an awareness of these ambiguities before September 11, 2001 and they increased significantly since.

One of the most eloquent expressions of the complex nature of protest policing before the terrorist attacks in the USA on September 11, 2001 comes from P.A.J. Waddington:

Mass action can be the defender or destroyer of democracy. Official repression can extinguish freedom and liberty or defend the weak and vulnerable. Liberal democracies must steer a precarious path between these opposing evils. In liberal democracies, those who repeatedly find themselves treading that path are the police. They in effect decide, within the law, the boundaries of freedom of protest.(P.A.J. Waddington, 1994)

Protest policing within democracies has been affected by those terrorist attacks. There is constant contingency planning for a terrorist dimension to large protest crowd events. In 2002, when Canada hosted the G-8 Summit, the venue was moved from Ottawa to Kananaskis in the Rocky Mountains of Alberta. The venue itself was made totally inaccessible to protesters and, because of the terrain, required protection by military troops.

In 2006 the G-8 Summit was hosted in Saint Petersburg where security forces repressed all protest, showing a combination of vulnerability and risk aversion. This phenomenon of protest repression is the norm in countries around the world that have not yet established secure democracies.

Beyond Current Forms of Democracy

At this point, there are only a few isolated examples of policing moving into the Mutual Respect Paradigm. If anything, governments are even less comfortable than the police with this new paradigm. In reaction, protest movements who are determined to bring about change are prepared to push the limits in terms of disruptive tactics. Considering the fear in the air since the terrorist attacks on September 11, 2001 and the commitment by governments to use whatever means necessary to combat violence, the behavioural and geographic boundaries of what might be allowed before decisive strong armed tactics are used have been pushed back in the direction of increased safety for the targets of protest. Paramilitary organized crowd control paradigms are very strong even though they are camouflaged by discursive control tactics.

Nicholas Charney has argued that occidental democratic institutions contain within them latent violence (Charney, 2006). He uses the mimetic theory of René Girard and the memetic theory imbedded in spiral dynamics as developed by Beck and Wilber to make his point. He argues that the discourse of political parties in Canada represents the first Tier thinking of the less complex levels of consciousness (this corresponds to the Crowd Control and Discursive Management Paradigms). As such they include highly partisan non inclusive forms of rhetoric. Not only do parties attempt to make scapegoats of one another during election campaigns, the election victory of one party, which in Canada almost never represents a majority of the population, makes scapegoats of all the others since the winner gets exclusive rights to power. Charney argues that democratic institutions as they exist today are products of lower levels of consciousness. As the level of consciousness of populations increases, at a certain point there will be the emergence of new forms of governance that are more inclusive of higher levels of participation in decision making and hence higher forms of complexity.

Richard McGuigan has argued that individuals who function at a higher level of consciousness can handle complex conflict competently (McGuigan, 2006). For them, the conflict is an occasion for creative thought and the generation of new policies and practices that satisfy multiple parties. For those who are willing to try, it is possible to integrate the positive aspects of diverse positions into something new—a whole that is greater and better than its parts. The orientation towards attempting this and the capacity to do it are indicators of a higher level of consciousness.

The Mutual Respect Paradigm coupled with a mimetic structure of blessing infusing the protest crowd–police relational system could be the beginning of the emergence of new forms of governance that reflect a higher level of consciousness, comfort with complexity, a willingness to exist for a time at the edge of chaos, and an openness to surprising insights that transcend the perspectives of any one party. Eventually political leaders who exemplify both a higher level of consciousness and a willingness to risk change will play a role.

The potential for these developments to occur is not without risk. However the risk of latent conflict turning violent if they do not occur may be greater. Any good goal, process and institution can be subverted in the interests of narrow partisan interests or of outright violence. The evolution of democracy has occurred gingerly in an effort to avoid a worst case scenario. The cautious warning of the chaos that would ensue should women be allowed to vote, for example, seems ludicrous at this point. But the subversion of democracy in the direction of tyranny and violence in Mugabe's Zimbabwe show that democracy in and of itself is not a panacea.

In the end, we conclude with a spirit of hope and optimism that a new paradigm will emerge to guide all of the stakeholders through the complex conflicts represented by protest crowds.

PART TWO

The Mutual Respect Paradigm in Practice

Overview of Part Two

The Mutual Respect Paradigm of protest crowd–police dynamics emerged from training as an intervention, which morphed into Participatory Action Research. The initial insights were generated without knowledge of the history of protest, crowds, and policing that inform Part One. The intervention took place between the Summer of the year 2000 and Spring, 2002; the historical and background research was completed in the subsequent years. The spirit of hope and optimism we hold for a new paradigm is nurtured by our experiences in which we witnessed the power of dialogue and creative scenario development that dissolved stereotypes and generated options that went beyond what we might have imagined.

The story of our experience is told in chapter eleven. It provides an account of the initial training seminars that brought representatives of protesters, police, targets and bystanders together for shared experiences. These seminars took place within a context and organizational structure that included an advisory council and eventually focus groups. Part of the story includes a G20 gathering of Finance Ministers in Ottawa, Canada during which the police–protest crowd dynamics went off track. Follow-up gatherings of police and protesters generated many new insights which informed the Mutual Respect Paradigm described in Part One and provided lessons learned for the intervention methodology in Part Two.

Our story is followed by essays from various representatives of the different stakeholder groups in chapter twelve which gives voice to some of those involved in the process. In chapter thirteen, we provide some practical suggestions for implementing a new paradigm. It provides a model and methodology for people who wish to initiate processes for stakeholders in protests to share understandings, generate insights, and develop scenarios for protests that can be effective in promoting justice and transforming institutions.

11. 'Getting the Dialogue Started': Crowd Management and Conflict Resolution—A Case Study

The Saint Paul University Crowd Management and Conflict Resolution Initiative had its genesis in the summer 2000. An ad hoc group met with the purpose of exploring an innovative approach to crowd management: one that would maintain public order in a non-violent manner while still protecting the democratic rights of citizens to protest and demonstrate lawfully and with passion. We held two developmental training sessions to test the validity of our approach. These sessions, along with Advisory council meetings, a myriad of phone calls, and two focus groups, constituted a Participatory Action Research Project. The participants' feedback on the training sessions was overwhelmingly favourable, providing the impetus to move ahead on the project.

Richard L'Abbé, President of Med–Eng Systems Inc. at the time, asked the question that gave rise to our initiative: 'Can you do anything about crowd control?' Med–Eng was a local Ottawa company that developed and manufactured protective equipment for use in fields such as de-mining, bomb disposal and public order. L'Abbé perceived that there might be insufficient training available to security forces, particularly in certain parts of the world, with respect to crowd control. Furthermore, he wanted to avoid the potential misuse of equipment designed to protect security personnel—misuse that would result in police exerting excessive violence against legitimate protesters. He believed that Canada was a leader in crowd management and in the protection of democratic rights, and thought that an opportunity existed to develop new approaches and training in the field of crowd management. He challenged Saint Paul University to do something on the subject at a meeting in the Rector's office on July 25, 2000. He offered to finance the first training session. Cynics among protest groups were critical of our accepting financing from Med–Eng. We knew L'Abbé's company had much money to make with the escalating violence and growing need for protective police equipment and we were convinced that the Med–Eng President's democratic and pacifist nature coincided with our values. We were not disappointed. We had full academic and practical freedom to proceed as independent researchers on the question 'How might police develop more peaceful means of dealing with protest crowds?'

Vern Neufeld Redekop played a lead role in the development of this initiative. He was President of the Canadian Institute for Conflict Resolution (CICR), became Director of Program Development for Conflict Studies at Saint Paul University and, subsequently professor of conflict studies at Saint Paul. Redekop directed the protest crowd–police research. The University agreed to undertake the initiative and gave it a home within the Faculty of Human Sciences. Shirley Paré joined the initiative as coordinator and co-trainer, bringing her experience with government organizations and her knowledge in public administration into the project. We formed an advisory council to oversee the initiative, the goal of which was to support the Canadian government's dedication to public order and peace, at home and abroad. This advisory council consisted of representatives from Saint Paul University, the Canadian Police Community, Med–Eng Systems Inc. and eventually, members of the activist community.

We will begin this chapter with a description of the Community-Based Conflict Resolution methodology and philosophy used in the initial training workshops. We will then describe the two three-day workshops, our challenges and successes, which provided the foundation for our project and research. We tested our methodology in a mini-seminar, one evening long, to prepare for the protest at the G20 finance ministers meeting in Ottawa. After the G20, protesters and police assembled for an evening of storytelling and brainstorming. We will tell the story and present a detailed analysis of the lessons learned. The mini-seminar de-brief provided extensive data and leads into a section on lessons learned. Brief discussions on reconciliation and building trust, provide a vision and foundation for developing a process; process suggestions are included at the end of chapter thirteen. Our project concluded with two focus groups that reviewed our initial manuscript, the practical aspects of which are presented in the first part of chapter thirteen.

Community Based Conflict Resolution

From CICR, Vern Neufeld Redekop brought extensive experience using training as an intervention to deal with deep-rooted conflict. Shirley Paré was a graduate of both the Third Party Neutral Program and the Seminar Series on Intervening in Deep-Rooted Conflict.

Created in 1988 as a non-profit organization, the CICR has been involved in studying deep-rooted conflict in Canada and abroad, and has developed a unique program to help uncover the sources of deep-rooted conflict and begin the process of reconciliation. The CICR experience, and indeed history, has shown that lasting solutions to deep-rooted conflict come from within communities or among the individuals at the centre of the dispute. The CICR program approach, therefore, focuses on bringing together the different stakeholders in a neutral environment to examine the underlying issues in the deep-rooted conflict in a non-judgmental manner and to develop potential solutions. Using this methodology, the CICR has experienced considerable success in resolving conflict and finding solutions, both within Canada (e.g., Cops and Kids Program, Queensway-Carleton Hospital amalgamation and more recently in the northern community of Sioux Lookout), and internationally (e.g., in Taiwan, the former Yugoslavia, and in Rwanda).

The CICR uses a Community Based Conflict Resolution (CBCR) process based on the underlying principle that 'in order to establish union or collaboration within a community, everyone must have access and understanding of the methods and principles used in conflict resolution.' (Birt, 2001) Applying this principle to protester–police dynamics, it became critical that the same information be available to the protest crowds, the police, those who were targeted by the crowds (usually government officials) and bystanders, including the media. Our process would be based on the same principles as those developed by the CICR. We needed a practical, efficient, effective and sustainable way to reach all groups in the equation. Because we were dealing with this issue on a community basis, the process needed to be inclusive, barrier free and positively-centred so that it would respond to the needs of those involved. World-wide, there had been significant uncertainty, tension and violence associated with protesting crowds. These principles would help to ease the tension and, hopefully, reduce the violence in future demonstrations. Protests would return to the issues; they would become less about violence with the police.

A key process in Community-Based Conflict Resolution is 'gathering,' which is used in tandem with training as a positively-centred activity that is non-issue based. Gathering starts with a social mapping of all those who are part of a community or of all those implicated in a conflict. Based on this analytical work, people are gathered for an initial process—planning meeting, training session or dialogue. After the initial analysis, a larger, open list is made of all those who should be invited. People are then contacted; the purpose of the initiative is explained; they are also told about others who are invited. In the process of gathering, we ask for the names of others who should be included to enhance the diversity of the group.

Community-Based Conflict Resolution (CBCR) is based on a number of principles. Robert P. Birt identified these in a speech on May 19, 1994 at the end of his three-year residency which was focused on developing a foundation for CBCR. He stated:

> where dignity and respect exist, trust will follow ... and that these are the conditions for the forgiveness and healing necessary to bring about peace.

> As a process it has no power, unless it is enabled by the human spirit and will. As a process it has no meaning, unless it can in turn empower its users with a sense of self determination and positive centred activity. It has no direction, unless it is motivated by an essence that transcends the barriers of doubt and touches much higher powers. Community-Based Conflict Resolution is at its fullest a peace making process. It's goal is: to bring from the chaos of conflict, order and the potentiality of peace. (Birt, 2001)

The positively-centered, inclusive gathering of CBCR combined with conflict resolution training produces resolution skills, a framework to deal with issues and, most of all, trust among community members.

We decided to apply the principles of Community Based Conflict Resolution to the crowd management domain. In our initiative we would gather participants from each part of the crowd system—protesters, police, targets, and bystanders. The variety of backgrounds, interests and experiences would reflect the communities from which the participants were gathered.

The First Training Session: November 31–December 2, 2002
After Richard L'Abbé's initial challenge, the first step was to secure a mandate to proceed, particularly from the policing community. The protest community is much less organized; it is difficult to know who actually 'represents' the protest community and, consequently, from whom to seek a mandate. An

ad hoc meeting was held at Saint Paul University on September 8, 2000. This meeting brought together people from the RCMP, Ottawa Police, the Canadian Forces (including a Military Chaplain committed to advancing reconciliation as a goal among chaplains), Med–Eng Systems Inc., and the University. It was decided to move ahead on a *Special Workshop: Crowd Control and Conflict Resolution* (later changed to 'Crowd Management') and an Advisory Council was appointed.

The Goal of the Workshop was 'to enhance the capacity of police and military, in conjunction with other members of society, to manage angry crowds in a conflict-resolving manner.' The objectives were:

1. To introduce conflict resolution approaches to those responsible for crowd control.
2. To provide a framework to analyze the reasons for crowd anger, violence and chaos.
3. To develop new creative possibilities for crowd control strategies and tactics.
4. To generate new understandings about crowd control.

The first workshop was also to pre-test and evaluate this new approach to crowd management, to see whether the above goal and objectives could be met. We directed the workshop towards operational police officers and tactical troop commanders, and included members of the RCMP, the Ontario Provincial Police (OPP), Metro Toronto Police, Ottawa Police Service and Department of National Defence (DND).

In keeping with our CBCR objective of working with a diverse group, other participants included selected representatives from the media and protestor/activist stakeholder groups. This was not easy in the beginning. Early concerns expressed by the police were that sharing with activists might compromise the security of police and their activities. Primarily, the needs and desires of the police drove the makeup of the pilot workshop as they felt they were the ones who had the responsibility to change the way they did their business. They were not convinced that activists could contribute to their knowledge of how to keep the peace. In the past, the purpose of police consultation with activists was largely to gather intelligence about the plans and build a strategy that would facilitate peaceful demonstrations. In response to our request for a diversity of participants, the police agreed to include activists they felt they could trust. Two of the activist participants did not share this trust with the police and left the workshop early. Similarly, the police knew the media representatives invited. The media participants were restricted in what they could write and publish about the workshop. They could use the information from the workshop but not attribute it to the workshop or participants. Consequently, to attend a three day workshop without a good story at the end was of questionable value for their time. Many police officers wished to attend; however, we had limited capacity. We anticipated that future workshops could provide access to more officers. After the first session, the response from the police was so positive about the presence of protesters that we were advised to have a balanced group in the future. The initial resistance had vanished; even the demand for large numbers of police officers to get the training did not over-ride the importance of the diverse make up of participants. We felt that our process was working at a deeper level—police no longer had to have all the answers and no longer felt they were totally responsible to come up with the 'right' strategy. Of course, none of this was articulated as such and, in fact, it was and is never quite that simple where emotions and deep-rooted conflict are implicated. We knew that it was a start.

Based on theories of deep-rooted conflict (Redekop, 2002), the training would become an opportunity to work out differences and become a key conflict resolving process in itself. It would allow participants to relate deep-rooted conflict to their personal experiences so that insights would belong to them and the learning would be very personal.

The three-day training workshop opened with a process known as census. In this process people work in groups of 4 to gather information from group members. Individuals from each group rotate in such a way that everyone receives information from all the groups. The purpose of census is to establish a collaborative spirit, make everyone feel included, get information about the group for both group consciousness and a sense of who is there. It starts people thinking about certain themes and brings latent ideas to consciousness. It shows up unexpected areas of commonality and it is fun.

Census gets everyone talking early on. It builds trust as everyone shares personal information in small groups close enough to look into one another's face. It demands collaboration. The census process creates a safe space in which participants move from a closed to the positive dynamic of an open community. It is effective in diffusing a complex community conflict where there is tension.

On the front of the census page we asked for name, role and leisure activity. The questions on the reverse were recorded anonymously and pertained to what was happening; in our case, they were related to crowd experiences. Participants recorded the information within their own groups and this was shared so that at the end there was a record of people's experiences and what challenges needed to be addressed.

The first day then dealt with deep-rooted conflict, mimetic theory and values through a combination of short presentations and interactive processes. The second day focused on conflict intensifiers, types of crowds, principles of neutrality; participants to try their hand at a conflict resolution role play. On the third day, participants worked in small groups on several protest crowd scenarios. They were encouraged to develop creative interventions. The final afternoon was devoted to planning follow-up actions.

The feedback from participants of the workshop was positive and there was overwhelming support for our process. Thankfully, the security representatives thought that there should be greater representation from the other stakeholder groups, particularly from protest and activist groups. They also believed that further development of the process was required for applicability to the operational environment. Participants suggested that the way to get support for the number of workshops that would be required for all police officers who wanted them was to interest the senior leaders of local police forces first.

The Second Workshop: Getting the Leaders Involved

As the Advisory Council deliberated on the next step, it became clear that if the approach and process were to catch on among the police, senior officers must get directly involved. Because of the approaching Summit of the Americas, all police concerned with public order were preoccupied so we decided to have the next workshop shortly after the Summit. At one meeting, representatives of the Advisory Council from the RCMP and Ottawa Police got out their cell phones and called their superiors; on the spot we were assured of significant representation, including the Deputy Chief of the Ottawa Police and a Superintendent from the RCMP. One of the most important successes in gathering is that people agree to participate when they know someone who is involved in the project. Once these notables agreed to attend it became easier to attract other community leaders.

The second workshop from May 6 to 8, 2001, was entitled 'Strategic Leaders' Seminar'. The sponsorship of the Solicitor General of Canada and the

Canadian Police Research Centre made this workshop possible. This time the Advisory Council agreed that we would gather leaders from all contributing communities. Participants included police leaders, community leaders associated with the issue and other stakeholder representatives. Gathering from the activist community was more difficult than we anticipated. One evening during the gathering process, we met with about fifteen activist representatives who were quite agitated about our project and were actively objecting to protesters becoming involved. We wanted to explain our objectives. This helped to ease the anxiety and several agreed to participate.

The Senior Leader's Seminar participants included an Anglican Bishop; local activists who had taken a lead role in organizing protest activities; police, including an RCMP Assistant Commissioner, a Superintendent, the local Deputy Chief, and representatives from Sureté du Québec, the Ontario Provincial Police and the Toronto police; military representatives including a Padre; media reps were a reporter for the Ottawa Citizen and a professor from the Carleton University School of Journalism; two people in leadership from Armour holdings came from the United States and a politician came from Saskatchewan.

We repeated the general format of the pilot workshop incorporating lessons learned and included an optional debriefing of the Quebec Summit of the Americas just recently held. A number of the participants had been in Quebec City—some on the side of the police and some on the side of the protesters. As we went around the circle, each told stories of what they encountered. Here are some examples.

- One protester told of tear gas going into the medical compound for protesters.
- A police officer responsible for tear gas talked about the inaccuracy of the tear gas launchers.
- A protester told about how the fence was turned into an object of creativity as some women threaded coloured pieces of cloth through the wires.
- A police officer talked of spending twelve hours straight in protective gear without being able to eat, drink or go to the washroom. He also talked of waves of different types of protest. All would be peaceful for hours and then in a few minutes a new group came to the space in front of him and started throwing rocks and Molotov cocktails.
- A protester talked of how a van she was riding in was attacked by a group of fellow-protesters.

- The story was told of a tense situation where parents of young protesters emerged from a bar where they had been waiting only to be confronted by police in riot gear. A police officer, sensitive to what was happening, removed his helmet to expose his face and immediately the tension dissipated.

Near the end of the evening it was observed that usually groups debrief a situation separately but this was much more meaningful.

As with the first workshop, the feedback was overwhelmingly positive. Again, the police representatives endorsed and validated the participation of the other stakeholder groups, noting that even more participation from the protest community was valuable and necessary. They also encouraged further development for the operational environment.

After the Quebec Summit and the success of the first two workshops, the University decided to pursue the objective of providing support to the upcoming G8 Summit in Kananaskis in June 2002. As this initiative was proceeding over the summer and fall of 2001, Saint Paul University looked for an opportunity to test the developing crowd dynamics process that would provide further credibility for the process. At the same time, another application would further our research and progress the evolving paradigm.

The G20 Mini-Seminar: Phase Three

The Fall, 2001 G20 gathering of Finance Ministers in Ottawa provided an opportunity to apply and further test the new crowd dynamics paradigm. Insofar as time was too limited to 'do it right,' it was not a complete test of what might happen if the new paradigm was made operable. However, as it did lead to significant interpersonal exchanges and the development of new insights, it confirmed for us the need and potential for what we now call the Mutual Respect Paradigm of crowd dynamics as a model to guide the planning, actions and follow-up to major international events that attract huge demonstrating crowds.

The G20 Summit of the International Monetary Fund and the World Bank originally planned to be held in the Indian capital of New Delhi fell victim to the events of September 11, 2001. Canada and then Finance Minister Paul Martin agreed to host the mid-November (16th to 18th) meeting just one month before it was to take place, and chose Ottawa as the location. On the evening of November 4, we agreed to hold a mini-seminar on November 8, the latest possible date before the G20. We scrambled to gather a balanced group for the event. In the end, there were 28 participants. Of these, 13 were police, 7 were from the activist community, 5 were from government and there were 3 'bystanders.'

We decided to start with dinner and work through the evening. The process started with small mixed groups of four dining together over a set of questions designed to get them talking about the issues of peaceful protest—a mini census. During the seminar, we presented key aspects of the 'Collaborative Crowd Dynamics Paradigm' (as we called it then) and provided opportunity for dialogue. At the conclusion of the November 8 mini-seminar, the participants requested a debrief with the same people. The date was set for November 27, however, this became a public gathering so the debrief with participants was held on the evening of December 4th.

The G20 Summit

The first evening of the summit, Friday November 16, started out peaceful enough. The terrorist attacks of September 11, 2001 on the World Trade Centre in New York resulted not only in a change of venue for the Summit but also, no doubt, contributed to a strong police presence among the crowds in Ottawa during the event. There was no fence, only moveable bicycle stands were used as a barrier around the government conference centre. Activists were pleasantly surprised to see that they were given access to the space surrounding the War Memorial, letting them come closer to the site of the Summit than they anticipated. Later in the evening, a handful of demonstrators turned violent, smashing the window of a McDonalds outlet.

That action triggered a change in operational plans on the part of the police for Saturday. It meant that some of the tactical troops were mobilized in the protective gear that protesters find intimidating. A number of factors increased tensions, leading to circumstances in which some demonstrators got hurt. Police arrested fifty-three people. The experiences of those directly involved and those who witnessed events resulted in deep emotions of hurt, anger and indignation. These negative emotions were apparently generated by a number of events.

- Police responded to a 'single incident' of violence by mobilizing the tactical troops.
- The prearranged path of a protest march had been blocked.

- A police dog got loose and attacked protesters.
- A protesting Quaker grandmother was hit in the face by a police officer.
- There were some violent arrests.

The trust that had been built in the activist community from our workshops had been damaged.

In response to these feelings, the Ottawa Police Services Board agreed to hear five-minute testimonials on November 26. Nearly twenty people spoke—many were well established members of the community. At the end of that meeting, it was announced that the following evening there would be a meeting of police and protesters at Saint Paul University. This error in communication resulted in the planned debrief meeting for participants of the November 8th mini-seminar being advertised on local radio. Rather than turn people away, the University chose to open its doors. Some 80 mostly local citizens and fourteen police attended the evening public meeting of November 27th. We will first provide an overview of the Public Meeting, follow with a summary of the G20 mini-seminar debrief then articulate some lessons learned.

The Public Meeting

The evening started at 7:00 pm with a presentation of a framework for discussion. There was virtually no trust so there was no possibility for any smaller sub-processes. Many demonstrators and a few bystanders told their stories and offered their interpretation of events. Periodically we created space for police perspectives. The stories were mostly from angry activists and it was a challenge to maintain the neutrality of the process; eventually, participants were challenged to not only tell their stories but to come up with constructive suggestions that could be recorded on flip charts. All told, there were some 93 suggestions for steps towards creating peaceful crowd dynamics in Ottawa in the future. These suggestions provided real value for the meeting.

The evening was emotional, cathartic for some and frustrating for others who were clearly in need of meaningful resolution. One professional psychologist in the audience thought that there was evidence of Post Traumatic Stress Disorder among both activists and police who spoke. Protesters were reined in from violence by other protesters in the audience so that while there were many angry and some vicious comments, there was no destructive violence. One young police officer responded to angry protesters with a catch in his voice saying that he had dedicated his life to his community and he was surprised and saddened to learn that his contribution to a peaceful democracy was viewed with so much hate and criticism. We wish to emphasize that people who spoke did so for themselves and from their own perspective. The comments may or may not have been representative of the stakeholder communities to which they belonged.

We work to resolve deep-rooted conflict within communities. It is not our purpose to air or deal with particular grievances. Nonetheless, the comments and suggestions made on November 27 raised a number of issues and questions that are important for the further development of a new paradigm for protest crowds–police dynamics. We have grouped the public meeting suggestions according to the following topics:

1. Purpose of demonstrations;
2. Pre-event dialogue between police and activist communities;
3. Community-based policing concept extended to demonstrations and protests;
4. Arrest process;
5. Humanizing and stereotyping;
6. Reconciliation; and
7. Rebuilding trust.

The purpose of demonstrations

Activists see themselves, among other more obvious and well-stated objectives, as supporting protests in Third World countries where respect for freedom of expression is not as high. Since some demonstrators have significant experience and insight about issues affecting both Canadians as well as others around the world, the question is what structures, mechanisms and attitudes would allow government to hear what they have to say. Further to that, what is the role of the police in expediting the communication process?

Pre-event consultations between police and activist communities

Pre-event consultations have been used for several years with excellent results in the Ottawa community. There are more than 600 demonstrations each year in the capital and most are without incident. Most of these are on a small scale. When it comes to major international summits a number of issues emerge from the G20 experience:

1. Ongoing good relationships need to be fostered.
2. If either side has had experiences that reduce trust, there must be a safe forum to work through the issues.
3. The larger and more complex the event, the longer the desired lead-time and the more preparatory consultations are necessary.
4. For a new collaborative paradigm to emerge, dialogue about motivation, roles, broad issues, goals and potential scenarios needs to take place. This goes beyond consultations about logistics and beyond simply 'communicating' with the other.
5. The processes of pre-event dialogue and intelligence gathering must be clearly differentiated.
6. Some pre-event issues that warrant further discussion and work include:
   - The need for clear and transparent ground rules for demonstrations that are publicly negotiated among all stakeholder communities. This should include a frank discussion of tactics used by both police and activists and their consequences.
   - Police have a responsibility to communicate which actions and tactics will result in a police response and possible detainment or arrest.
   - A focus for further discussion is the impact of sounds and music to create a mood. For example, some drumming sounds are soothing and others energizing. One protestor suggested that police beating on shields energized demonstrators and, in itself, escalated violence.
   - Activists carrying potential weapons such as mirrors which could be used as projectiles or to reflect the sun and impair sight should be aware that they could be considered to be impeding police responsibilities and, consequently, they could be detained. Even if their intentions are honourable, they may be easily misinterpreted, making the risk to the security of the event unacceptable to police.

Community based policing concept extended to demonstrations and protests

The concept of setting up and using a collaborative, community approach to policing has been extremely successful in Ottawa. Several examples are indicative that this success can be extended to crowd dynamics.
- Ottawa's branch of the organization, Non-Violent Peace Force, reported incidents at the G20 of surrounding angry or vulnerable protesters to

inhibit the violence erupting or to stop what they saw as unwarranted aggression on the part of police.

- In case there are incidents in which activists feel unjustly treated by police, a variety of conciliatory processes could be put into place to supplement the public complaints system that tends to be cumbersome, time-consuming and adversarial in nature.
- Processes could also be put in place to mobilize the public as bystanders to reduce violence all around.
- A neutral body could be given a mandate to observe crowd dynamics, receive reports from activists and make a report after the event.
- Guidelines could be agreed upon to keep demonstrations away from vulnerable areas such as Ottawa's Byward Market.
- Plans could be agreed upon whereby non-violent protesters can dissociate themselves from violence. This includes a discussion of the meaning of 'red zones.'
- Self policing and marshalling within groups of demonstrators is to be encouraged and supported by police.

Arrest Process

Treating those arrested with dignity and respect is important. There is a need to publish clear and transparent guidelines for the arrest process to clarify for the protestors what they should expect. Police need to make distinctions between protestors' processes like 'going limp' which is a tactic in non-violent civil disobedience and hostile belligerent behaviour. At the very least, the following are important issues worth further discussion:

- How to develop a common understanding of behaviour that could result in arrest;
- How to make the process of arrest more transparent;
- Who would be acceptable professional, neutral witnesses to the arrest process; and
- How to ensure that those arrested are provided the opportunity to phone their legal counsel.

Humanizing and Stereotyping

The propensity of people in conflict to stereotype the opponent has several negative consequences. Earlier parts of this book explore the concept of stereotyping and, at the public meeting, it was apparent that stereotyping contributed to aggression on both sides. Bringing a personal, human dimension to each side of the crowd dynamic has potential to add clarity and an enhanced perception of fairness to the process. Some of the suggestions include:

- identify all police officers with clearly visible numbers, (this is still an issue—it was a problem at the UK G20 summit in April 2009)
- identify protesters wearing balaclavas,
- humanize police officers,
- recognize humanity of all, and
- ask police to imagine if one of the protesters going through the line was one of their 'own.'

Several comments at the public meeting reflected support for the process:

- the effort to put together the public meeting on short notice spoke well of the legitimacy of the process;
- the meeting was a good gesture; and
- it is important that 'intervention activities' like this not be supported financially by the police. In fact, it was a voluntary activity by the authors and the university.

The G20 Mini-Seminar De-brief

On December 4, we had a debrief meeting with the group from our G20 mini-seminar. Several participants from the mini-seminar were absent, notably the government representatives. We asked participants to pose questions they would like to ask in the wake of the G20 demonstrations in Ottawa. They asked many questions, each person honestly wanting to understand the dynamics of what they found to be baffling. What went wrong? The questions themselves revealed the need for on-going dialogue.

Questions Raised at the De-brief of December 4

For the activists present, there was a clear focus on planning for the event and confusion on how much latitude police on the spot have regarding their use of force. There were questions concerning:

- the authority to do what was done in terms of 'use of force' options,
- the chain of command for decisions seemingly made on the spot,
- who decides on security zones, and
- will security zones be a military decision for the G8 in Kananaskis?.

The police present looked for more organization among those in the activist community. There were questions about:

- how to get protesters involved in the planning?
- do protesters agendas change with the forum of the event?
- is it possible to have a mechanism to develop guidelines for peaceful protest?
- how police can protect international protesters?
- how best to give the benefit of police expertise to the crowds?
- what education do police need from the point of view of protesters? and
- is more general knowledge needed on both sides?

Additionally, there was much interest and seemingly some confusion about the use of violence:

- what are anarchists and hard line protesters trying to achieve through violence?
- why are they violent (it destroys the effectiveness of peaceful demonstrators)?
- why are peaceful protesters not more forceful in condemning violence of others? and
- why do activists scale barricades (undermines police trust of protesters)?

From a government representative:

- why do protesters think they deserve a seat at the table when they are not elected?
- whom do they represent? and
- what is their constituency?

People from each side were given a chance to respond. One police office who was responsible for the path of the march told about how they made their preparations at night. He mentioned that he should have walked the whole route himself at the end to be sure it was done right—it wasn't and somebody had mistakenly put barriers up at the wrong place to block the route. Police also mentioned that because it was such a big event organized at the last minute it was difficult to fully coordinate police coming from a number of different police services.

During the G20 intervention, we showed once again that the conflict resolution process is indeed applicable to the issue of protest crowd–police dynamics. The importance of a neutral intervention is crucial to the process of re-creating a non-violent, peaceful demonstration that is both honourable and respectful of our democracy.

What did we Learn about Protest Crowd–Police Dynamics Research?

First, our involvement in the process revealed a deep-rooted conflict that has developed involving activists, police, and government. It is characterized by distrust, mimetic structures of entrenchment, deep-feelings, and very different perceptions and interpretations of the same events. If anything, it has deepened our conviction that conflict-resolving dialogue processes will be instructive in furthering the understanding of protest crowd–police dynamics that could lead to a new paradigm within democracies. A positively centered process led by a neutral third party can transform deep-rooted conflict.

Second, we have learned that a three-day process is a minimum needed to transform relationships, develop understandings about a new paradigm and generate helpful scenarios. One of the members of the advisory council openly mused about whether more harm than good came of having a mini-seminar of only one evening. Both sides were willing to give the other a chance but neither had the confidence to allow small infractions to go unnoticed. One small infraction led to many more larger ones until chaos reigned. It is clear to us that we have to persevere; it takes so little to raise doubt and questions.

Third, notwithstanding the need for more time, protest crowds and police can make significant changes through any face-to-face encounter in a positively centered process. After the mini-seminar, police communicators informed us that they were reframing their press releases because of new understandings. After the G20 protests and resulting aftermath were over, police planners said that they had changed their operational plans because of what they had learned.

Fourth, we recognized that stereotypes are misleading. One of the 'youth dressed in black' who would have been marked as a violent troublemaker disclosed that he worked for a high-tech firm and had a high security clearance; he also felt strongly about global issues and the demonstration. In historical understandings of protest crowds, he would have been stereotyped 'riff-raff.'

Fifth, we learned that people act in ways that make sense within their own frame of reference. For example, on the Saturday morning of the demonstration, the Black Bloc had promised the pregnant mothers that they would do nothing to incite violence. Demonstrators worked on the presumption that everything would be peaceful. The violent incident at McDonalds the night before triggered among the police a contingency plan B that called for the deployment of tactical troops making it unsafe for families. Violence is returned by violence with interest.

Sixth, we learned to flow with the process. When the planned debrief for former participants turned into a public event, our temptation was to cancel everything. We decided canceling would do more harm than good and that the best decision was to welcome all who came. The many positive suggestions generated and the large number of people who came forward with their names and coordinates at the end showed that we had indeed made a difference in attitudes at least towards our process.

Seventh, we learned that violence in the course of a demonstration can be traumatizing and cause a deep-rooted conflict to surface. Reconciliation is not easy particularly since there are structural constraints on apologies. Nevertheless, in a safe confidential environment, the kind of communication and gestures of understanding needed for reconciliation are possible.

The Aftermath to the G20 Demonstrations

Since the incidents between the police and citizens at the G20 demonstrations, citizens have chosen to deal with their perceptions of wrongdoing by the police in two ways. First, because of some incidents, a group of Ottawa citizens organized a 'Citizens Panel on Policing and the Community.' They held public meetings in late February. The Citizens Panel listened to the stories of many people affected by the events of that day. They hoped to help us all understand what happened on the streets of Ottawa, and to make recommendations on ways to improve relationships between police and the community in the future. After considering the submissions, the Panel published a report. Secondly, some individuals have decided to pursue the formal process to lodge a complaint against police. Each of these initiatives is important to clarify just what happened at the demonstration and to hold accountable anyone responsible for wrongdoing.

Additionally, it will be important to rebuild the trust and to reconcile the anger and entrenchment between protestors and police. Until those who feel betrayed regain their capacity for trust, they will find it difficult to move forward. The formal complaints process may provide some relief; however, it is time consuming and adversarial in nature. As one person at the public meeting said, feelings are facts—we need to recognize that these feelings are serious even if the legal facts do not support them in the formal process. Those involved need to deal with negative emotions adequately or they will continue to affect future events.

Often the people with the greatest tendency toward violence, those categorized as the 'violent two per cent,' are marginalized young people who have themselves been severely victimized. They often feel that they have no voice; that no one has been listening to their concerns. If ways could be found to give them an effective voice as part of the humanizing process, their own perceived need for violence would possibly be diminished.

The Advisory Council was convinced that the Crowd Management and Conflict Resolution Initiative offered significant potential as an approach to public order that could conceivably reduce the increasing level of violence observed at recent anti-globalization demonstrations. One of the principal objectives of this initiative was the development of enhanced awareness amongst police, protesters, the media, politicians, government officials and citizens at large of ways to de-escalate conflict when crowds gather.

Reconciliation

The process of reconciliation has been touched on only briefly in this book. To provide some background for understanding the G20 discussion, it is helpful to note that reconciliation involves emotions and a recognition of the humanity and validity of the perceptions of the 'other.' The process of reconciliation has several steps; it is sometimes sequential, sometimes iterative, it can be circuitous or sometimes quite simple and quick. It requires commitment from both sides in the conflict. There must be an acknowledgement of the conflict (name the demon), an openness to see the human face of the 'other,' and some teaching so both sides learn that reconciliation is a good thing and can imagine how it could happen. The Graduated Reciprocal Initiatives of Tension Reduction (GRIT), an interactive dance of communication, then follows. Each side needs to see signals of remorse and forgiveness; they need opportunity to rethink their perceptions, integrating new truths, understanding and values. It is helpful to reframe the experience and discover a higher perception. Then there needs to be room for ritual and a process to re-establish the relationships, room for healing to establish new emotional pathways and room for re-creating a new way of being together including structure, norms, laws, story and teaching.

The activists at the G20 public meeting put great emphasis on the importance of apology and admission of wrong-doing on the part of police as a first step in the reconciliation process. There are constraints imposed by the legal and adversarial nature of the public complaints process that make it difficult or impossible for police to apologize outside of that formal process. Reconciliation outside of the formal process holds earlier and more effective promise. Some of those at the public meeting showed good understanding of the process. For example, the following points could all contribute to restoration of previously good relationships:

- listen to each other,
- be willing to break the tension,
- all sides agree to one thing about which to let guard down a little,
- remove 'arms' on both sides,
- agree on tactical de-escalators to be used during demonstrations,
- all sides tell the truth.

Rebuilding Trust

Rebuilding trust has also been only touched upon briefly in the book. An integral part of reconciliation is to rebuild trust where it has been broken. Most of us know very easily when we trust and when we do not. We sometimes lack the vocabulary to talk about what constitutes trust and just how it is built and how it is broken. Consequently, what surfaces when trust is broken is often anger and frustration. Similarly, we know when we have been betrayed yet many of us find it difficult to deal with betrayal in a productive way. Those who have experienced betrayal and recovered are better equipped to deal with it a second time. Others who have never fully recovered can be psychologically damaged by a second betrayal or even the perception of one. Experiencing a major betrayal is like experiencing a death—we have feelings of loss of trust in others and maybe feelings of loss of trust in ourselves.

The public meeting allowed for an airing of many grievances against police originating at the G20 demonstrations and, as such, started the recovery process. It may not have been the process of choice at the time, nonetheless it was a beginning and a good one. Hearing the views of the 'other side' provided the information that can eventually allow those who feel betrayed to reframe the experience, forgive and move on. The protagonists deserve support from the community to do this. The activists and others at the public meeting asked for relationships with integrity. This demands open communication about changes in plans and expectations along the way. If a pre-demonstration consultation has resulted in a given set of shared expectations and if unexpected events necessitate a change in strategy, operations and tactics along the way, the more this is communicated with an explanation, the better.

Focus Groups

After the G-20 event, we organized two focus groups to involve participants from our various seminars to have a voice in the shaping of a document that was to give expression to the emerging new paradigm. Their important contributions helped shape the original manuscript. Much of chapter thirteen comes from the original text and formed the manuscript that underwent significant scrutiny by the focus groups.

Conclusion

In this chapter, we have presented an account of some of the experiences that led us to the conclusion that a new paradigm is both needed and available when it comes to relationships between protesters and police at a primary level and between these groups and media, bystanders and targets at a secondary level. This realization functioned heuristically as we did the research on the histories of protest, crowds and policing in Part One. It became evident as we witnessed true dialogue occurring between those from the policing and protest communities, that it was possible to generate mimetic structures of blessing within this relational system. As we listened to the creative ways police and protesters developed scenarios, it became clear to us that given the chance people can work together to develop possibilities that transcend individual imaginations. In the next chapter, a number who participated in these processes will give their reflections.

12. Hearing from the Players

Introduction

Of the many people who have participated in our seminars, several have kindly agreed to share their experiences and ideas. These are presented below in the interest of extending the interpersonal dialogue. They have each been asked to take us into their worlds, to let us know how crowd dynamics touch them personally. There has been no attempt made to try to harmonize what they say with the overall perspective presented in this book. Indeed, the overall message of the collaborative approach is that we must speak candidly and listen with an open spirit. Structures need to be put in place whereby stakeholders in demonstrating crowd dynamics encounter one another in dialogue. Until that happens, written accounts like those presented below provide a glimpse into how crowds are experienced 'on different sides of the fence.'

The context is 2002, closely following the seminars and events described above. They come before the historical and social scientific research and subsequent reflections that generated a distinct Mutual Respect Paradigm developed in Part One. As such, they provide historical indicators of why such a paradigm is needed; they supply hints of what might be entailed and what pitfalls to avoid. The different voices from the perspective of very diverse stakeholders also highlight how the same phenomenon—a protesting crowd being confronted by police—is understood in such different ways. Some allude to the Québec City Summit of the Americas, the descriptions and reactions are important for historical context. They provide a benchmark, if you like, by which to measure what happens in the future.

Julia Fleming speaks about her fear during the demonstrations in Quebec City, her experiences with the Crowd Seminar at Saint Paul and her hope for the future of the dialogue. Carl Stieren comes from a lifetime of demonstrations and puts current demonstrations in Ottawa and his participation in the seminar in the context of history and his overall crowd experience.

Gary Nelson is a veteran police officer. He also has extensive experience with conflict resolution and alternative dispute resolution. He speaks personally about his policing career and reflects on the impact of recent crowds on his life.

Leonard Stern not only tells us about the media's roles but also provides food for thought and possibly a warning about the potential for bureaucratization and choreographed pseudo-events—both of which detract from effective protest.

Peter Coffin was an Anglican Bishop with experience working for social justice in places like the Philippines where he witnessed crowds in a context very different from Canada. His conclusion highlights the importance of meeting for dialogue.

Raymond Laprée was a professor in the *Animation Sociale* program at Saint Paul University. He stresses the importance of theoretical understandings to move us ahead in our construction of social concepts and relations.

Their contributions are largely unedited and come from their hearts. What they write is their personal perspectives and must not be construed to represent 'teachings' or, even, common learnings coming out of the seminars. The seminars themselves seek to reveal individual and personal experiences behind the positions commonly taken by different communities who have a stake in this issue. From these personal experiences the participants themselves work creatively together to develop possibilities for a better future. These essays are representative of just some of these communities and some of the communities within communities.

Healing Dialogue to Rebuild Active Democracy
by Julia Fleming

In 2001 I had the opportunity to be a voice during the Summit of the Americas in Quebec City. I was an individual and also part of a credible organization that collaborated in developing a week-long conference (during the week prior to the FTAA meetings) that brought together individuals, politicians, specialists as well as many diverse non-governmental organizations, faith groups and labour representatives from all across Canada and around the world. Our common ground was our great concerns with the fundamental motivation of international trade agreements. The deals and decisions that lead to top down profits to further corporate agendas by the development of disturbing policies that threaten the health, environmental sustainability, local economies, democracy and basic community and human rights such as clean water.

I could not believe how much preparation took place in the full spectrum of society to have the FTAA meeting occur. Millions of dollars were poured into the creation of the most extensive security plan Canada had ever initiated within its own borders. The sheer volume of equipment mobilized from both inside and outside of Canada seemed like the preparations for a war. The older section of Quebec City was closed off. The summit was designed to have ministers from all across North and South America except Cuba to come together and discuss a variety of issues concerning the FTAA agreement. Yet, this operation also inspired more than 60,000 people from Canada and across the world to gather and communicate their opposition to the oppressive international trade agreement policies.

I was able to see the security operation in full force during the summit, yet the police presence in Quebec City had started months earlier. Through the media, articles exposed one of the police tactics building Quebec City's second fortress wall, this time to 'protect' the government from its own public. This divisive wall inevitably stirred a reaction in the public, leaving many feeling marginalized, created a climate of distrust and no room for opposing opinions or democratic discussion. I felt this tactic contributed to the development of a conflict far before the actual event. This fence controversy inspired thousands of people to mobilize and gather to be a physical reminder to the politicians that they were not acting with our approval or in the best interest of Canadians and global citizens.

This summit was a life changing experience. Personally this was the closest I have ever been and want to be to a war situation. I felt the choice of security tactics played a large role in escalating violence and fear on all sides, with little attempt to use non-violent de-escalation techniques. Thousands of chemical tear gas canisters, along with water cannons, pepper spray, rubber bullets, attack dogs, unconstitutional searches and excessive abuse were all tactics that were used and I feel promoted conflict. For a week I was on the streets and in public initiated conferences. I witnessed tens of thousands of peaceful protesters and only a few hundred individuals with more of an aggressive style of dissent, for example throwing the tear gas canisters back at the police lines and dismantling the fence. Yet of course, these actions dominated the media more than the messages of the 60,000 other people lining the streets kilometers thick. Also the police somehow felt these aggressive few, warranted the use of thousands of tear gas canisters (8000 was a figure I remember hearing at the seminar), which choked the entire city. I personally experienced the scare of an unmarked police car nearly running me over, stopping and then a male officer patted me down with no reason he felt necessary to communicate to me. At this point I was just walking with a girlfriend down the street quite far away from the center of the protest. Throughout the course of the few days I saw all the forceful tactics I mentioned above at use and still can remember the sensation of burning eyes from the gas. I met people who shared their experience of having the citizens' independent media center smothered in tear gas to interfere with reporting. In another building, mainstream reporters were in a lock down with no external access for several hours. I saw seniors being evacuated from senior homes, overcome with the toxic gases. A weary volunteer medic shared her shocking experience of the citizen's medical center being over taken by police at gunpoint. She recalls the heart pounding experience of having the clinic fill with tear gas, she scrambled to take whatever medical supplies she could get a hold of as she removed a patient out to the back ally. She was treating the patient for an emergency tracheotomy, as a result of a rubber bullet. A member of parliament was shot with a rubber bullet. In addition, support centers to provide food, shelter and medical support for the 60,000 new arrivals were shut down. These many examples of the miss-use of power and police violence I will never forget. Is this the way a crowd is managed in a progressive democratic country? Is this the reaction from the government and security forces to opposing political views from voting citizens demonstrating dissent? Is this the Canadian way? During this week I truly witnessed the ingredients of fear, anger and absolute lack of trust and accountability of behalf of my government and my 'public' police force. This was part of the motivation behind choosing to attend and speak about my experience at the seminar in May 2001 presented by St. Paul's University on Crowd Management and Conflict resolution.

Trust is the number one ingredient to effective dialogue. The unfortunate reality is there are millions of people around the world who have witnessed or been victims of police and military violence and political abuse. Unfortunately we cannot change history but we can learn and move forward to create effective change and dialogue which is critically needed. I feel that the largest challenge for this initiative is rebuilding the trust to effectively bring people to together and open up to a progressive and honest dialogue. Personally being an 'activist' or I prefer an average out-spoken Canadian citizen, I was very skeptical of the seminar, especially because it was so soon after my experience of Quebec City. The fact is I had very little trust. I would not give over my contact information; I was watching my back and what I said, as if it was going to be added to my local police file of photos and video of non-violent actions and trainings I have been involved with. The fact that some of the police officers greeted me by knowing my name and the colour of my clothing during the last Ottawa action did not comfort me.

Yet all said and done, I am very glad I attended the seminar. As I went through the days, personal barriers came down and I met real people behind the masks, people I never thought I would be sitting in the same room with. At the beginning I was a little defensive, then I became more of an active listener, continuing to speak my truth of my experience. The result, I felt a very positive exchange occurred and common ground and understanding was met on both sides of the 'fence.' I felt the possibilities and need in continuing the debates and dialogue. I feel the reason why it was so effective was because of the diverse cross section of society, which was the key. It is only effective by offering a neutral space (including funding) which includes not only security force and activists but also accountable politicians local and federal, human rights observers, corporations, medics, both provincial and community based volunteers, bystanders, members of labor and faith organizations and of course the media (both independent and main stream) who play a huge role in developing wide spread public perceptions. This debate of crowd management style and actions needs public exposure and inclusion. With all this wealth of experiences and perspectives coming together, facilitated though focused dialogue, great results can manifest.

I feel this is a very good starting point in building effective political and public inter-relations, policing and activism that will strengthen democracy and accountability. The veils of mistrust can be slowly dissolved. We can choose to change the destructive patterns and move forward from old lessons.

I feel these seminars have the potential to offer an international template and are the foundation to further understanding of the complicated dynamics and rebuilding of trust between citizens, police, media and politicians, which inevitably will bring issues to the surface in a reflective process. I wish you all the best during this adventure, we really need to heal many wounds and this is a process we must engage in.

Bridging the Gap: Conversations among Demonstrators and Police on the Right to Dissent
by Carl Stieren

The invitation to a meeting at St. Paul University had two strange words in its title: 'Crowd Management.' Hearing those words, my mind flashed to the writings of Gustave Le Bon, that conservative 19th Century French political theorist who reckoned that crowds had a tendency to do evil things. The use of the word 'crowd,' as Le Bon did, winds up tarring democracy by the same brush as the worst crowds—using one term which could today lump together a racist lynch mob in the U.S. South with Gandhi's Salt March to the Sea. Those two groups are far from the same type. And surely there is also a difference between the one million nonviolent peace demonstrators who gathered in New York City in 1982 to support the United Nations Second Special Session on Disarmament, and the French crowds who called for guillotining of opponents during the French Revolution.

I didn't go to the first seminar of the series at St. Paul's, but I did go to subsequent ones, starting in the summer of 2002. What was new was to meet police representatives who were not in uniform and were not on camera. Instead, they were in a place where they could tell us what they thought or perhaps even what they felt. By the time the later seminars got under way, the words in the title of the series had changed to 'Collaborative Management of Crowd Dynamics', something that was better, but really more like a compromise hammered out by Canadian diplomats—awkward and unpronounceable, but offending no one.

There are real differences, even in what words mean and when they are used, that separate police and demonstrators. In the worst case, we can wind up with differences such as the following:

Description by demonstrators	Description by police
demonstration	crowd, mob
holding the line	refusing to move
solidarity	conspiracy
expressing righteous indignation	having a riot

For me, the chance to build bridges and open channels of communication could not only help reduce violence but might even save lives in future crises. For, as my linguistics professor at the Illinois Institute of Technology used to say, there are three levels of communication: formal, informal, and scientific.

If communication is blocked or becomes impossible on any one level, it will move to another level. Thus, when parents in the United States from the 1930s to the 1950s were too embarrassed to talk about sex on a formal or informal level, they gave their children the Van de Velde marriage manual, a scientific explanation of the reproductive act, something that even a sexually explicit novel could have done better.

Communication may become blocked or even impossible on the formal level during a demonstration. When a policeman's 'Don't move any further!' doesn't get across and neither does the demonstrators' 'We are going to cross the line and thereby commit nonviolent civil disobedience,' communication has broken down. At that point, the old alternative used to be to move to scientific or legal level and read the Riot Act. Today, it's 'You've got 60 seconds to leave this area.' Following that, communication ceases, and force or violence may occur as police spray tear gas or beat protesters. Ironically, the arrest of a co-operative suspect can be almost nonviolent. Instead of such behaviour, there was escalation and provocation by the police during the November 17, 2001 G-20 demonstrations in Ottawa when police went into the crowds to apprehend specific individuals. During these attempted arrests, some of which were unsuccessful, at least one police dog got loose from its leash (accidentally, one police officer told us) and went after a suspect.

How can we bridge the gap between demonstrators and police, a gap that has become so confrontational since the World Trade Organization meetings in Seattle and the onset of globalization? Specifically, how can Canadian society in the post-September 11 era, with Bills C-35, C-36, and C-42 now on the books, allow for peaceful dissent during international conferences in Canada? If the police, the politicians, and the courts decide to interpret these bills as 'Internationally-Protected-Persons-Über-Alles,' there may be no hope for democracy.

Were there disappointments in the meetings? Of course. The failure of the police to live up to their agreement to keep their actions peaceful during the G-20 protests was the biggest one. Yes, the police blame the single demonstrator breaking windows in a McDonald's Restaurant on Rideau for their donning their Darth Vader gear and releasing tear gas, and they blame the snake march of a small group of demonstrators. I somehow find that like saying that one man, Gavrilo Princip, caused World War I, or that his Black Hand group in Belgrade was the cause. There's a lot more to it than that, and the Austrian and German Empires—and the police in Ottawa on November 17, 2001—had/have a lot to answer for.

Were there positive outcomes from the contact group meetings? Absolutely. I can think only of one member of a police force who shall not be named speculating to me in the hallway, 'Carl, what if we had at Kananaskis what they have on July 1 on Parliament Hill? Two huge televisions screens, with a representative of the G-8 on one screen debating a member of the demonstrators on the other?' I could only say, 'If only!'

Should we encourage Vern Redekop and Shirley Paré to continue this experiment? Certainly. Should the governing board of this project be more representative of both demonstrators and ordinary members of civil society? I think that's essential to keep the process from either becoming or being seen as tilted toward the side of the police.

Collaborative Management of Crowd Dynamics
by Gary Nelson, Retired Police Officer

Reflections:

Having completed over thirty seven years of police work I felt that I had grown accustomed to conflict as normally every call the police respond to involves some form of conflict. Violence becomes part of every police officers day, but I had never given up hope that a difference could be made. In the aftermath of the conference in Quebec City in 2001, I nearly gave up hope. I never expected or dared to dream that such an event could occur in our peaceful/peacemaking country. Many people were injured, many people felt victorious, however, I suspect that many more were disappointed that this occurred in Canada. I know that I was not alone when I expressed my sorrow and disbelief in seeing a wall erected in such a beautiful city in Canada. Those that were bent on destruction and violence made their point. Many of them will be held accountable through the most democratic justice system in the World, but surely everyone that participated in this event was not bent on destruction and violence? I listened to stories of people who were demonstrating with their children and were afraid for themselves and their children. I also listened to stories of police officers who were afraid that they might not get home safely to their families. How is it those two groups were afraid of each other and forced to face one another in such a manner?

Policing Environment:

Generally speaking, conflict impinges on police work at every turn: between community members, between police and community, and within the Police Service. Most of the calls for police assistance in the community feature some form of conflict. Most crimes involve conflict. Often, police intervention generates a conflict between police and community. Some conflicts have a short duration and some are long and drawn-out. Some are intense, violent and visible, while others simmer beneath the surface.

The vast majority of Police Officers have become officers in order to help others and do, what the majority view as, what is right for society. Considering this, they are otherwise normal community members who have their share of hopes, beliefs and dreams. Because of their constant exposure to conflict, police officers are generally able to deal with conflict, albeit, there are instances when the standard reaction by police can be somewhat problematic. Conflicts can take the form of disputes over rights or events, underlying conflicts over interests and deep-rooted conflicts over identity. Whatever the form of conflict, it can create problems for the entire community and if not properly dealt with, this conflict can be costly in both time and money. Furthermore, some of the hidden costs to conflict come in the form of harmed relationships because of physical or emotional wounds. Larry Hill, Deputy Chief of the Ottawa Police Service, has shown leadership in his path to understand and allow community members to be heard. This has provided the opportunity for police to directly hear the concerns from community members and likewise communicate to community members the perspectives from police on community conflict. Does this not reflect favourably in our initiatives on establishing partnerships with the community in problem solving policing? One of the basic principles of communicating effectively is to listen to understand. To avoid community-based conflicts which may from time to time get out of hand, we must all listen to understand.

Since the mid 1980s, there has been tremendous growth in emphasis and understanding of both community-based policing and crime prevention. It has been recognized that long-term effectiveness is based on getting at the root causes of fundamental community problems.

If we are to rely on adjudication to determine that what we did was right, then we are utilizing the wrong end of the conflict resolving spectrum because the decision making body of adjudication does not allow for relationship building, it is merely a process for identifying who was right and who was wrong. A relationship building exercise would utilize the negotiation end of the conflict resolution spectrum in which the conflictant parties have more control over the process and the outcome. It is also less formal and is based on preserving relations. Where long term relations are seen as desirable, this end of the spectrum would appear to be the ideal context for resolving conflict. At the opposite end of the spectrum where the courts render decisions, the parties have no ownership in the outcome. This requires the outcome to be enforced by some other party and the conflict is not resolved. However, rights must be preserved and the adjudication end of the spectrum is necessary in relation to persevering rights.

In view of the recent and pending 'G' conferences, we must be mindful that conflict management is about continuous improvement, learning, growth and also about having the courage to do what is right. Police officers often find themselves weighted down with the concerns of the quiet majority. It is my belief that we must show courage in order to build a strong link to the community in these hard and changing times. The main focus of crowd management training is developing an understanding that enables us to do something or decide things. Conflict resolution training involves the transfer of skills and knowledge in such a way that people accept and use those acquired skills. Crowd management offers a change in the way police go about their business. We all know that change is an ongoing process in everyone's life, that it is sometimes uncomfortable and it is a well-known fact that people tend to resist change. A less well-known fact is that people don't tend to resist change as much as they resist being changed.

Dr. Vern Redekop and Dr Cheryl Picard, both academics, have had a large influence on how I try to deal with conflict and lead my life. It is now my intention to pass these teaching on to others through various venues.

As a guiding light the question I continually ask myself is 'would I lead my life differently if I could'?

Covering Conflict: A Media Perspective
by Leonard Stern

The Ottawa Citizen

An important ethical principle in journalism is that reporters report the news rather than manufacture it. On occasion this code has been violated. Most famously, in the heyday of yellow journalism, William Randolph Hearst dispatched a staffer to Havana to cover the Spanish-American war. When the man noted that there was no war yet, Hearst replied, 'You supply the pictures and I'll supply the war.' A more recent case: A photographer for a Canadian newspaper was lurking outside the apartment building of a noted pedophile who had just been released from prison. Another tenant asked what was going on and the photographer told him. When the pedophile emerged, unaware he was being stalked, the tenant punched him in the head. A photograph of the vigilante assault appeared on next day's front page, along with a story to the effect that tenants were enraged a sex offender had moved in. The article neglected to mention that there would never have been any story had the photographer not revealed the pedophile's identity in the first place.

These exceptions aside, respectable media organizations try not to shape, distort, or otherwise interfere with the events they are supposed to cover. News gathering, once considered a trade, is now a profession. The day of the high school dropout who works his way up from copy boy to reporter is over. At large metropolitan daily newspapers, new recruits more often than not have graduate degrees. Along with higher salaries and increased social status is a growing sense of professional pride and responsibility.

Manufacturing or sensationalizing events is simply unacceptable.

The noisy, often violent street demonstrations that mark the anti-globalization movement—perhaps the most significant protest movement since the Vietnam War—pose a serious challenge for thinking journalists. Covering public demonstrations of any kind is a tricky business. The basic problem is this: Even the most upright journalist who would never spin the facts to make a better story cannot help but notice that his or her presence influences the way actors in a crowd behave. Anti-globalization protesters who a moment before were milling about looking bored will, upon the approach of a television camera, spring to life as though on cue, waving signs and shouting 'No Justice, No Peace!' When the camera leaves it's as though a stage manager shouts 'cut!,' and the protesters return to whatever they were talking about before the interruption.

No doubt the police also perform for the media. When practicing crowd control, security services employ methods that vary in their degree of physical coercion. The presence of media probably makes police adopt softer methods than they otherwise might. The notorious image of an RCMP officer dousing university students with pepper spray at the 1996 APEC demonstrations in Vancouver served as a lesson in bad publicity. It is conspicuous, nowadays, that there are often no reporters around during moments when police brutality is alleged. At the November, 2001, G20 meeting of finance ministers in Ottawa, a number of anti-globalization activists claimed that, after being arrested, police roughed them up or engaged in gratuitous intimidation. True, the activists may well have invented some of these claims in an effort to demonize police as tools of state oppression. But it is also conceivable that these abuses occur beyond the range of television cameras precisely because police now understand what does and doesn't play well on the evening news. Evaluating the competing claims of protesters and police is difficult. In the end the media satisfy no one. Protesters see us as agents of the right wing corporate establishment while police see us as liberal, left wing muckrakers.

In truth, reporters in my experience are fairly adept at restraining personal, political biases. These are conscious biases, and as such are easy to set aside while on assignment. More problematic, at least in the context of street demonstrations, is the journalist's instinctive attraction to human conflict. The most compelling stories, as playwrights and novelists know, involve some form of conflict. Because physical violence is the most dramatic expression of conflict, these stories are the ones that make the front page. But does the predilection for conflict constitute a bias, one that could lead the media to behave irresponsibly? It would be instructive, I suspect, to analyze news coverage in the days leading up to a demonstration at a summit of the World Bank or International Monetary Fund. Do the media treat the upcoming protest as a legitimate political event or do they frame it as a violent spectacle performed by the protesters? The media's understandable preoccupation with conflict might create the impression that violent confrontation is inevitable. By draining protests of their political content, by seeing them only as theatre, the media could be unwittingly acting like a casting director. The crowd, frustrated because its concerns are not taken seriously, accepts the role that has been assigned to it.

Through my participation in the Crowd Management initiative at Saint Paul University I have come to believe that crowd behaviour is very much influenced by legitimacy needs—and that crowds often resent the media for our power to confer or withhold legitimacy. With this in mind, when the G20 meeting came to Ottawa, I spent an entire day with various activist groups, interviewing members at length, in an effort to give them an honest hearing. It was disappointing. Although union leaders and other semi-official spokespeople talked a serious political agenda, raising issues of poverty, the environment and child labour, the majority of front line demonstrators—the ones who had been bused in from out of town—had either come for the party or to voice truly marginal ideas. Many in the crowd, for example, told me that the September 11 terrorist attacks had been orchestrated by the CIA (to provoke a 'racist' crusade against Muslims) or by the American 'military-industrial complex' (which would supposedly profit from a convenient war in Afghanistan). The crowd was seeking legitimacy, but I was unable to provide it.

Those who theorize about crowd dynamics and who practice crowd management do not generally concern themselves with whether a given crowd is protesting a real or perceived injustice. The fact that it is real to the crowd is sufficient. If demonstrators converged to riot against a Beatles reunion, it would matter little to police as they tried to keep the peace whether the Beatles were really getting back together. But to members of the wider community, who are alarmed and inconvenienced by street closures and security fences, these are not irrelevant questions. The media has a public obligation to investigate and analyze the motivations of the crowd.

In some instances, unfortunately, this may hinder efforts to manage crowds peacefully. If the crowd is judged to be without legitimate grievance—to be a nuisance—the community's patience will wear thin and the security apparatus will be pressured to exert a heavier hand. Those who envision the media as partners in collaborative management of crowds might, in the interest of harmony, prefer the press to extend a certain generosity. After publishing an article detailing the bizarre conspiracy theories among demonstrators at the G20, I was accused of reckless journalism. Organizers of the demonstration said I ought to have restricted my reporting to what they themselves had said in their polished speeches. To me that is asking a bit much. Activist leaders wanted to claim the crowd as their own (as evidence of a mass movement, or 'people power') and yet expected the news media to ignore what the crowd was saying.

Still, the concept of collaborative crowd management, as being developed at Saint Paul University, holds great promise. Even the simple, preliminary step of gathering activists and police in the same seminar room, on neutral ground, to see each other for the first time without their respective uniforms, softens adversarial reflexes. But is unclear to what extent collaborative crowd management—whereby demonstrators, targets (politicians, say) and police jointly plan events—will bureaucratize public protests. One challenge will be persuading crowds that the exercise is more than an attempt to co-opt them. As for the media, journalists are wary of what historian Daniel Boorstin has called 'pseudo-events'—events that are not spontaneous but manipulated and planned. The idea of collaborative crowd management was borne out of a commitment to inclusion, safety and civility. But the interest and attitude of media workers will depend on whether demonstrations choreographed along the collaborative model are perceived, or not perceived, as pseudo-events.

Reflections of a 'Bystander'

by The Rt. Rev. Peter R. Coffin, Former Anglican Bishop of Ottawa

It has been a long time since I have been involved in a street demonstration opting instead for other ways of engaging in issues for which I feel some passion. I might, therefore, be termed as a 'bystander' in relation to demonstrations though it is becoming more difficult not to be involved with a variety of issues that they evoke. This has become increasingly more apparent with those around globalization throughout the world and particularly in Canada.

The issues that have taken people to the street have become eclipsed by what happens when they get there. Media coverage and the behavior of some demonstrators and some charged with 'crowd control' as well as some bystanders drawn in have turned the 'sideshows' into the 'main show' and this is unfortunate in the extreme. One of the results has been 'terminal identification.' Simply stated it is the feeling that if someone is not for us they must be against us. To see and maybe even appreciate the positions of various parties is to be 'soft' and therefore biased towards a particular one. Polarization is inevitable and not to align is seen, by some, not to be an option. Or is it? It is a dangerous place to be and one runs the risk of being vilified if one says that they understand or appreciate, even if not unreservedly, the positions of, say, the police or the demonstrators or some other 'stakeholder.'

I would contend that the uncritical 'typing' of parties and a blanket laying of blame is simplistic and probably unfair and unhelpful. To some that may seem like a 'cop out' or being 'soft' and maybe even a heresy but there are deep issues at stake here that require consideration if we are to respect the rights, freedoms and responsibilities that we hold dear. I have some questions.

What really are the issues? Are we talking about 'crowd control' and tactical questions or are there deeper things at stake in this conversation? Who are the stakeholders and can they come to agreements and in ways that do not violate each other? Is there a possibility of collaboration that allows for valid and peaceful dissent and deals fairly and appropriately with those whose behavior compromises the common good and hijacks the good motivations of others and reduces them to the status of those 'needing to be controlled'? Is dissent interpreted as a loss of order and therefore something to be 'controlled'? Have the objectives of crowd control changed given a perceived and possibly inappropriate estimate of threat and, if so, who makes that determination? Could a collaborative approach by all of the stakeholders provide a better and more accurate assessment and a more positive outcome? Can we deal with each other in a way that ensures our rights, freedoms and responsibility to dissent, or not, without particularly destructive levels of alienation which only serve to exacerbate anger and distrust to almost unresolvable levels? Is there something in the global, regional and national political climate that has changed and has formed or informed dissent and ways of dealing with it? Is the presenting issue of demonstrations and 'control' not simply a harbinger of something more and worthy, if not essential, to this conversation?

As a citizen and as a reluctantly involved bystander I cannot let the media alone influence my concern for the issues around dissent in general and demonstrations in particular. I make no apology for my respect for our police. This is not something conditioned by my experience of police in other parts of the world for that would be damning with faint praise. My personal experience is that they do serve and protect our citizenry and though not exempt from the need of accountability our police forces are, for the most part, made up of people called to a noble and serving vocation. I also have deep respect for peaceful demonstrators and those who take the just cause of others in other ways as well. While they may not be given much credit, due to the widely publicized antics of a few, they do, in fact render a public service by exercising democracy which often involves taking the cause of those who are marginalized and otherwise have no voice. That seems to be a responsible thing to do in a world where many are disenfranchised. I am concerned for those, like shopkeepers for example, who, in the course of dissent have their livelihoods disrupted and compromised. They are understandably angry and are very much stakeholders who need a voice. And I am concerned when damage appears to have been done and people retreat into fixed and defensive positions and a blame game that pits citizen against citizen and makes conversation and 'rapprochement' even more difficult. I am concerned about those who might be called 'loose cannons' who compromise the best of endeavours and hog the spotlight and define the public perception. Surely it is naive and even dangerous, on all kinds of levels, to allow them to unduly influence the conversations and agreements that need to happen and can happen, maybe with some brokering and ways of accountability, between responsible citizens.

I work with a religious organization with a long history and a fair share of not getting it right and sometimes doing wrong despite what we would regard as a good cause. We have come to a realization of what we need to do in order to get back on track with integrity. We meet! This does not always mean that we achieve a resolution but we have come to know that it takes us a whole lot further than if we do otherwise. We have also taken some lessons, long overdue, from brothers and sisters of the First Nations, and that is patient and respectful listening.

A Reflection from the Academy
by Raymond Laprée, Professor Saint Paul University (retired)

Translated from the French original by Susan J. Roche

René Girard's approach regarding violence, its rapid escalation and subsequent control by a symbolic act of purification of unhealthy spirits is an interesting seminal hypothesis. Nevertheless, it remains a literary perspective on the human tragedy involved. Anthropological reflections based largely on a particular interpretation of the mythical stories also come into play. Vern Redekop enriches and brilliantly articulates the ideas of the great philosopher Girard, combining this approach with the theory of human needs satisfiers as well as the most recent management concepts, in a process applicable to concrete situations of conflict. Various people from law enforcement agencies involved in public security in Canada and even abroad recognize there is foundation for the implementation of these ideas. They as well as members of pressure groups, who challenge police barricades during large-scale demonstrations, have made equal contributions in the consolidation of the fundamental Girard-Redekop ideas. Thanks to this concurrent effort, we can now count on an original, universal explanation with regard to crowd behaviour. This is definitely the most significant break-through since Gustave LeBon's time-honoured theory on the psychology of crowds.

Saint Paul University will benefit greatly from this intellectual contribution developed at its core and which, from now on, will enrich teaching in the Master's Programme in Conflict Studies (Faculty of Human Sciences). In this university context, conflict theory and in particular conflict resolution and even the healing of wounds will continue to develop along collaborative lines while taking on other schools of thought.

For example, it would seem to me that Georges Dumézil's sociological studies have something to say about the prevention of the causes of conflict or their interpretation. This researcher, looking into the foundations of Indo-European culture, has shown that the societies studied flourished for as long as the 'functional tripartition' was in harmony. The decline and fall of the Roman Empire, for example, could be explained by the subordination of the priestly and production functions to the warrior function. In light of this theory, it would be interesting to study the role of the popular masses in the fall of the Soviet Empire at the end of the last century, as well as current world-wide terrorism and the subsequent spin-offs into war.

As for the parallel that Redekop draws between Girard's ideas and the human needs theory, it seems to me apt to add to this perspective Gilbert Durand's ideas on the anthropological structures of the imaginary. While the 'functional tripartition' of Dumézil would benefit from it, opposition among humans appears 'natural' as does their harmonization. The whole notion of struggle for social justice could be grafted there. We would realize, for example, that demonstrators who shout angrily in the street are necessary to wake our sleeping conscience, when, due to the unequal distribution of goods in the world, three times more victims die of hunger every day than died in the attack on the World Trade Centre. Is not ONE person in one location worth as much as ONE person in the other location? Yet, instead of mobilization, the arsenal of war is brought out! The same veiled violence became evident at home during the 2001 Christmas season. The shelters for the homeless announced they no longer knew where to house the ever increasing number of 'users,' while a few days beforehand, the greater part of Federal budget adjustments had been allotted to the Department of National Defence.

Again let us stress that the concept of 'collaborative management' used by Redekop can be effectively converted into a valuable apprenticeship only by including scholarly reflection on the psycho-sociology underlying group dynamics.

In conclusion, let us mention the following rather unique phenomenon: In developing their respective ideas, the authors Girard, Dumézil and Durand have drawn their inspiration largely from the great myths of humanity. The profound symbols of these grandiose stories bear proper names, those of the gods 'of a thousand faces' (Joseph Campbell) found in all cultures or civilizations. It is not entirely by chance that a university whose mission statement is firmly committed to research of individual and social significance through the plurality of the religious phenomenon should become the place of a renewed discourse on 'Conflict Studies.'

Certain players who make up the active forces in our society have already begun to benefit from this through workshops on crowd dispersal management given by one of the community services at Saint Paul University. It is to be greatly hoped that this participatory movement in the permanent reconstruction of peaceful conditions in our communities and in society will grow.

13. Practical Suggestions for Community-Based Initiatives

The word 'practical' and its cognate 'practice' are derived from the Greek word *prassein*, meaning to do or to act (Barnhart, 1971). Those that have reflected on the meaning of action have shown that an action is complex (Melchin, 1998; Ricoeur, 1992). It takes on meaning within a certain cultural context. In includes, embedded within it, intended consequences. Actions, looked at in hindsight, are revealed to have many consequences that were not intended. Actions may be simple or they may be part of action chains or they may become ongoing practices (MacIntyre, 1981). Those who deliberately take certain actions to affect change, usually do so out of a significant analysis and reflection about what is going on (Freire, 1970). There evolves a pattern of action and reflection such that subsequent actions reap the benefit of accrued wisdom.

Processes leading to this book can be seen from this perspective. First came the challenge from Richard L'Abbé to do something. The initial action did not come out of a vacuum. Rather it meant taking a well developed methodology, Community-Based Conflict Resolution, and applying it to a new situation. Advisory council meetings provided occasion for reflection on what had happened and planning subsequent actions. The chain of actions described in Part Two became the basis for a much more profound reflection, including years of research, resulting in Part One.

Readers of this book will be from many contexts around the globe. They will be playing any of the various roles described above. Hence, the practical suggestions, suggestions meant to enable people to start to take action, start with questions that prompt initial reflections about who should and could do what. Eventually we will get to more precise descriptions of possible actions based on our experience. These are not meant to be recipe cards or techniques that guarantee certain results. Rather they should be thought of as imagination stimulators—as ideas that can generate ever new ways of approaching the challenge of bringing to life the Mutual Respect Paradigm of Protester–Police Dynamics.

We are not alone in suggesting a process approach to relationships between police and others in the community. In November, 2008, the Lokahi Foundation in the United Kingdom sponsored a two day residential event marked by large and small group processes. It included police and community members. The focus was not on protest crowds but rather on relationships between police and the Muslim community. Evaluations of the event were overwhelmingly positive. (Lokahi Foundation)

We will begin this chapter with an overview of the roles of the parties involved in the crowd relational system; crowd organizers, targets, security, media, and bystanders. We follow with a set of principles developed during our seminars which could represent a first draft of principles that would be adapted to serve the reader's community. We then provide some suggestions for the Mutual Respect Protest Crowd–Police Process that is about how to use this book and how to proceed designing your own project or intervention. We provide two sample processes to get you started. This chapter concludes with our heartfelt wishes for your democratic, non-violent and passionate expression of your unique self, your unique opinion, your unique difference.

What are the Roles of the Different Parties?

There is first of all a shared role for all the parties to come together in a neutral spot and in good faith interact with one another to first understand each other's perspective and then to work together at defining what mutually respectful creative dynamics might mean practically. Within any relational system, people are uniquely empowered by their roles and positions to say and do things appropriately that others could not say or do. What follow are reflections on potential roles of different groups of people.

Role of Crowd Organizers

Crowd organizers are generally leaders within activist organizations. They are usually highly motivated, with a strong concern for their cause. Because of past interaction with security forces, many of them have been subjected to physical violence by being beaten, tear-gassed, sprayed or arrested. By agreeing to enter into cooperative relationships that involve police, they risk losing credibility among their own people. On the other hand, if they see the validity of some new approaches, they are probably the only people with a capacity to convince other activists to enter into a new approach. If they go out on a limb to try a new approach and their goodwill is used against them, it could be extremely difficult to try something new again.

Activists generally like to proceed on the basis of consensus; they try to communicate with one another about what is going on and avoid (where possible) what others might be opposed to. Processes of arriving at consensus provide a useful backdrop for relationally creative dynamics. The challenge is to engage enough activists in dialogue with other stakeholders to really effect a new way of doing business. Since the style within many protest groups is not a top-down command structure but an engagement with grass-roots, it is not sufficient for leaders to simply decide that a new approach can be implemented. Enough opinion leaders from the diverse groups committed to demonstrating at a given event need to have a positive experience interacting with police and politicians in order to create widespread acceptance of a new way of doing things.

Since buy-in is not based on a command structure, communication is very important—a new approach must be communicated clearly and accurately. Communication is a back and forth motion such that leaders quickly get feedback from others in their groups and leaders of other groups. Consensus oriented processes can be time consuming. Any consensus position never reflects all the individual opinions on a given subject—activists are not unified in their opinions—but their opinion usually does reflect what people can live with. A given consensus position among activists includes the right to dissent and to express oneself publicly. There is also general agreement on the types of injustices that need to be exposed. Diversity of opinion is found when talking about strategies and tactics.

Demonstrators have an interest in getting their message across effectively to political and business leaders and to the public at large. They also have an interest in not getting hurt in the process of communicating their message. In many respects the onus is on the target groups and the security groups to convince them that their interests will be truly served through a cooperative approach.

Role of Target

Targets are generally people or groups of people who believe that they have a legitimate right to make decisions on the subjects that are being considered either by virtue of being democratically elected, duly appointed or otherwise in a position to take action (e.g. corporate executives). They study, consult and discuss with as many people and organizations as they feel necessary and are able to, by virtue of time, before entering into decision-making discussions.

From the government perspective, there is a time and place to listen to public opinion and, at the time of a Summit, negotiation or decision-making meeting, the duly responsible individuals feel they consider fairly all opinions they have gathered prior to the meeting. Each activist does not need to be listened to at the time of the meeting for his or her opinion to be considered. Furthermore, arriving at a conclusion contrary to one or more groups' opinion does not mean that their opinions have not been considered fairly. The issue for many activists is that they do not trust that they have been heard sufficiently for their opinion to receive fair consideration.

Targets of crowd protest may feel defensive and out of the defensiveness try to protect themselves. In *Dealing with an Angry Public*, the authors point out that often, angry protesters have very good reasons to be upset. They offer a set of principles for business and government leaders, which if implemented, would help significantly in reducing the level of emotion within crowds. These are:

- Acknowledge the concerns of the other side.
- Encourage joint fact finding.
- Offer contingent commitments to minimize impacts as they occur; promise to compensate knowable but unintended impacts.
- Accept responsibility, admit mistakes, and share power.
- Act in a trustworthy fashion at all times.
- Focus on building long-term relationships. (Susskind and Field, 37–38)

(With appropriate adaptations these could be applied to activists, media and police as well.)

Certain individuals in the target community believe that crowd violence is strictly a police issue. This has contributed to the perception that target communities (e.g. politicians and government officials) are avoiding responsibility and puts them in danger of being scapegoated and dismissed by the wider community. If the underlying perception of some activists is that they do not feel represented by the democratic process of the country then the participation of elected and other government officials becomes critical to the resolution process.

It is always a temptation for target groups to hire media consultants who can frame issues in such a way to get public support. They can be quite adept at getting appropriate experts lined up for media interviews who can slant information in their favour in an attempt to discredit the message of protesters. If the ethical vision guiding business and government is shaped by a desire to create long-term mimetic structures of blessing such that the well-being of all will be enhanced, it becomes in their interests as people on the planet to listen carefully to those messages from protesters that are based on good research and a thoughtful assessment of current trends, even though the message may be critical of their institutions.

Beyond acting on these principles, political and business leaders can play a constructive role in developing communication processes that enable effective dialogue with crowd protesters. This dialogue could involve meeting with groups of representatives, using closed circuit television to have a two-way exchange or having a series of consultations in advance of a major event. They can also work creatively on new systems, institutions and structures that can attend to the needs and interests of all parties.

Some activists observe that governments are extremely responsive to the influence of people in the business community. To them, policy regarding the environment seems to be developed to protect the economic interests of large corporations which happen to be major contributors to political parties. The Mutual Respect Paradigm opens up the issue of what really influences public policy and what is perceived to have an influence. Trust is extremely important and trust begins with dignity and respect.

Role of Security

As public employees, security personnel have the responsibility to protect everyone in the crowd scenario from harm and violence. Additionally, they must protect the democratic process of decision-making while at the same time facilitating the legitimate expression of dissent. As long as crowds are peaceful the role of security can be peaceful. Security personnel have experiences and memories of violent activists and are wary of the possibility of someone who appears peaceful becoming violent. They also have information about those intent upon using violence and a public responsibility to act upon that information in the interest of the public peace. However, there is always the possibility that their information is inaccurate or that their interpretation of that information may be faulty.

It is risky for security forces to let down their guard. It is risky for them to abandon the tactics that have proven effective in getting the jobs done in earlier times. It is risky for those who want to give a cooperative approach an honest try to stand up to the *status quo* and lead the way. When the old approach has been seen to be efficient and effective in quelling disturbances it is difficult to replace it with an untried and unproven approach. Sometimes a show of strength has intimidated members of a crowd and quelled the mimetic violence that may have been instigated by the 'two percent.' Many security personnel are seeing the spiral of escalating violence with the use of crowd control tactics and are willing to take whatever risk is necessary to turn around the dependence on defensive tactics. One police participant at Quebec reported that the fence reduced the incidence of toe to toe confrontation with angry protesters and that this was a good outcome—one that allowed them to remain more neutral. Few on the other side who were angry at the fence and demonstrated in a haze of tear gas would agree that the fence was a good thing.

Security services have been thrust into the forefront of dealing with crowds that feel passionately about local and global injustices. They have been asked by leaders to control crowds, shielding leaders and the buildings they are using from those who might wish to make their voices heard, and perhaps occupy buildings and/or disrupt sessions. They have used a variety of techniques—from intelligence gathering, to passive security structures, to negotiations and the use of less than lethal instruments of control, to more aggressive ways of holding crowds in check. The combination of the violence of protesters and the matching violence of police, or to some the initial violence of police and the angry response of crowds have succeeded in introducing a growing mimetic structure of violence into the relational system involving protesting crowds and police. Within this climate, even well intentioned initiatives by police to communicate with protesters in advance of an event are held suspect. Some police are caught in an internal conflict between doing their job, which involves following orders, and sympathy with the issues which protesters are flagging. For example, a police officer, who is a strong supporter of his own union, might have to act against violence on a picket line.

The Mutual Respect Paradigm poses a number of challenges for police. First, if a given scenario has been agreed upon by all parties, there may be unexpected factors that warrant an abrupt change of tactics calling into question the good faith involved in the agreement. These factors could include intelligence reports concerning anticipated violence, legal requirements invoked by new realities or commands issued by those not understanding the Mutual Respect Paradigm. Second, in the post

September 11 reality there is an ever present fear of terrorism. Some of the actions on the part of security might be more to prevent terrorism that to deal with demonstrators. Third, police often cannot talk about what they know because information is classified. The Mutual Respect Paradigm suggests that ways can be found to address these challenges through new communication structures.

There are now in place police negotiators who embody the Mutual Respect Paradigm as they work to facilitate the effective communication of protesters' issues. Their mandate should be strengthened. Police leaders should learn from their experience. All those involved in public order policing and critical incidents should be trained in a way that gives precedence to this paradigm and reinforces the role of police negotiators. This training should include workshops run by third parties and that include representation from the protest community. A key issue to be on the agenda for the training sessions is how to be respectful without institutionalizing protest to the point that it becomes banal and ineffective.

Media

The media are the eyes and ears and sometimes the brains for people in the general population who are not close enough to physically watch the action. They determine what is to be seen on television, heard on the radio, or described in print. How they frame the coverage determines what gets emphasized as being significant and what gets passed over or mentioned in a way that trivializes it. Often politicians base perceptions on what the public feels about a given situation on what is covered in the press and broadcast media and how it is framed. This means that besides covering the news, the media also indirectly make the news. Given this power, different sides manipulate the media as events are staged for the camera. The reality is that media needs stories; journalists have tight deadlines; the easiest way to get a good story on time is to focus on violence or on a clear polarization of positions.

However, given their very crucial role, it is important that media personnel be included in explorations of the Mutual Respect Paradigm and understands what it is all about so that if there is a new reality it can be 'seen,' 'heard,' and presented. Media can play an important role in contributing to mutual understanding of the different parties involved through coverage that brings to light the deeper motivations behind various actions. In fact, the General Conference of UNESCO passed a declaration of fundamental principles urging media to work actively to promote peace and international understanding. One of its principles is the following:

> With a view to the strengthening of peace and international understanding, to promoting human rights and to countering racism, apartheid and incitement to war, the mass media throughout the world, by reason of their role, contribute effectively to promoting human rights, in particular by giving expression to oppressed peoples who struggle against colonialism, neo-colonialism, foreign occupation and all forms of racial discrimination and oppression and who are unable to make their voices heard within their own territories.[21]

The spirit of this principle would serve to reinforce the role of media in promoting a culture in which relationally creative crowd dynamics would work. As well, it emphasizes the importance of giving expression to many of the voices of oppressed people that are taken up by many of the activists.

Journalists try to be balanced in their reporting by talking to those on the different sides of an issue. They have discretion about the questions they ask and the particular answers they report. Used in the interests of mutual understanding and creativity, this discretion could lead to an examination of underlying interests and perhaps overlapping interests that could be met creatively in such a way that neither side would lose. If, in their questioning, they would ask about solutions to the problem, they might get some interesting answers. The 'good story' then would be about why some obvious mutually beneficial solutions are not being implemented.

Role of Bystanders

Bystanders are those not directly involved in crowd action but who are affected by the dynamics. As Ervin Staub points out, bystanders can have a huge impact on the behaviour of other stakeholder groups by voicing encouragement or discouragement of certain actions. After the November

21 Article II-3, DECLARATION ON FUNDAMENTAL PRINCIPLES CONCERNING THE CONTRIBU-TION OF THE MASS MEDIA TO STRENGTHENING PEACE AND INTERNATIONAL UNDER-STANDING, THE PROMOTION OF HUMAN RIGHTS AND TO COUNTERING RACIALISM, APRTHEID AND INCITEMENT TO WAR (1978) Adopted by the General Conference of the United Nations Educational, Scientiric and Cultural Organization on 22 November 1978. Taken from Albert Blaustein, Roger S. Clark, Jay A. Sigler, Human Rights Source Book (New York: Paragon, 1987) 338.

2001 G20 gathering of finance ministers, for example, the police report received far more commendations than criticisms for their efforts from the public in a 10 to one ratio, even though a number of demonstrators got hurt in the process. This reflects a public preoccupation with security. The responses to the police have an impact on what they do in the future.

Bystanders are not a coherent group. They are implicated in different ways so we will describe potential roles for different bystander groups.

Immediate Bystanders

Immediate bystanders are those living in close proximity to the crowd–target–police dynamics. In the case of major events like the Quebec Summit of the Americas or the G8 meeting in Genoa, their living and working areas may be cordoned off and they may need security passes to get to home or work. There is also the possibility that tear gas comes into their windows or that protesters smash windows and engage in looting. They may be sympathetic to the concerns of activists, they may support the positions of political leaders on a particular issue or they may be neutral. Since they are affected, it is fair that their concerns be taken into account in managing crowd–target–police dynamics.

Society

Sometimes large communities of people are affected by the violence associated with crowd dynamics since these dynamics are a reflection of society as a whole. People are led to ask, 'Is this the kind of society I wish to live in?' Such questions may be prompted by the actions of any of the parties.

The Mutual Respect Paradigm can be seen as enhancing the development of civil society.

Moral Authorities

Moral authorities and religious leaders have a role to play in interpreting what is happening and offering teachings, paradigms and arguments in support of new constructive and cooperative approaches. The Anglican Bishop at the Strategic Leaders Seminar played a valuable and constructive role.

Role of Neutral Leadership Institutions

In instances where feelings are strong and distrust high, there is a need for trusted third party institutions to be involved in creating a safe space for dialogue, creative scenario development and debriefing. Our experience has been that a university offers a safe space for interaction. People working on developing cooperative approaches to crowd dynamics must be able to maintain the trust and esteem of all affected parties. No one is ever neutral, but it is possible for people to conduct themselves with sufficient neutrality that both sides continue to feel comfortable. Those trained as Third Party Neutrals make a point of doing reality checks to be sure that neither sides perceives them as favouring the other side.

People accept new paradigms if they help understand the truth of a situation. Actions based on new paradigms will continue if they are effective and will die out if they are not. A good understanding of a new approach and suitable processes of dissemination are important for them to take hold. In the case of the Mutual Respect Paradigm, it is important that people of the different stakeholder groups be gathered together in a neutral place and be allowed to explore each others' experiences and understandings in a climate of safety and through processes guided by a neutral trainer. For this to happen, initiatives need to be launched by neutral institutions such as universities in order to create the new climate needed for a new approach.

In addition to broad-based initiatives to enhance cooperation, some people are needed on the ground to attend to particular conflicts that might arise. In his book *Getting to Peace*, William Ury writes about those who 'witness' as a means of creating a third side in a conflict situation. He writes, '… destructive conflict does not just break out but escalates through different stages, from tension to overt conflict to violence. By watching carefully, we can detect warning signals, which, if acted on, can save lives.' Witnesses may be there simply to try to pacify the situation or to enhance communication and reduce violence. Groups like the Non-Violent Peace Force work systematically to create a safe neutral space for those in conflict. In some parts of the world there are Civilian-Based Peace Forces that do not use violence. Christian Peacemaker Teams play an important role as witnesses. Any of these groups might have a role to play in protest crowd–police dynamics. There may be other forms of third party intervention involving processes such as mediation or conciliation to deal with conflicts within particular relational systems. People in this situation get unique glimpses into the life situations of various parties and hence can present a perspective sensitive to the experiences and feelings of both sides of an issue.

It is important that leaders with a broader vision be engaged in the process since there are bound to be setbacks and pitfalls. An example of someone of vision working on a new approach is Sheriff Douglas Call of Genesee County, New York. In the 1980s, he had a vision for victim-offender reconciliation in the case of serious crime. The first case they attempted failed. Instead of giving up, he chose to work on victim support. The result was that when victims' needs were attended to, nine times out of ten they wanted to meet with the perpetrator. The result was creative and constructive sentences that enabled offenders to take steps to make things right with victims and the community.

What are the Rules?

In order for Mutual Respect to work, the various parties have to come to terms with the basis on which they can work together. One way to accomplish this is for them to agree on principles of engagement. These following principles are a first step only and should be developed through facilitated processes involving all stakeholders.

Principles
1. Treat everyone with dignity and respect.
2. Engage a neutral process leader to lead joint planning and debriefing sessions.
3. Develop creative scenarios, with each stakeholder group participating, on how to handle contingencies; communicate these widely to groups.
4. Hold joint debriefing sessions after major events to develop lessons learned.
5. Put in place joint problem-solving structures to handle unforeseen circumstances
6. Share as much information as possible.
7. Clarify the meaning of terms and actions such as violence and non-violence.
8. Respect role specific codes of conduct.

In his book, *Living with Other People*, Ken Melchin (1998) makes a number of observations that are helpful in thinking through how we should act within a Mutual Respect Paradigm. First, as the title suggests, we must acknowledge that we all need to live together on this planet. We are not simply going to get rid of any of the groups described above. Second it is important to note which direction we are going in terms of progress or decline. Third, when we think of what is right and good we think in terms of different levels—what is important to me, what is important in the relationship and what is important in terms of social structures.

As people think through their approaches to crowd dynamics from their own perspectives, it is important that they think about what kind of society or community they would like to see evolve and what kind of relationship they might like with each of the players implicated in crowd dynamics.

Mutual Respect Protest Crowd–Police Process Suggestions

Ultimately Mutual Respect involves people from different stakeholder groups working together. This book could be used as a catalyst to bring people together for a process in which they accomplish several things together:

- They develop a common understanding of the concept of Mutual Respect in Crowd Dynamics
- They get to know and understand one another better
- They generate new ideas around what it would mean for them to collaborate.

There are several potential uses for this book over and above the pure learning of the concepts contained. First, the book could be distributed strategically to people and informally people could start talking about what they thought about it. Second, the book could be used for a process to establish a basis for working together. If it is to be used for a process, the following questions need to be addressed: Whose process is it? Who should be there? Who will lead the process? How long is the process? What happens in the process? We will offer some ideas about what to consider in relation to each of these questions. The answers are meant to give you ideas about how to proceed.

- ### *Whose process is it?*
  Use of this book starts with you being concerned about crowd dynamics in some particular context. You could be an activist, a police officer, a bystander or a government leader. Whoever you are, you would do well to find like-minded people in each of the stakeholder groups who might work with you on an ad hoc steering committee. Talk to people about the book; give it to

them to read; find out if they are interested in exploring the concept with you. Ideally you would find some institution that everyone feels comfortable with to sponsor the process. With an initial small group of 4–8 individuals you may wish to try out your own process (see below for options).

- ### Who should be there?
Initially it is important to involve people with considerable leadership skills who are respected within their own organizations or communities. It is desirable to have a good sense of balance among the stakeholder groups. Out of a group of 20, the following would be a desirable group: 6 activists, 6 police, 2 politicians, 2 civil society moral authorities (respected elders, religious leaders, academics, leaders of service clubs, judges, etc.), 2 journalists, 2 business people, residents or community association leaders from the vicinity of a potential crowd. There should be a gender balance.

- ### Who will lead the process?
The process should be led by a neutral facilitator with whom all of the participants will feel comfortable. There should be a neutral co-facilitator who acts as observer, attending to how people in the group are doing and taking notes to be included in a report on the process. This frees the head facilitator as well as the participants.

- ### How long is the process?
The process could be one segment of about three hours, three days or a series of segments spread out over a period of time.

- ### What happens during the process?
The purpose of the process is to facilitate dialogue among members of each of the stakeholder communities. We will give a sample process of three hours, The Crowd Dynamics Dialogue, that will allow community members to assess the potential value of the Mutual Respect Paradigm as presented in this book. We will also provide a sample process for three days, The Crowd Dynamics Seminar, with 12 segments. The Mutual Respect process is evolving and with each successive seminar new approaches are incorporated into the training. We are committed to ensuring that you have the newest and latest information.

Crowd Dynamics Dialogue

The Crowd Dynamics Dialogue is a three hour process. It is assumed that everyone has read the book in advance. *The crowd dynamics dialogue process is confidential unless individuals agree to talk about it outside of the process.* We will outline supplies and equipment needed, make suggestions for ground rules, provide process details including welcome, check-in, opportunity for discussion of the book, four tasks, and circle closing.

Needed: flip chart and markers, Tape, 30 Coloured stick-on dots or 10 pieces of paper.

Ground rules:
1. Treat one another with dignity and respect.
2. Speak the truth with an attitude that you may not have the total picture yourself.
3. Listen carefully.
4. Respect the process and the guidance of the process leader.
5. If you need to leave before the process is over, let the facilitator know in advance. Explain to the group if it seems appropriate.
6. Give one another equal air time.

Process:

Welcome and introduction—5 minutes

Circle Check-in (Each person explains briefly why they are there)—20 minutes

Ask: What are your overall impressions of the book? Discuss—10 minutes

Ask: Are any concepts unclear? Discuss and clarify.—15 minutes

(If someone does not understand a word or concept ask who in the group thinks they understand. Let them explain. Ask the group if this is clear to everyone. Go on to the next question.)

First Task: Pair people up by chance: Divide the number of participants in two, number them off to that number and then number them off again. Those with the same number are to work together.

Turn to the chart comparing the Crowd Control, Crowd Management and Mutual Respect paradigms. Discuss with your partner each of the items of comparison and work together at selecting the three you think are most significant. Write the three numbers on a slip of paper. When the time is up, give the paper to the facilitator.—20 minutes

Break:—15 minutes (During the break, the facilitator puts the results of the vote on a flip chart. Alternately the chart can be enlarged to 11x17 inches. Each pair can be given three coloured dots which they then stick beside their three choices.)
Review the results of the vote. Let people comment.—10 minutes

Second Task: Number people off into groups of four. Each group appoints a reporter. Ask each group to work on the following questions*—30 minutes (give 5 minutes warning before end-time)
What difference would the Mutual Respect Paradigm make in your community?
What are the possibilities for working together as you prepare for the next event?
What are the challenges to working together and how could these be addressed?
Gather the group together and ask each group to report on what they came up with in 3 minutes or less. Total discussion time—15 minutes.

Third Task: Ask the group if there are any actions that need to be taken as a follow-up to this session. Record on the flip chart. Ask who should follow-up. 10 minutes

Fourth Task: Ask the group, if there were another similar session, who should else should be invited. Record on flipchart. 5 minutes

Circle debrief. Go around the circle letting each person talk about insights, dreams, questions, thoughts about the process or feelings that they might have.—20 minutes
*Note: Remember that dialogue among participants is a primary goal and if a good dialogue begins, that may be more important than covering all of the questions.

The Crowd Dynamics Seminar
The Crowd Dynamics Seminar is a three-day process. As with the Crowd Dynamics Dialogue, it is assumed that everyone has read the book in advance. *The crowd dynamics seminar process is confidential unless individuals agree to talk about it outside of the process.*

The following table gives an overview of topics that could be covered. We recommend a selection of topics customized for the particular participants and contexts of the seminar. The person leading the process should have training as a Third Party Neutral and as a trainer. Such training can be obtained at institutions like the Canadian Institute for Conflict Resolution (information is available at www.cicr-icrc.ca).

	Day 1	Day 2	Day 3
Segment 1	Introduction Census	Roles of crowds, security and government within society	Creative scenario development
Segment 2	Human Needs	Why is there violence	Lessons learned
Segment 3	Paradigms	Dreams and challenges: Crowds and targets	Action plan
Segment 4	Questions you always wanted to ask	Dreams and challenges: Crowds and security	Answers to questions and closure

Census: On the front page census includes names, roles and favorite something (suggest something neutral such as a book/ favorite holiday/ favorite piece of furniture). On the back page the questions could be to list protest situations you have known; what is the most important/ difficult aspect of the crowd relational system? As these questions are not attributable to individuals they provide the opportunity to bring up topics that could contribute a dialogue on the issue later during the seminar process. It creates safety by not requiring depth of conversation in the beginning.

Human Needs: An overview of Redekop's Human Identity Needs Theory provides common language and a foundation upon which to discuss emotions.

Paradigms: Differentiating among the control, management and mutual respect paradigms provides brief historical background, opportunity for questions and clarification about experiences, roles and goals.

Questions: Many times security personnel and activists have never had an opportunity to exchange ideas in a safe space. These questions provide for that opportunity early on in the training so additional opportunities will be more likely to be taken later on.

Day Two

Roles: Links back to Paradigms and provides a common model upon which to base questions and clarification. Defines the 'us' and 'them' of the conflict and differentiates between the issues being protested and the conflict on the streets between security and activists framing the roles and players.

Why violence?: An opportunity for deeper introspection about roles. Facilitator cautions about blaming. Theory about structures of violence provides clarity about the consequences of violent incidents.

Dreams—crowds and targets; crowds and security: Begins to develop a concrete positive objective and focus for future relationships within the mutual respect paradigm for activists, targets and security. It also provides a framework for media stories.

Creative scenario development: brings the dreams into more tangible potential as real possibilities are explored.

Lessons learned: can be personal or theoretical.

Closure: can include exchange of contact information

Event Preparation

With adequate preparation time both dialogue and seminars can be used to prepare a community for an international event such as a G8 or G20 in which major demonstrations are expected. The following guidelines represent possibilities. They require a committed cadre of people including seasoned trainers (two of which are experienced with training content), adequate funding, facilities in which to train/ conduct dialogue(s), and community support. Some suggestions include:

1. Establish a steering committee or advisory council that reflects the diversity of the relational system as much as possible.
2. Plan the funding, marketing, media coverage, ongoing research and evaluation of project.
3. Establish timelines.
4. Manage media and marketing.
5. Establish gathering process with one coordinator.
6. Start the project with one or more dialogues. This establishes a cadre of people who are aware of the paradigm and from which to draw for subsequent seminars.
7. Conduct one or more strategic seminars to establish community support and from which to draw potential trainers.

8. Conduct train the trainer training, if necessary.
9. Gather for operational seminars and conduct as many as possible. The objective is to include everyone who wants to be included.
10. Conduct ongoing research and evaluation during the project.
11. After the event, conduct debriefings, focus groups and post-event evaluations.
12. Conduct follow-up interviews with participants.

Train the trainer sessions could also be conducted so that organizations can conduct their own internal dialogues and seminars. Pre-event preparation is aimed at exposing the maximum number of people to the Mutual Respect Paradigm so that a single untoward incident will not result in excessive reaction by anyone in the relational system. Conflict is inevitable—how we deal with it can be respectful and fair.

Conclusion

The world over, citizens have opinions that differ from those of their governing bodies be they democracies or not. They want to express these differences not only during election time but also at times when they believe they can influence decisions that will bring irreversible change to their communities. They want to be safe when they speak out. The freedom to express difference varies from one community to the next, from one democracy to the next and even among dictatorships, and the ability to do so is a measure of the respect and dignity afforded a community. The continuum of dynamics between protest crowds and police that we have presented as three paradigms provides for perspective so that communities can measure how they fit into the world of protest activities. We hope that in learning about how to work out effective protest crowd–police dynamics, community leaders can choose to make less violent choices.

Protesters use a range of strategies and tactics from peaceful marches to violent, chaotic activities to bring attention to their message. Police have responded in ways that ensure they keep the peace, sometimes with a very heavy hand. Targets have both ignored protesters and learned from them. Bystanders have sometimes taken on leadership roles that further the dialogue. The media have learned to frame police–protester crowd conflict in ways that build trust. At Saint Paul University, we have worked out a process that supports safe peaceful interaction among all community stakeholders; a process that respects differences and different opinions and provides for community members to work together to effectively place their dissenting opinions in the public domain. We were pleasantly surprised at how little effort it took to bridge the gaps in our own community, not that our own community is totally 'there' but that significant dialogue created the will for our community members to work together for safe peaceful expression of opinion. We were confident that the CBCR process dealing with communities in conflict was transferable to many venues and now we have demonstrated that it readily applies to communities in conflict over protest. The process is recommended for all communities with the will to support peaceful protest.

As we researched the literature, we learned that what we did intuitively is totally supported and we found answers for some of the reactions we observed. As the global community comes together, activities in one part of the globe influence all of the rest. We have described the mimetic contagion and concepts of complexity and levels of consciousness that makes this so. In a complex world that can no longer rely on cause and effect the only recourse for peaceful coexistence is dialogue and creatively building relationships. Exactly how this is done will differ from community to community and it will be up to community members be creative in their efforts.

It has been an honour to work in this area. Our belief is that people the world over have the ability and creativity to protect communities from repressive violence associated with their expression of difference and, with the will to do so, every community can provide for peaceful passionate protest.

Bibliography

Bar-Siman-Tov, Y. (2004). Dialectics between Stable Peace and Reconciliation. In Y. Bar-Siman-Tov (Ed.), *From Conflict Resolution to Reconciliation*. Oxford: Oxford University Press.

Bar-Tal, D., & Bennink, G. H. (2004). The Nature of Reconciliation as an Outcome and as a Process. In Y. Bar-Siman-Tov (Ed.), *From Conflict Resolution to Reconciliation*. Oxford: Oxford University Press.

Barlow, M. C., Tony, C. (2001). *Global Showdown: How the New Activists are Fighting Global Corporate Rule*. Toronto: Stoddart.

Barnhart, C. (Ed.). (1971). *The World Book Dictionary*. Toronto: Field Enterprises Educational Corporation.

Birt, R. P. (2001). Community-Based Conflict Resolution. In *Foundational Process: Principles, Process, Techniques and Tools* (Version 3.0 ed.). Ottawa: Ridgewood Foundation for Community-Based Conflict Resolution (Int'l).

Björk, M. (2005). Between Frustration and Aggression: Legal Framing and the Policing of Public Disorder in Sweden and Denmark. *Policing and Society, 15*(3), 305–326.

Bohm, D. (1997). *On Dialogue*. New York: Routledge.

Bole, W., Drew Christiansen, S., & Hennemeyer, R. T. (2004). *Forgiveness in International Politics. An Alternative Road to Peace*. Washington, D.C.: United States Conference of Catholic Bishops.

Boulding, K. E. (1999). Nonviolence and Power in the Twentieth Century. In S. Zunes, L. Kurtz, and S. Asher (Eds.), *Nonviolent Social Movements: A Geographical Perspective*. Malden and Oxford: Blackwell.

Bouton, C. A. (1993). *The Flour War: Gender, Class, and Community in Late Ancien Régime French Society*. University Park, PA: The Pennsylvania State University Press.

Brewer, J. D., Guelke, A., Hume, I., Moxon-Browne, E., & Wilford, R. (1996). *The Police, Public Order and the State: Policing in Great Britain Northern Ireland, the Irish Republic, The USA, Israel, South Africa and China* (Second ed.). London, New York: MacMillan Press, St. Martin's Press.

Brown, J., & Waters, I. (1996). Force versus service: a paradox in the policing of public order? In C. Critcher & D. Waddington (Eds.), *Policing Public Order: Theoretical and Practical Issues*. Aldershot: Avebury.

Cerrah, I. (1998). *Crowds and Public Order Policing: An Analysis of Crowds and Interpretations of their Behaviour Based on Observational Studies in Turkey, England and Wales*. Aldershot: Ashgate Dartmouth.

Charney, N. (2006) The Centrality of Latent Violence and the Spiraling Dynamics Within Contemporary Canadian Parliamentary Democracy. Unpublished M.A. Thesis in Conflict Studies. Ottawa: Saint Paul University.

Ciacccia, J. (2000). *The Oka Crisis: A Mirror of the Soul*. Dorval: Maren Publications.

Cummings, G. (1993). Black Theology and Latin American Theology. In D. Batstone (Ed.), *New Visions for the Americas: Religious Engagement and Social Transformation*. Minneapolis: Fortress Press.

Dalai Lama; Goleman, D. (2004). *Destructive Emotions: How Can We Overcome Them?* New York: Bantam Books.

Deibert, R. J. (2002). Civil Society Activism on the World Wide Web: The Case of the Anti-MAI Lobby. In D. R. S. Cameron, Janice Gross (Ed.), *Street Protests and Fantasy Parks: Globalization, Culture and the State*. Vancover: UBC Press.

della Porta, D., & Reiter, H. (2006). The Policing of Transnational Protest: A Conclusion. In D. d. Porta, A. Peterson & H. Reiter (Eds.), *The Policing of Transnational Protest* (pp. 175–189). Aldershot: Ashgate.

della Porta, D. and Reiter, H. (1998). Introduction: The Policing of Protest in Western Democracies. In D. R. della Porta, H. Reiter (Eds.), *Policing Protest: The Control of Mass Demonstrations in Western Democracies* (pp. 302). Minneapolis: University of Minnesota Press.

Eng, S. (2005). Policing for the Public Good: A Commentary. In D. Cooley (Ed.), *Re-imagining Policing in Canada*. Toronto: University of Toronto Press.

Epstein, B. (1993). *Political Protest and Cutural Revolution: Nonviolent Direct Action in the 1970s and 1980s*. Berkeley: University of California Press.

Faber, Digna. (2003) *From Revolution to Reconstruction: Biography of Adam Smith (1723–1790)* http://odur.let.rug.nl/~usa/B/asmith/adams1.htm

Ferguson, N. (2002). *Empire: The rise and demise of the British world order and the lessons for global power*. London: Allen Lane.

Freire, P. (1970). *Pedagogy of the Oppressed*: Continuum Publishing Company.

G8 Research Group, University of Toronto, *What is the G8* http://www.g7.utoronto.ca/what_is_g8.html July 15, 2005 accessed August 16, 2009.

G20 United Kingdom 2009, *About G-20, What is the G-20* http://www.g20.org/about_what_is_g20.aspx accessed August 16, 2009.

Gabriel-Doxtater, B. K., & Hende, A. K. V. D. (1995). *At the Woods Edge*. Kanehsatake: Kanesatake Education Center.

Gell-Mann, M. (1994). *The Quark and the Jaguar: Adventures in the Simple and the Complex*. New York: W. H. Freeman and Company.

Girard, R. ([1978]1987). *Things Hidden Since the Foundation of the World*. (S. Bann, M. Metteer, Trans.) Stanford: Stanford University Press.

Girard, R. ([1972]1988). *Violence and the Sacred*. (P. Gregory, Trans.) Baltimore: Johns Hopkins University Press.

Girard, R. ([1982]1989). *The Scapegoat*. (Y. Freccero, Trans.) Baltimore: Johns Hopkins University Press.

Girard, R. (2000). *A Theatre of Envy: William Shakespeare*. Leominster and New Malden, UK: Gracewing and Indigo.

Girard, R. ([1965] 1990). *Deceit, Desire and the Novel: Self and Other in Literary Structure* (Y. Feccero, Trans.). Baltimore: The Johns Hopkins University Press.

Gladwell, M. (2000). *The Tipping Point: How Little Things Can Make a Big Difference*, Boston, New York, London: Little, Brown and Company.

Goleman, D. (1997). *Emotional Intelligence*. New York: Bantam Books.

Gonzales, P. B. (2001). *Forced Sacrifice as Ethnic Protest: The Hispano Cause in New Mexico and the Racial Attitude Confrontation of 1933* (Vol. 5). New York: Peter Lang.

Goodman, J. (2002). Defeating the OECD s Multilateral Agreement on Investment. In J. Goodman, ed. (Ed.), *Protest and Globalisation: Prospects for Transnational Solidarity* (pp. 276). Sydney: Pluto Press Australia.

Gora, J. M., Goldberger, D., Stern, G. M., & Halperin, M. H. (1991). *The Right to Protest: The Basic ACLU guide to Free Expression*. Carbondale: Southern Illinois University Press.

Gramsci, A. (1968). *The Modern Prince and Other Writings*. New York: International Publishers.

Grix, J. (2000). *The Role of the Masses in the Collapse of the GDR*. New York: St. Martin's Press.

Hayes, P. (1992). *The People and the Mob: The Ideology of Civil Conflict in Modern Europe*. Westport, CT: Praeger.

Herman, J. (1997). *Trauma and Recovery*: Basic Books.

Hermann, T. (2004). Reconciliation: Reflections on the Theoretical and Practical Utility of the Term. In Y. Bar-Siman-Tov (Ed.), *From Conflict Resolution to Reconciliation*. Oxford: Oxford University Press.

Hochschild, A. (2005). *Bury the Chains: Prophets and Rebels in the Fight to Freee an Empire's Slaves*. Boston: Houghton Mifflin Company.

Holland, J. H. (1995). *Hidden Order: How Adaptation Builds Complexity*. Reading, Mass.: Perseus Books.

Home Affairs Committee, House of Commons (UK) (2009). *Policing of the G20 Protests*. London: The Stationery Office Limited. http://www.statewatch.org/news/2009/jun/uk-hasc-g20-policing-report.pdf accessed August 6, 2009.

Huyse, L. (2003). The Process of Reconciliation. In D. Bloomfield, T. Barnes & L. Huyse (Eds.), *Reconciliation After Violent Conflict: A Handbook*. Stockholm: International Institute for Democracy and Electoral Assistance.

James, P. (2002). Principles of solidarity: beyond a postnational imaginary. In J. Goodman, ed. (Ed.), *Protest and Globalisation: Prospects for Transnational Solidarity*. Sydney: Pluto Press Australia.

Jasper, J. M. (1997). *The Art of Moral Protest: Culture, Biography, and Creativity in Social Movements*. Chicago: University of Chicago Press.

Jefferson, T. (1990). *The case against paramilitary policing*. Philadelphia: Open University Press.

Joyce, P. (2002). *The Politics of Protest: Extra-Parliamentary Politics in Britain since 1970*. Houndmills: Palgrave Macmillan.

Juergensmeyer, M. (2001). *Terror in the Mind of God: The Global Rise of Religious Violence*. Berkeley: University of California Press.

Kauffman, S. (1995). *At Home in the Universe*. New York: Oxford University Press.

Killam, D. (2001). *The Royal Canadian Mounted Police and Public Order: An Evaluation*. Queen's University, Kingston, Ontario.

King, E. G. (1990). *Crowd Theory as a Psychology of the Leader and the Led* (Vol. 7). Lewiston: The Edwin Mellen Press.

King, M., & Waddington, D. (2005). Flashpoints Revisited: A Critical Application to the Policing of Anti-globalization Protest. *Policing and Society, 15*(3), 255–282.

King, M., & Waddington, D. (2006). The Policing of Transnational Protest in Canada. In D. D. Porta, A. Peterson & H. Reiter (Eds.), *The Policing of Transnational Protest* (pp. 75–96). Aldershot: Ashgate.

Klandermans, B. (1997). *The Social Psychology of Protest*. Cambridge, MA: Blackwell Publishers.

Klein, N. (2002). *Fences and Windows: Dispatches from the Front Lines of the Globalization Debate*. Toronto: Vintage Canada.

Kratcoski, P., Verma, A., & Das, D. (2001). Policing of Public Order: A World Perspective. *Police Practice, 2*(1–2), 109–143.

Kriesberg, L. (2004). Comparing Reconciliation Actions within and between Countries. In Y. Bar-Siman-Tov (Ed.), *From Conflict Resolution to Reconciliation*. Oxford: Oxford University Press.

Laville, S. and Campbell, D. (2009). Baton charges and kittling: police's G20 crowd control tactics under fire. The Guardian, 3 April 2009. Retrieved August 13, 2009 from http://www.guardian.co.uk/world/2009/apr/03/g20-protests-police-tactics/print

Le Bon, G. ([1986]1930). *The Crowd: A Study of the Popular Mind*. London: Ernest Benn Limited.

Lederach, J. P. (1997). *Building Peace: Sustainable Reconciliation in Divided Societies*. Washington, D.C.: United States Institute of Peace Press.

Lederach, J. P. (1999). *The Journey Toward Reconciliation*. Scottsdale, Penn.: Herald Press.

Lerhe, E. (2004). *Civil Military Relations and Aid to the Civil Power in Canada: Implications for the War on Terror*. Retrieved July 25, 2006, from http://www.cda-cdai.ca/symposia/2004/Lerhe,%20Eric-%20Paper.pdf

Lewis, P. Video reveals G20 police assault on man who died. *The Guardian*, 7 April 2009. Retrieved August 13, 2009 from http://www.guardian.co.uk/uk/2009/apr/07/video-g20-police-assault

Lewis, P. and Vallée, M. (2009). 'UK plc can afford more than 20 quid,' the officer said. *The Guardian*, Saturday 25 April 2009. Retrieved August, 13, 2009 from http://www.guardian.co.uk/uk/2009/apr/25/police-informers-tape-recordings-gifford

Linger, D. T. (1993). The Hegemony of Discontent. *American Ethnologist, 20*(1), 3–24.

Lokahi Foundation (2008). *Final Evaluation Operation Nicole South Yorkshire1st/2nd November 2008*. Unpublished.

MacIntyre, A. (1981). *After Virtue: A Study in Moral Theory*. Notre Dame: University of Notre Dame Press.

Mackenzie, I., & Plecas, D. (2005). Policing Public Order in Canada. In D. K. Das (Ed.), *Public Order: A Global Perspective* (pp. 45–61). Upper Saddle River, NJ: Pearson Prentice Hall.

Mansbridge, J., & Morris, A. E. (2001). *Oppositional Consciousness: The Subjective Roots of Social Protest*. Chicago: The University of Chicago Press.

Manwaring-White, S. (1983). *The Policing Revolution: Police Technology, Democracy and Liberty in Britain*. London: The Harvester Press.

McAllister, P. (1999). You Can't Kill the Spirit: Women and Nonviolent Action. In S. K. Zunes, Lester R.; Asher, Sarah Beth (Ed.), *Nonviolent Social Movements: A Geographical Perspective*: Blackwell.

McGuigan, R. (2006). *How Do Evolving Deep Structures of Consciousness Impact the Disputant's Creation of Meaning in a Conflict?* Union Institute and University, Cincinnati, Ohio.

McPhail, C. (1991). *The Myth of the Madding Crowd*. New York: Aldine de Gruyter.

McPhail, C., Schweingruber, D., & McCarthy, J. (1998). Policing Protest in the United States: 1960–1995. In D. R. della Porta, Herbert (Ed.), *Policing Protest: The Control of Mass Demonstrations in Western Democracies*. Minneapolis: University of Minnesota Press.

Melchin, K. (1998). *Living with Other People: An Introduction to Christian Ethics Based on Bernard Lonergan*. Ottawa: Novalis.

Metropolitan Police Authority (2009). Policing of the the G20 Summit 2009. Report: 6a, 30 April 2009. Retrieved July 25, 2009 from www.statewatch.org/news/2009/apr/uk-met-police-authority-report-on-g20-protests.pdf

Niehoff, D. (1999). *The Biology of Violence*. New York: The Free Press.

Noakes, J., & Gillham, P. F. (2006). Aspects of the 'New Penology' in the Police Response to Major Political Protests in the United States, 1999–2000. In D. della Porta, A. Petersen & H. Reiter (Eds.), *The Policing of Transnational Protest* (pp. 97–116). Aldershot: Ashgate.

Osgood, C. (1966). *Perspective in Foreign Policy*. Pal Alto: Pacific Books.

Paré, S. (2002). Aid of the Civil Power: Military Force in the Resolution of Conflicts within Canada (pp. 27).

Paré, S. (2003). Crowd Dynamics: A Clash of Cultures (pp. 44). Ottawa.

Pert, C. (1997). *Molecules of Emotion: The Science Behind Mind-Body Medicine*. New York: Touchstone.

Peterson, A. (2001). *Contemporary Political Protest: Essays on political militancy*. Aldershot: Ashgate.

Polanyi, M. (1964). *Personal Knowledge: Towards a Post-Critical Philosophy* (Harper Torchbook ed.). New York: Harper and Row.

Randall, A. C., Andrew. (2000). The moral economy: riots, markets and social conflict. In A. C. Randall, Andrew (Ed.), *Moral Economy and Popular Protest: Crowds, Conflict and Authority*. New York: St. Martin's Press.

Redekop, V. N. (2002). *From Violence to Blessing: How an Understanding of Deep-Rooted Conflict Can Open Paths to Reconciliation*. Ottawa: Novalis.

Redekop, V. N. (2007a) 'Reconciling Nuers with Dinkas: A Girardian approach to conflict resolution,' *Religion—An International Journal*. 37, 64–84.

Redekop, V. N. (2007b) 'Teachings of Blessing as Elements of Reconciliation: Intra- and Inter-Religious Hermeneutical Challenges and Opportunities in the Face of Violent Deep-Rooted Conflict,' *The Next Step in Studying Religion: A Graduate's Guide*, edited by Mathieu E. Courville. London: Continuum, 129–146.

Redekop, V. N. (2008) 'A Post-Genocidal Justice of Blessing as an Alternative to a Justice of Violence: The Case of Rwanda,' *Peacebuilding in Traumatized Societies*, edited by Barry Hart. University Press of America, 205–238.

Redekop, V. N., Paré, S.L. (2001). Crowd Dynamics and Conflict Resolution: Getting the Dialogue Started. Report submitted to the Ministry of the Solicitor General of Canada and Canadian Police Research Centre, 42 pp.

Reina, D. S., & Reina, M. L. (1999). *Trust and Betrayal in the Workplace: Building Effective Relationships in your Organization*: Berrett-Koehler Publishers.

Reiter, H. and Fillieule, O. (2006). Formalizing the Informal: The EU Approach to Transnational Protest Policing. In D. D. Porta, A. Peterson & H. Reiter (Eds.), *The Policing of Transnational Protest* (pp. 145–173). Aldershot: Ashgate.

Ricoeur, P. (1992). *Oneself as Another*. Chicago: University of Chicago Press.

Rigacos, G. S. (2005). Beyond Public-Private: Toward a New Typology of Policing. In D. Cooley (Ed.), *Re-imagining Policing in Canada*. Toronto: University of Toronto Press.

Rigakos, G. S. (2005). Beyond Public-Private: Toward a New Typology of Policing. In D. Cooley (Ed.), *Re-imagining Policing in Canada*. Toronto: University of Toronto Press.

Rogers, N. (1998). *Crowds, Culture, and Politics in Georgian Britain*. Oxford: Oxford University Press.

Rucht, D. K., Ruud; Meidhardt, Friedhelm. (1999). Introduction: Protest as a Subject of Empirical Research. In D. K. Rucht, Ruud; Meidhardt, Friedhelm (Ed.), *Acts of Dissent: New developments in the Study of Protest*. Lanham: Rowman & Littlefield.

Rudé, G. (1999). *The Crowd in History: A Study of Popular Disturbances in France and England, 1730–1848*. London: Serif.

Schirch, L. (2005). *Ritual and Symbol in Peacebuilding*. Bloomfield, CT: Kumarian Press.

Sheldrake, R. (2003). *The Sense of Being Stared At*. New York: Crown Publishers.

Sheptycki, J. (2005). Policing Political Protest When Politics Go Global: Comparing Public Order Policing in Canada and Bolivia. *Policing and Society, 15*, 327.

Shriver, D. W. (2001). What Is Forgiveness in a Secular Form? In S. Raymond G. Helmick & R. L. Petersen (Eds.), *Forgiveness and Reconciliation: Religion, Public Policy, and Conflict Transformation*. Philadelphia and London: Templeton Foundation Press.

Sites, P. (1990). Needs as Analogues of Emotion. In J. W. Burton (Ed.), *Conflict: Human Needs Theory*. New York: St. Martin's Press.

Sluzki, C. E. (2003). The Process Toward Reconciliation. In A. Chayes & M. Minow (Eds.), *Imagine Coexistence: Restoring Humanity After Violent Ethnic Conflict*. San Francisco: Jossy-Bass.

Smith, P. T. (1985). *Policing Victorian London: Political Policing, Public Order, and the London Metropolitan Police*. Westport: Greenwood Press.

Sopow, E. L. (2003). *The Age of Outrage: The Role of Emotional and Organizational Factors on Protest Policing and Political Opportunity Frames*. Fielding Graduate Institute.

Soros, G. (2002). *George Soros on Globalization*. New York: PublicAffairs.

Staub, E. (1992). *The Roots of Evil: The Origins of Genocide and Other Group Violence*. Cambridge: Cambridge University Press.

Sunstein, C. R. (2003). *Why Societies Need Dissent*. Cambridge, MA: Harvard University Press.

Susskind, L., & Field, P. (1996). *Dealing with an Angry Public: The Mutual Gains Approach to Resolving Disputes*. New York: The Free Press.

Sword, D. (2003). *Complex Conflict Analysis of Public Protest*. Doctoral thesis.

Taylor, M. (2009). Campaigners monitored by civil servants. The Guardian, 1 May 2009. Retrieved August 13, 2009 from http://www.guardian.co.uk/uk/2009/may/01/liberty-climate-protesters-campaigners/print

Times, T. S. o. t. L. A. (1992). *Understanding the Riots*. Los Angeles: Los Angeles Times.

Townshend, C. ([1993]2002). *Making the Peace: Public Order and Public Security in Modern Britain*. Oxford: Oxford University Press.

Vejnovic, D., & Lalic, V. (2005). Community Policing in a Changing World: A Case Study of Bosnia and Herzegovina. *Police Practice and Research, 6*(4), 363–373.

Vitale, A. (2005). From Negotiated Management to Command and Control: How the New York Police Department Polices Protests. *Policing and Society, 15*(3), 283–304.

Volkan, V. (1990). An Overview of Psychological Concepts Pertinent to Interethnic and/or International Relationships. In D. Julius, J. Montville, and V. Volkan (Eds.), *The Psychodynamics of International Relations*. Lexington and Toronto: Lexington Books.

Waddington, D., Jones, K., & Critcher, C. (1989). *Flashpoints: Studies in public disorder*. London and New York: Routledge.

Waddington, P. A. J. (1991). *The Strong Arm of the Law: Armed and Public Order Policing*. Oxford: Clarendon Press.

Waddington, P. A. J. (1994). *Liberty and order: Public order policing in a capital city*. London: U.C.L. Press.

Waddington, P. A. J. (1998). Controlling Protest in Contemporary Historical and Comparative Perspective. In D. R. della Porta, Herbert (Ed.), *Policing Protest: The Control of Mass Demonstrations in Western Democracies*. Minneapolis: University of Minnesota Press.

Warcry. (2001). My Family Wears Black: A Manifesto on Militancy and Anarchism in the Anti-Globalization Movement. In N. Welton & L. Wolf (Eds.), *Global Uprising: Confronting the Tyrannies of the 21st Century—Stories from a New Generation of Activists*. Gabriola Island, BC: New Society Publishers.

Welch, M. (2000). *Flag Burning: Moral Panic and the Criminalization of Protest*. New York: Aldine de Gruyter.

Welch, S. (2004). *After Empire: The Art and Ethos of Enduring Peace*. Minneapolis: Fortress Press.

Wilber, K. (2001). *A Theory of Everything: An Integral Vision for Business, Politics, Science, and Sprituality*. Boston: Shambhala.

Wink, W. (1992). *Engaging the Powers*. Minneapolis: Fortress Press.

Zunes, S., Kurtz, L. and Asher, S. (Eds.). 1999. *Nonviolent Social Movements: A Geographical Perspective*. Malden and Oxford: Blackwell.

Index